IT HAPPENED TO
AUDREY

IT HAPPENED TO
AUDREY

A Terrifying Journey from Loving Mom
to Accused Baby Killer

AUDREY EDMUNDS
with Jill Wellington

Title Town
PUBLISHING

IT HAPPENED TO
AUDREY

A TERRIFYING JOURNEY FROM LOVING MOM
TO ACCUSED BABY KILLER

AUDREY EDMUNDS
WITH JILL WELLINGTON

TitleTown Publishing, LLC
P.O. Box 12093 Green Bay, WI 54307-12093
920.737.8051 | titletownpublishing.com

Editor: Claire Gerus
Cover Design: Erika L. Block
Interior Layout and Design: Erika L. Block
Cover and Author Photos: Jill Wellington

PUBLISHER'S CATALOGING-IN-PUBLICATION DATA:

Edmunds, Audrey (Audrey Ann), 1961-
It happened to Audrey : a terrifying journey from loving mom to
accused baby killer / Audrey Edmunds with Jill Wellington. -- 1st ed.
Green Bay, WI : TitleTown Pub., c2012.

p. ; cm.
ISBN: 978-0-9857998-0-9

Summary: Audrey Edmunds was a happily married young Wisconsin mother of two with a baby on the way, providing casual childcare, when the unthinkable happened. Accused of killing a baby in her care through shaken baby syndrome, she spent 11 years in jail before her conviction was overturned. She was finally exonerated after updated science showed her innocence. Audrey shares her story of hope and redemption in the face of unrelenting odds.--Publisher.

1. Edmunds, Audrey (Audrey Ann), 1961- 2. Shaken baby
syndrome--United States--Cases. 3. Shaken baby syndrome--
Diagnosis. 4. Judicial error--Wisconsin--Cases. 5. Prisoners--
United States--Biography. I. Wellington, Jill. II. Title.
RA1122.5 .E36 2012
616.85/8223--dc23 1211

Printed in the USA

I dedicate this book to my three beautiful daughters Carrie, Allison and Jennifer. I love being their mom and thank them with all my heart for staying strong during the cruelest times. They are my glowing inspiration in moving forward with positive intentions and hope that no other family has to suffer what we lived.

Audrey Edmunds

I lovingly dedicate this book to my husband Mark and children Lindsay and Mark. Their support throughout the long process of writing this book was unwavering and I am eternally grateful.

Jill Wellington

Me finally released from prison on February 6, 2008. I was wearing my friend Shelley's coat and boots because I didn't have any of my own.

(Courtesy Hank Snyder/Daily Citizen)

CHAPTER ONE

"Our life is going to be great!"

My husband Dave's excited voice and soft lips on my cheek roused me from a peaceful sleep. I squinted at the clock: five a.m. The room was still dark except for the bathroom light that sliced into the bedroom.

Dave's employer, Edward Kramer & Sons, had recently promoted him to manage operations in Burnsville, Minnesota, which meant a big move for our family. Now, he zipped his suitcase on the bed beside me as he prepared to return to his job 260 miles away. We always enjoyed his weekend visits back home, and I smiled groggily at his boyish enthusiasm as he contemplated our family's bright future.

Dave is a modern-day Fred Flintstone, working in the rock quarry business. When we began dating, I'd always pictured him sliding down a dinosaur's tail, like Fred, at the end of his shift! Then, one day, he put me into a jeep and we lurched over heaps of stone deep inside the quarry, and he explained the colossal business of mining rock. The rocks were interesting, but I was far more fascinated by this burly, blond fellow who had come into my life at the perfect time.

Now, seven and a half years later, we were married with two little daughters and a baby on the way. Our little family was happily nestled in Midwest suburbia in the tiny village of Waunakee, Wisconsin, the only Waunakee in the world--at least, that's what the town sign says welcoming visitors to this wholesome slice of Americana. We'd moved here from Toledo, Ohio almost three years before.

As I stayed snuggled under the covers, I hugged my five-month baby bump, watched as Dave swept out of the bedroom with his suitcase, then rolled over to grab another hour of sleep.

At six-fifteen that morning of October 16, 1995, I bounced out of bed. Dave's excitement over his new job lingered. We'd sold our house in September in preparation for our move next month.

The thought of moving the girls to a new city and starting a fresh life seemed like an exhilarating adventure.

Like Dave, I was thrilled about his promotion—he'd worked hard for years to earn it, and the advancement would bring us more money and a bigger house for our growing family. That morning, I felt unusually energetic, despite my expanding waistline. I bounded to the bathroom to grab a quick shower before the girls awoke.

The boisterous hubbub of my neighbors' babies and toddlers would soon take over my day. I felt like the luckiest woman in the world, with my life revolving around Dave and the kids and the babysitting I did for some working moms in the neighborhood.

I had quit working when we moved from Toledo to Waunakee; our eldest daughter, Carrie, was eighteen months old at the time and I wanted to be home to share her childhood. I soon became the neighborhood mom, and other mothers began asking if I would watch their children during the day.

That was how my home daycare business began. I didn't mind a bit: I could be home with Carrie and my soon-to-arrive second daughter, Allison, while tending several children from my neighborhood. It also brought in a bit of extra income.

Watching children was a perfect solution for me to be with the girls and fulfill my love for children, and I constantly planned activities for the lively brood.

Now, I scooped up eighteen-month-old Allison, who toddled into the bedroom to say good morning. Four-year-old Carrie was close behind, wiping wisps of blonde hair like both Mommy's and Daddy's from her sleepy eyes. I hugged them both close to me, still feeling the excitement of our move and Dave's promotion.

At seven o'clock, we were in the kitchen, the kids chattering at the table while I poured cereal into their bowls. The doorbell rang just after seven-thirty and I left the girls to greet my neighbor, Cindy Beard, at the front door. I'd been watching her seven-month-old daughter, Natalie, for the past five weeks.

"Mornin', Cindy," I said, holding the door open for her.

Natalie was crying loudly from her car seat and Cindy looked exhausted. "She was fussy during the night," Cindy told me. "I was up with her twice and she wouldn't take her bottle this morning."

Natalie usually drank a seven-ounce bottle of formula before she arrived at my house in the morning. Cindy told me Natalie had been on an antibiotic for an ear infection for the past four days, but now she seemed inconsolable. My kitchen was right by the front entry, so Cindy placed the baby carrier on the kitchen table, removed Natalie's jacket, put it in the diaper bag, and picked her up to calm her fussing.

Meanwhile, I put the baby's bottles in the refrigerator, leaving out a partial bottle in hopes that she would let me feed it to her for breakfast.

At around seven-forty a.m., Cindy placed her daughter back in the car seat and left her with me. As I listened to the baby's shrieks, I thought, *Poor Natalie. I'm sorry you're so unhappy.*

The doorbell rang again, and I left the girls while I opened the door for Jim Henning and his two-year-old daughter, Jessica. I just loved the Hennings, and Jessica felt like a daughter to me. I'd been watching her two or three days a week for more than a year and had babysat her older brother, Matthew, before he entered school. I talked with Jim for a moment in the front hall and we both spoke of Natalie's nonstop crying in the kitchen.

After Jim left, Jessica hopped up on a kitchen chair and joined my daughters for cereal. I prepared toast with jelly and filled sippy cups with juice and milk. With the girls eating and chatting happily, I picked up a still-wailing Natalie and offered her a bottle. I was pleased that she began sucking and swallowing tiny amounts of formula. But then, she spit the nipple out of her mouth to resume her howling. Gently, I smoothed her dark, wispy hair. Natalie was a pretty baby with a lovely olive complexion and chocolate eyes that now overflowed with tears.

Handling all those kids in the morning was routine for me. I was adept at holding and feeding infant Natalie while helping the older kids with their breakfast. I was also familiar with Natalie's odd feeding pattern. I had even mentioned to Cindy how slowly she fed when I first started caring for her daughter. Natalie would suck a little formula, cry and fuss, and then suck a bit more. It always took her at least half an hour to consume seven ounces of formula. She was almost seven months old and never held her own bottle, but when I mentioned this, Cindy told me it was simply Natalie's feeding pattern.

The phone rang and I grabbed it in the kitchen, then smiled as Dave's cheerful voice came through the line. "Honey, I'm driving west right now on I-94 toward the Twin Cities."

I felt a flutter of love for this man whom I'd met eight years before in Minnesota's Twin Cities. I'd been working as a secretary at MSI Insurance Company when a mutual friend set us up. The connection was instant and our romance progressed quickly. We married thirteen months after we met.

Dave loves the outdoors and thrives on living near Minnesota's "land of ten thousand lakes." His hair bleached to a pale blond every summer as he fished, boated, and hunted. Best of all, I adored his mischievous sense of humor. After a few dates, I knew I didn't want to spend my life without this man.

As he talked, I glanced down at Natalie, still fussing, and told Dave she was having a difficult morning. I'm sure he heard her crying over the phone.

"I'll call you tonight," Dave promised, and we hung up, confident that all was well in our world.

Because Natalie was recovering from an ear infection, I dismissed the fact that she didn't seem interested in feeding. I knew she needed gentle care and quiet surroundings—she'd always been that way. She had been slow to develop her mechanical skills, and at nearly seven months she still didn't roll over easily; nor did she sit up on her own.

I accommodated her sensitivities and often urged the other children to be calm with her. Sometimes I put Natalie into the infant swing, which helped soothe her when she was restless. I had only a few weeks left with her because Cindy planned to quit work at the end of the month to stay home with Natalie when we moved our family to be with Dave.

That October morning, with Natalie still crying, I had to rethink her feeding schedule. I usually fed her at ten-fifteen, but I thought she'd be hungry earlier because she'd missed the morning bottle Cindy usually fed her. I put the car seat in an upright position on the floor in our master bedroom—it was a more peaceful environment away from the rowdy toddlers. Cindy had told me Natalie needed tranquility to calm down and eat, and the room seemed a perfect sanctuary at the time.

Our house in Waunakee, a single-story ranch with pale gray vinyl siding, matched the other houses that lined our suburban street. The neighborhood overflowed with young families and numerous children. I enjoyed the company of many friends in the neighborhood, including that of my best pal, Shelley Murphy.

When we first moved to Waunakee, Shelley's youngest daughter, Melissa, was five. If she saw me outside playing with Carrie, she ran to join us. After a few times, I strolled down the street to her house and introduced myself to Melissa's petite, blonde mother. Shelley's luminous blue eyes danced, reflecting her lively personality, and we hit it off immediately.

Soon, we were shopping together and scouring garage sales. Shelley was a fashion maven and I learned the latest clothing styles and trends from her. Our husbands bonded, too, and enjoyed golf and football games. Our families shared many delicious dinners and barbeques together, with the guys at the grill and the women inside preparing side dishes. I loved Shelley's warm enthusiasm and friendship, which expanded and would sustain me in the trying years to come. Having to say goodbye to the Murphy family seemed impossibly difficult, but we promised to keep in touch from our new home in Minnesota.

Our bedroom was right off the gray carpeted Great Room, which made it easy to keep an eye on the kids. I carefully lay Natalie down in the car seat and held the bottle's nipple in her mouth so she would know it was there. Then, I grabbed a spit-up rag and folded it several times to prop up the bottle.

I didn't like propping a bottle and didn't usually do it, but this was an unusual morning. Natalie hadn't eaten before she arrived and was still fussy, so she was probably hungry. I figured that if she got something into her stomach, she might feel better.

I then moved to Carrie and Allison's bedroom to watch the girls play. "Can I brush your hair?" Carrie asked Jessica. Allison, still in her nightgown, rolled on the floor as Carrie ran the brush through Jessica's mop of dark blonde curls.

"That hurts!" Jessica squealed. With that, the trio burst into laughter and tumbled out of the room. I patted Allison's wispy mane as she scurried past me. Born bald, she was finally, at eighteen months, sprouting light brown locks. My precious Allie, born on my April 27th birthday, wouldn't be a baby much longer.

As the girls played in the Great Room, I quickly loaded the breakfast dishes into the dishwasher. A normal day with the kids was now underway in the Edmunds home--or so I thought.

"Carrie," I called to my four-year-old. "Come get ready for school."

Carrie bounded into the room with excitement. She loved being the big girl in the house and was enjoying preschool. After Carrie dressed herself, we walked back to the Great Room, where we could hear Natalie still crying. The girls scampered to the master bedroom and burst through the door and we all entered. Natalie continued to wail, so I shushed the girls and led them out of the room, leaving the door open a bit so I could keep an ear on Natalie. She was so often like this, I wasn't really concerned.

Then it was back to the living room to dress Allison and help the girls into their jackets. My morning routine was to load the younger children, and baby Natalie into my big stroller and walk Carrie to preschool. Up the street, we would join my neighbors, Tina Hinz and Patti Larson, who were also day care moms. Together, we enjoyed walking our group of kids to the same preschool.

My pleasant mood continued as I padded the back section of the stroller with a thick quilt for Natalie. I knew the baby was extremely sensitive to any bumping movement, so I always cushioned the stroller for her.

Allison and Jessica would ride side-by-side in the front. I thought ahead to Halloween and the fun I would have with the kids.

Mid-October has long been my favorite time of year, when the green leaves give way to the dazzling reds and fluorescent oranges, the color spectacular of autumn. Fall was the reason I loved living in Wisconsin, and I knew it was much the same in Minnesota. My husband was on his way to our new city, our house had been sold, and the weather was still warm enough to walk Carrie to school. It really was a happy day!

Right on time, I thought, as I raced into the house to get Natalie. My clock said eight-forty, which gave us plenty of time to stroll to the school. I was relieved when I entered the bedroom to find that Natalie was no longer crying. I heard a slight whimper, and as I drew closer, I noticed her eyes were closed with her head tilted to one side. Her bottle was lying on the floor.

Hopefully, she can sleep on our walk, I thought and placed Natalie's jacket on the floor, ready to put it on her. I gently lifted the drooping child and placed her on the opened jacket, but as I put one of Natalie's arms into her sleeve, I was startled to see formula dribble out of her nose! Instantly, I picked her up and softly patted her back, expecting her to burst into tears, but she was unresponsive.

My heart hammered and I knew something was dreadfully wrong. Had she choked on her formula? Adrenaline pulsed through me as I raced through the house, the garage and across the front yard with the baby in my arms, screaming for help. I had never been so afraid in my life. It was obvious Natalie was in serious trouble.

My neighbor, Tina, waiting for me down the block with her kids, heard my shrieks and ran up the street.

"My God! My God!" I screamed hysterically and held Natalie upright in front of Tina. "I…I think the baby choked…I was putting on her jacket. She's…she's…not responding to me."

"Go inside and call 9-1-1!" Tina shouted.

I barely remember getting to the phone, and in my overwhelming panic, I sputtered to the 911 dispatcher that Natalie had choked and was now limp. *Pant…pant…suck in a big breath.* I was now hysterical.

The dispatcher tried to calm me and told me to lay Natalie on the floor. She began to explain the steps for infant CPR. With trembling hands, I followed the instructions and Natalie gasped lightly. I was horrified when more formula flowed out of her small mouth. *This cannot be happening*, my mind raged. An overpowering force took over my body as I performed the thrusts for infant CPR. I knew I had left Natalie with a propped bottle and I felt the full impact of having that baby's precious life placed in my hands.

Within minutes, two Waunakee police officers, including Police Chief Robert Roberts, arrived. I was crying so hard that Roberts shooed me to sit at the kitchen table so he could assess Natalie. Shortly afterward, I was hugely relieved when EMT's Lorraine Endres and Shirley Nelson pulled up in an ambulance to take over and work on the wilted child. Surely, they were experts at this. They would know how to save a choking baby.

I stumbled into the kitchen, collapsed onto a chair at the table and prayed with all my heart. Now I could fall apart, and I did. My body wracked with sobs as I started to pray that now Natalie was in good hands. Safe hands.

While EMT Endres worked on Natalie, I showed EMT Nelson Natalie's bottles and amoxicillin in the refrigerator.

"We need to contact the baby's parents," Nelson said. In a daze, I found Cindy's number in a file cabinet. Nelson asked me to leave so they could continue to work on the baby. Shock took over and I was on autopilot, feeling very confused, panicked, almost out-of-body.

Suddenly, my friend Shelley was with me on the back porch, and I remember Nelson ordering us to move the patio furniture to clear the entryway through the master bedroom into the house. I had no idea what was happening inside because the police told us nothing. Soon after, I heard a loud whirring sound above us and instinctively ducked. It was the Med Flight Helicopter swooping in like a giant locust. It landed in the vast field right behind our house, and to me, it felt like a Black Hawk arriving at a war zone.

Shelley led me, stunned, across the street to her house. In my foggy state, I had no idea where the other children were, but learned later that Tina and Patti took them and drove Carrie to preschool.

I remember Shelley pulling me by the arm as I was floating… floating. Next, I remember being on her couch and hearing her talking with Dave on the phone, explaining that Natalie had choked on her formula and was now in a helicopter on the way to the hospital. Was she breathing normally? Would she be okay? I didn't know.

"Dave is driving back to Waunakee right now," Shelley said. "Tell me everything that happened."

I tried to explain the hideous morning but I couldn't think clearly through my sobs. I truly felt lightheaded and disoriented. Shock is a very strong shield against reality.

Shelley figured they had flown Natalie to University of Wisconsin Hospital in nearby Madison, and we later learned that Natalie was stabilized when they removed her from my house. But when Shelley called, the hospital had no information on her condition. She did her best to comfort me and was concerned about my pregnancy--which I had virtually forgotten.

Just after nine o'clock, Tina and Patti arrived with Allison and Jessica. Everyone was disturbed as we talked about the dreadful morning. The next few hours are a blur of conversation and concern. Someone fetched Carrie from preschool and just before noon, Shelley walked me back to my house, where in my robotic state, I fixed lunch for the kids.

Natalie's mother, Cindy, finally called me around noon and I told her what had happened. Cindy was kind and concerned about me, and after our conversation, I melted onto a kitchen chair. I was extremely relieved to know that Natalie was receiving the best care possible from medical experts. I told Cindy I would meet her at the hospital later.

Despite the news that Natalie was alive, I felt a deepening gloom, wondering how my perfect morning had deteriorated into a glimpse of Hell.

Little did I know that Hell is a deep, dark hole.

CHAPTER TWO

A million times since, I have thought over the details of that fateful morning and wondered why I didn't sense anything amiss. I remember standing at the bathroom sink before the day care kids arrived that morning. As I ran a brush through my hair, I hadn't a smidgen of foreboding. That happy, lanky woman gazing into the mirror had no premonition that this promising, sunny day in October was the beginning of a long, long nightmare.

Early that horrible afternoon as Allison and Jessica napped and Carrie played outside with neighborhood friends, the doorbell rang. I opened the door to a sandy-haired man in uniform and immediately recognized him as Waunakee Police Chief Robert Roberts.

"How are you doing?" he asked with genuine sympathy.

Through tears, I told him I was still an emotional wreck and couldn't believe what had happened to Natalie that very morning.

"I'm waiting for word from the hospital," I told Roberts. "I will go this afternoon to see the baby for myself."

Roberts was extremely empathetic and told me that when his own son was about six months old, his wife had been feeding him a bottle when he, too, choked and was rushed to the hospital, where he was unconscious for several hours.

"I can understand your agony," Roberts said. "We were so relieved when our son awakened, and we took home a healthy child several hours later."

The police chief's story and kindness soothed me.

"I am trusting Natalie will have the same outcome," I said. "But I'm absolutely numb with shock."

"I'm concerned about you and the Beards," Roberts said. "I will let you know if I hear anything about Natalie's condition."

After the police chief left, I called my church and talked with Doris Porter, who heads the prayer chain at Crossroads United Methodist Church. She spread the word and soon prayers, hope and caring poured from my church family for Natalie and her parents.

Meanwhile, I got a call from a doctor at University Hospital.

"I'm Dr. Gregory Holman," he introduced himself. "Did Natalie seem normal to you when Cindy Beard dropped her off at your house?

"Yes," I answered.

He did not elaborate any more on this. Little did I know the stress Natalie was in when she was crying that morning. Nor did I have any idea how my simple answer to his vague question would drastically change my future. He didn't ask me much more. His brief "investigation" became crucial later.

Still in my shocked state, I answered the door at two-thirty for Chris Henning, who arrived to pick up Jessica. The sparkly two-year-old hopped into her mother's embrace, oblivious to the chaos that surrounded her day.

My voice trembled as I told Chris what had happened to Natalie, and she was understanding and concerned. The Hennings lived across the street from the Beard house, and Chris liked both of our families.

"Please call us with any updates," Chris said. She hugged me warmly before leaving with Jessica.

At three o'clock, Dave arrived and found me in the kitchen, weeping. It was a huge relief to fall into his sturdy arms. "I'll do anything I can to help you," Dave said firmly. His solid embrace and loving, supportive words were just what I needed.

Dave helped me gather the kids and take them over to Shelley's house so they could play while we drove to the hospital. We arrived at the UW Madison Children's Hospital about four o'clock. Cindy came out of Natalie's room and hugged me, and we both dissolved into tears.

"Natalie is being prepared for a test," Cindy told us. "Nobody is allowed in the room right now."

I asked Cindy about her husband, Tom, and she said he was sitting in an area with his parents.

I talked with Cindy and shared how upset and concerned I was about Natalie. I understood a mother's fear when her child is ill. I thought back to my own surprise entry into the world in Stevens Point, Wisconsin on April 27, 1961. I wasn't due until the end of June, so when my petite mother, Jean Ann Glasbrenner, plunged into labor that morning, she was terrified to deliver me two months premature. My parents were stunned yet elated when teensy me, Audrey Ann Glasbrenner, entered the world, looking like a shriveled raisin and weighing a scanty three pounds, fourteen ounces.

My older brother Fred was only two years old when I was born, so my parents stretched themselves between their responsibilities at home and worrying about their tiny daughter living in an incubator at the hospital. After two weeks, I was moved to the nursery, and after another week my parents finally brought me home to meet my big brother.

All was happy and fine until that autumn when my mother took me for my six- month check-up. The doctor measured my head in a routine baby exam and found it was enlarged. They performed tests and learned I had hydrocephalus, or what is often called "water on the brain." The condition is sometimes a complication of a premature birth and can cause brain damage or even death if left untreated.

That November, a doctor performed surgery and inserted a shunt to drain the excess fluid away from my brain. Oddly, the surgery was performed in Madison where, all these years later, doctors were just as valiantly trying to save precious Natalie Beard.

Now I was standing beside her mother, who must be as terrified as my own mother had been. I know I'd have been sobbing with grief if one of my daughters were in this horrifying situation. My heart twisted with empathy for Cindy. I wanted so much to turn back the clock to the joyous beginning of the day, when everyone was happy and healthy.

After fifteen minutes with Cindy, she promised to call us if Natalie's condition changed. My pregnant body felt heavy and clunky as I lumbered with Dave out of the hospital.

Dave was concerned about my health and insisted we stop at a restaurant, where he coaxed me to eat. We picked up Carrie and Allison from Shelley's around six o'clock, but their innocent play and laughter that evening clashed with my chaotic state of mind. I wept off and on, waiting for a phone call about Natalie's condition.

Around eleven p.m., I let go of the stress enough to settle into a shallow sleep. Since I hadn't received any updates from the Beards or the hospital, I hoped it meant Natalie was improving, and that I would awaken to promising news in the morning.

Dave was up early the next day to go to work in nearby Plain, Wisconsin. "Call me with any news," he told me as he hugged me tight. "I'll come home whenever you need me."

His words were comforting, but what I really needed to hear was that Natalie was recovering and on the road back to health. Carrie and Allison awoke and after breakfast, played around the house as they did every other morning. How I longed to enjoy their laughter and a normal routine. Instead, a dark, menacing cloud hovered above me, and I feared the storm would break at any moment.

The phone rang at nine o'clock. It was Shelley asking about Natalie. I cried as I told her there was still no news, and Shelley promised to come over soon to keep me company.

When she arrived, the girls jumped into her arms to show off their new outfits. I was grateful to Shelley, who played enthusiastically with them in the front yard. Shortly after eleven, she and I took the girls to the local McDonalds, where the girls could enjoy a Happy Meal and Playland and I would have a change of scenery, too.

Nearly two hours later, Shelley and I brought the kids back to my house and put Allison down for a nap. My heart jumped when I saw the red light blinking on the answering machine. Was it news about Natalie? I pushed PLAY and listened to warm messages from my church pastor, Dave Werner, my husband, and a neighborhood friend, Jodi Siehoff. As I was finishing up with the phone messages, the doorbell rang.

I opened the door to find Pastor Werner and his wife, Barb, standing before me. As they entered the house, Barb pulled me into her arms and hugged me close.

Pastor Dave's face was somber. Taking my hand, he told me in a quiet voice, "I'm so sorry, Audrey. Natalie passed away last night. Tom and Cindy Beard agreed to let doctors take Natalie off life support around nine o'clock, and she died soon after."

Overwhelming grief engulfed me like a tidal wave, and I felt physically ill. I burst into heavy sobs, and Barb helped me place my pregnant body in a chair at the kitchen table.

Within minutes, a social worker from Dane County was at

the door. Shelley spoke with him, and he took Shelley, Carrie and Allison to the Murphy's house to talk with them.

Through the murky fog of pain, fear, and confusion, one blaring question rose in my mind: What had caused Natalie's death?

Pastor Dave and his wife prayed with me and offered comfort. After awhile, the social worker returned and asked me questions. I answered as clearly as I could, and then he left.

Within the hour, Dave bolted into the house and I fell into his arms. We both collapsed, moaning with grief and shock.

That afternoon, Detective Giese from the Waunakee Police Department came to the house to take pictures of the living room, kitchen, master bedroom and indents in the carpet where Natalie's car seat sat. He was polite as he gathered more details and said he was doing the same thing at the Beard's house.

As the evening passed, neighbors came by to offer prayers and support. A daycare provider named Pat, who lived a few blocks away, brought me a small plant. Taking my hand, she told me I was in her thoughts and prayers.

"This could happen to anyone caring for children," Pat said.

I was truly grateful for the outpouring of support and the caring, kindness and sympathy that also flowed to the Beards.

Dave called my parents, John and Jean Glasbrenner, and they jumped in the car and zoomed the four hours from Hudson to be with us.

Later, Dave and I sat at the kitchen table. For once, we had no words for each other. I stared out the window but couldn't even force a smile as I watched Carrie and Allison merrily playing on the front lawn with Mom and Dad. I called the Beards several times, but they never returned my calls. I could only imagine how they were feeling.

That evening, my friend Jodi Siehoff stopped by. She lived in the house next door to the Beards. I so appreciated everyone who offered prayers and sympathy during that time.

"I talked with Cindy today," Jodi said. "She wanted me to tell you that she hasn't returned your phone calls because after Natalie died, county investigators told Cindy and Tom not to talk to you. They are investigating Natalie's death."

I found that news unnerving. An investigation? And now I couldn't talk with Tom and Cindy? But I wanted to find out what had caused Natalie's death, so instead of calling again, I wrote them a card offering my thoughts and prayers. I wanted to go to their house, hug them and extend my heartfelt sympathy, but that was clearly impossible.

The next day, Grandma and Grandpa entertained the kids as I continued to wonder why this baby had died. Did she die from choking on her formula? What else could it be? I was absolutely overwhelmed with anguish.

In the afternoon, Dave insisted I go to my doctor for a check-up. What was all this trauma doing to our baby inside me? I told Dr. Kenneth DeVries the details of Natalie's death.

"It sounds like she aspirated," Dr. DeVries said.

"What does that mean?" I asked.

"That's when a person inhales a liquid into their lungs. In infants, this liquid is often vomit."

I cringed. My biggest fear was that Natalie had choked on the formula after I left her with a propped bottle. Now, the emotion I'd been holding away from me, guilt, entered every pore of my being, filling me with despair.

Dr. DeVries patted my shoulder. "This is a tragedy for all involved."

With my heart pummeling inside my chest, the doctor examined me and checked the baby's heartbeat. Fortunately, the baby's was normal. Mine certainly was not.

"The baby is fine," the doctor said. "But you should rest and try to stay as peaceful as possible."

Little did he know his Rx was impossible: I had a meeting the next day with police investigators to unearth more information about Natalie's death.

CHAPTER THREE

Thursday morning, my mom and dad packed their things and gathered clothes and toys for Carrie and Allison. They were taking the girls back to Hudson with them and Dave and I planned to join them on Friday.

I remember hugging Carrie tightly.

"Mom, let's rub noses!" she said gleefully. It was our ritual and she giggled with delight as we swished our noses back and forth. I loved the smell of her sweet shampoo.

I scooped up Allison, who wrapped her legs around my jutting belly. She pressed her nose against mine, mimicking Carrie. "I love you, precious girl," I whispered into her soft hair, and immediately I flashed on the Beards, who would never rub noses with their only child.

With my parents and the girls on their way to Hudson, the house was harshly quiet. I had nothing to do but think about the upcoming evening meeting with two Dane County investigators in downtown Madison. I still had so many questions about Natalie's death, I was eager to share whatever I could to help solve the mystery.

Dave's boss recommended we have a lawyer present and suggested the corporation's attorney, Dale Peterson, and we gratefully agreed. We met Dale that evening at the Dane County Municipal Building. The investigators summoned Dave first. I saw his jaw clench. He did not understand why we were being interrogated and felt angry. But he held himself in check to support me. He wanted to speak the truth and close this process as quickly as possible.

I was surprised when the questioning crawled on for an hour and a half. It was a long wait for me, with Dale Peterson sitting in with Dave. I wanted so much to know what was going on.

I would learn soon enough. I sat before investigators Dawn Johnson and Dave Bongiovioni while they tossed questions at me for more than two hours. Everything I did to love and care for each of the girls at my house that day was now dissected and examined.

They wanted exact times, which threw me. I was bustling about with four children that morning, not looking at my watch every few minutes. I had no idea what time the girls finished breakfast or the exact time Dave called me.

I was puzzled by this heavy barrage of questions, which to me seemed unrelated to Natalie's death. However, I did my best to remember and respond to them with full descriptions of each event. I was exhausted when the session ended late in the evening. Dale assured us it had gone smoothly and both Dave and I had been consistent with our answers.

"You both said pretty much the same thing," Dale said. "That's definitely a strength. I'll let you know if I need to assist you more in this process."

At this point, I didn't know what else we could tell them, so I thought our role in the investigation was complete. Dave and I climbed into his truck, and again I fell apart crying. Everything felt so dark and heavy.

Dave held me against him and assured me, "This will be over soon."

How soon? I wondered.

We drove back to Waunakee where we both fell into a sound and desperately needed sleep.

Friday morning, Dave made coffee. The house was oddly quiet without the girls around and we showered and prepared for what I knew would be one of the saddest days in my life: Natalie's funeral. Despite Jodi's news that Tom and Cindy were not allowed to talk to me, I never even considered missing the service.

My tummy was quickly expanding and I had to dig through a box of packed clothing to find my purple maternity dress. I hadn't planned to wear it before our move, and as I ironed the dress, I couldn't believe we were going to a funeral for the beautiful little girl I'd so lovingly cared for. I thought of her shining dark hair and striking brown eyes. I so adore babies, and she was special indeed. I couldn't imagine what Tom and Cindy were feeling as they prepared to bury their beloved baby girl.

Later that morning, we arrived at the Methodist church in Sun Prairie, Wisconsin, about fifteen minutes from our house. Tom and Cindy had baptized Natalie there just a few weeks before her death. They were new to the church, and since they didn't know many people there, Tom remembered the pastor from my church who had called with prayers when Natalie was in the hospital. Tom contacted Pastor Werner after Natalie's death and asked his advice on songs and Bible verses for the funeral. I was grateful that my church opened its arms to the Beards to help them through this horrific time.

Many friends and neighbors mingled outside before pouring into the church. Inside, everyone was weeping and sniffling as the minister spoke about Natalie's brief life and how she had, in such a short time, touched so many people.

"God says, 'Let the children come to me,'" he declared from the pulpit. "I have no answers why God took her home so soon."

Relatives of the Beards spoke and asked *Why?* I was wondering the same thing, with such overwhelming sadness that I thought the agonizing service would never end.

After the funeral, Dave and I trudged to the foyer and hugged friends and neighbors. Tom and Cindy avoided me, but I understood. My heart was filled with sorrow as I battled my need to hug and comfort them in some way. Suddenly, Dave grabbed my arm and led me aside.

A tiny, white casket was carried out of the sanctuary and brushed past me. It was too much for me to bear, and again I wept, picturing beautiful Natalie inside that airless box. Dave pulled me to him and walked me out a side door and back to our vehicle.

When we arrived at home, Dave and I changed into more comfortable clothes, then packed and headed to Hudson. We had a dinner meeting Saturday night about Dave's new job in Minneapolis, and I needed to hold Carrie and Allison, to share stories about their dolls, watch *Little Mermaid*…and to just keep them close to me.

***

The rest of October and most of November were a blur of packing and caring for the girls. The horror of Natalie's death was always in my thoughts, even as my own womb expanded with a new life inside.

The movers arrived in late November, along with a heavy snowfall. The stinging air whipped through our open doors as the movers packed our possessions into the cavernous van. I was both exhausted and relieved when the last piece of furniture was finally placed in the vehicle.

Dave and I settled the girls into our car and headed to my parents' house four hours away in Hudson. We were all looking forward to moving into our beautiful new house in Lakeville, Minnesota in January. I felt I needed to move forward with my life despite the horror of Natalie's death.

Our Christmas that year was subdued, since we weren't in our house yet and I was seven months pregnant. I managed to force a happy face for the girls, who were ecstatic over Santa Claus and eagerly expecting his slide down the chimney at Grandma and Grandpa's house.

But the shadow of Natalie's death still hovered over me. I wondered if the ache would ever lift. I hadn't read the autopsy report yet and I still feared that Natalie had choked from the bottle I'd propped for her that day. I needed to learn the cause of her death. Only then could I move on emotionally and try to achieve "normalcy" again.

Shortly after New Year's, we moved into our new home in Lakeville, Minnesota. Soon after, Dave got a call from Attorney Dale Peterson. Dave looked grim when he sat me down to tell me the news. "Dale said they are going to charge you with Natalie's death," Dave explained, a catch in his voice.

My worst fear had just been realized. The baby had choked and it was, after all, my fault. My body felt numb as my mind absorbed the shock of Dave's words.

"The preliminary autopsy report is back and the results are shocking," Dave said softly. He read from notes he'd jotted on a piece of paper. Apparently, Dr. Robert Huntington, the pathologist, had performed the autopsy and found that Natalie suffered subdural, subarachnoid and retinal hemorrhages. Dave and I didn't totally understand the technical medical jargon, but we did realize the baby had bleeding in the brain and the retinas of her eyes.

I shook my head in disbelief. How could this be? She had choked on her formula, hadn't she? I was the one who had picked her up and seen the formula dribble out of her nose and mouth. Now they're telling me she had brain injuries? My own brain was having trouble following what Dave was telling me.

"The pathologist declared that Natalie's injuries were so severe, they had to be caused by some intentional force equal to an automobile accident or a fall from a two-story building," Dave explained. "These three types of bleeds are considered a classic result of 'Shaken Baby Syndrome'."

What? Where was this coming from? I could not imagine how Natalie could have incurred such catastrophic injuries. "Shaken Baby Syndrome"? I had heard of that on the news, but nobody had shaken Natalie, at least not at my house!

Dave took my hand in his and I felt him trembling. He told me that Dale had said both the pathologist and Dr. Gregory Holman, the doctor on duty when Natalie was brought to the hospital, agreed that the injuries were so severe they had to have been inflicted just before the baby began showing symptoms. They determined that this meant the injury had occurred while Natalie was in my care!

Dave's face swam before me, and I gasped, "But I never hurt Natalie. I would never hurt a child. Shake a baby? Never!"

"I believe you," Dave said firmly. "It sounds like they're trying to pin this on somebody, and you were the last person with Natalie."

"She was at our house for less than one hour before she became limp," I said. "Do you really believe me? I did not hurt her. I told you exactly what happened that day and I'm telling the truth."

I felt indignation rise, but I also believed in our justice system. It wouldn't put an innocent mother in prison. Impossible!

"I can't believe this will ever go to trial," Dave agreed. "They have absolutely no evidence that you shook Natalie. It's purely circumstantial. They can't possibly charge you without evidence."

He told me that Dale recommended we contact Steve Hurley, an excellent defense attorney in Madison, Wisconsin. Afterward, I plunged into a tailspin of anxiety. Here I was with two daughters under age five, and was almost eight months pregnant with our third child. I could barely shift in my chair with the weight of my pregnancy. My babies needed me. How could I possibly deal with these atrocious accusations or undergo the trauma of a criminal trial? Dear God, what was going on here?

February arrived, living up to Minnesota's reputation for brutal winters, but now my body shivered from more than the cold. I forced myself to settle into our new house, meet new neighbors, and care for Carrie and Allison. But I was terrified for the baby inside me. What was the steady flow of fear and adrenaline doing to my unborn child?

Bitter cold moved in on the third week of February, and I awoke on the eighteenth to new snowfall lightly covering the ground. I arose, dressed Carrie for Sunday school, and off we headed to church. Our new friends patted my protruding stomach, knowing the baby was due any day. It felt as if we were really beginning a new life, with kind, loving people around us.

Then, on our drive home as we exited off the highway onto the Lakeville exit, I felt a strong cramp stab my side. *Hmm*, I thought, *the baby must be changing position.* However, as the day progressed, so did my contractions. By mid-afternoon we called my parents, who drove in from Hudson to watch the older girls.

At six o'clock, Dave drove me to the hospital, and in less than one hour, our adorable daughter, Jennifer Ann, arrived into this world. Dave and I wept, thrilled at the prospect of a new life, and new hope.

I was in the hospital for one glorious day, breathing in the softness and sweet fragrance of baby Jenny. Dave came to pick us up, and as we exited off the highway the light from a water tower caught my eye. Suddenly, tears began to flow. This should have been one of the happiest moments of my life, but the upcoming charges against me suddenly loomed large before me. How could this be happening to me? All I had done was to lovingly care for a baby. I looked at my beautiful, tiny Jenny all bundled up in her car seat and sent up a prayer that we would never be separated. "Please, God, send me a miracle," I whispered.

CHAPTER FOUR

The weeks after Jenny's birth were both blissful and harrowing. I cuddled my three healthy, beautiful girls close to me. They were all so young and needed their mother's touch, stability and guidance. But I was also breastfeeding, so shortly after giving birth I was hormonal and highly emotional about my pending legal battle.

Flowers continued to arrive at my door from concerned friends and neighbors from Waunakee, and I deeply appreciated the letters, cards, phone calls and prayers that poured in. Nobody could believe this was happening to me, and everyone thought it would be impossible to take me to trial. After all, I had a reputation for a deep love for children, and there was no witness—and no evidence—linking me to Natalie having been shaken.

I spoke with my attorney, Steve Hurley, on the phone several times and was still incredulous that I was being charged with first degree reckless homicide. It sounded so ugly—and in fact, it's the second most serious crime in the state of Wisconsin, right below first degree murder!

Steve and I had received only a brief, preliminary autopsy report, and I was still unaware of how Natalie had sustained such severe injuries. I ran the fateful morning through my mind a million times, focusing on that propped bottle as the culprit. But that was not reckless murder! And at that point, we had no detailed medical findings to offer an alternative scenario.

My arraignment was scheduled for March 21, 1996. I flipped through my closet, studying all the nice outfits I still owned from my working days, and hastily pulled an ivory-colored dress from the hanger. I have always eaten healthfully and exercised regularly. Now, under all the stress, I had to force myself to eat. After only three weeks since giving birth, I already fit into my regular clothes.

Dave and I loaded the kids into the car for the five-hour drive from our new home in Lakeville, Minnesota, back to our old neighborhood in Waunakee, Wisconsin. We dropped off Carrie and

Allie with some former neighbors, and tiny Jenny stayed with my friend, Betsy Adams.

Struggling to find strength and composure, I walked into the courthouse with Dave through a side door. Later, I learned that dozens of my friends were marching with picket signs out front supporting me. One affirmed: *We Love You, Audrey.*

My parents and relatives drove in from Hudson, and a few friends took time off from work to drive hundreds of miles from the Twin Cities to support me. My heart swelled with gratitude for every loving supporter out there.

I talked to my attorney before the arraignment, who instructed me to enter the courtroom just before the hearing, and then come to the front and sit at a table next to him. I was a wreck waiting outside the door, and when the time came to enter the room, my heart was pounding so hard I was certain everyone could see it hammering beneath my ivory dress. On one side of the room, I saw a window and a row of photographers with cameras pointed at me. Family and friends were packed into the rows of wooden seats. Dave gave my arm a squeeze as, on trembling legs, I managed to get to the table and slide into the seat next to Steve.

I felt almost out-of-body, awash in shock and disbelief. *Surely*, I thought, *these people will see they are wrong, and this horrible nightmare will soon end.*

Of course, I was totally ignorant of the American judicial system. I'd never had a run-in with the law--not even a traffic ticket! I'd always been a law abiding citizen who loved caring for children.

The session began in Dane County Circuit Court, Branch 11 with Honorable Judge Daniel Moeser presiding. Steve entered my "Not Guilty" plea.

My God, I thought. *Didn't anyone hear me say I did not do this? Why am I here?* I maintained my composure, but inside I was frantic, confused by all the legal jargon and the courtroom process. I was immensely thankful for Steve, who was knowledgeable and professional. I trusted his expertise.

The judge set a date for a "preliminary hearing." I had no

idea what that was. "Bail is set at five thousand dollars," he declared, and with the pounding of his gavel, the session was abruptly over.

Steve stood up and said, "Follow close behind me. I'll block the media from getting pictures."

We met Dave in the hallway, and he took me in his arms and embraced me. I fought back my tears-- I knew if I started crying I wouldn't stop for days.

We had known ahead of time about the five thousand dollar bond. My dear parents insisted on paying it--they would do anything to protect their only daughter from the madness surrounding her. After posting the bail, Steve sat down to talk with us.

"I now have the medical and the autopsy materials," he reported. "I'll comb through it all and talk with you very soon." Steve and I were eager to learn why I had been charged in Natalie's death.

As Dave and I left the courthouse, I was relieved not to see any cameras, and I noticed that Tom and Cindy Beard were also missing; they had not attended the arraignment. The pain surrounding this whole experience was extreme for everyone involved, especially since I was charged with first degree reckless homicide on what would have been Natalie's first birthday!

Dave and I were silent as we drove the fifteen minutes back to Waunakee. I asked him, "Why do they think they can charge me when I clearly told the authorities I wasn't guilty? Why do the doctors think I intentionally hurt Natalie?"

Dave and I picked up our precious Jenny, who was sleeping soundly in her car seat, and as I watched her slumber peacefully, my heart nearly burst with love. Her eight-pound body was so tiny!

We returned to Patti and Jeff Larson's house. The couple lived on our old street, Dorn Drive, where Natalie had fallen ill. Carrie and Allie swarmed into our arms as we entered Patti's house, eager to see their baby sister. Many of our friends gathered at the Larsons' to offer hugs, words of hope and support and I felt peace and solace just being among these loving supporters. Then, Jenny woke up and I lifted her into my arms, unable to bear the thought of losing her or her sisters.

We stayed for a few hours to visit with these caring friends, but Dave had to get back to work the next day in Minnesota and I wanted to be home again in my warm, secure nest with my babies and my husband. Of course, I knew this was only a fantasy. I was returning home as a person wrongly accused of the second worst crime in Wisconsin...recklessly killing a baby.

Once at home, a friend sent me a copy of the article that had appeared in the Wisconsin State Journal. The headline sickened me: *Baby Sitter Faces Infant-death Charge.* The article was actually fair and accurate and quoted several of my supporters. It stated that Cathy Frischmann of Waunakee had held a sign that said, *Audrey Edmunds, Gentle and Kind.* "I'm here to show support of Audrey. I think she's an upstanding and caring person," the paper quoted her as saying.

I had taught her daughter in my Sunday school class.

Barb Rowe said, "We think she's innocent. She's one of the most kind, gentle, considerate people we've ever met. Her own children are bright and happy people."

These comments warmed me and I reasoned that if others believed this was true, surely a jury would, too. I would be home less than a month before I was due back in Wisconsin for my preliminary hearing.

"That's where the state will briefly present its main reasons and evidence for charging you," my attorney Steve had explained. "If the judge thinks there is enough evidence against you, he will bind you over for a trial."

One night in early April, a booming clap of thunder awakened me from a deep sleep. I immediately heard the familiar patter of tiny footsteps running toward our bedroom and the door burst open as Carrie screamed, "Mommy!" Carrie had feared thunderstorms for years and she woke up and scurried into our room when they occurred.

I scooped her into bed with us and cuddled her next to me. "You are safe, my precious girl," I whispered into her ear. But I knew that wasn't true. She was actually in grave danger that her mother would be stolen from her life. I tried to hold back my tears as the rain outside pounded against the window.

On April 17th, we made the five-hour trek back to Wisconsin for the preliminary hearing. Once again, my supporters filled the courtroom; this time, they were all wearing yellow ribbons. Although I was still frightened and confused, I was curious to finally learn more about what had killed Natalie.

Waunakee Police Chief Robert Roberts was first on the stand and told the same story I remembered about arriving to my house after I had called 9-1-1. He explained that he'd found me hysterical and had asked me to leave the room because I was crying so loudly, he couldn't assess Natalie's condition.

He testified that Natalie had mucous around her mouth and that her eyes were fixed and dilated when he arrived, her breathing labored. When he'd asked me what happened, I had said the baby choked on formula.

"When I got Natalie on her side, additional formula came out of her mouth and onto the floor," Roberts testified. "I picked Natalie up and laid her in my arm, cradling her and gave her two upper back blows between the shoulder blades. Additional formula came out from Natalie's nose and mouth out on to the floor."

This information about the baby formula was disputed later, but the above is an exact quote from the transcript of the preliminary hearing.

When I heard him say it in court that day, my heart fluttered in fear, knowing I had left Natalie with a propped bottle before she went limp. But that was the only thing I was guilty of in Natalie's death. I had not shaken or struck her, and her injuries just didn't add up in my mind. Now, I was anxious to hear the medical testimony.

The next witness on the stand was Dane County Detective Dawn Johnson, one of the detectives who had interviewed me three days after Natalie's death. I recognized my statements that Natalie was crying when she had arrived at my home that morning and how I had tried to feed her, but she had eaten only a bit, and then fussed again.

Johnson testified how I took Natalie into the master bedroom and propped her up with a bottle to get her away from the other children's commotion in the kitchen. "Maybe that was upsetting Natalie," the detective said on the witness stand.

I wanted to stand up and object when Detective Johnson said that Natalie had been crying when I returned to the room to get her. I only remembered her whimpering, not full-out crying.

My attention perked up when Dr. Gregory Holman finally took the stand. He was the Director of Pediatric Emergency Services at the University of Wisconsin Children's Hospital and had treated Natalie when she was brought up from the emergency room that grim day. I remembered his call to me that day.

He testified that Natalie was on a ventilator when she was transferred into the pediatric intensive care unit from the emergency room around eleven o'clock in the morning. The emergency room doctors had told him Natalie suffered a cardio- pulmonary arrest, meaning she had stopped breathing and her heart had slowed to almost no pulse. Holman had performed various tests, but Natalie had no response to verbal or painful stimulation.

"Her pupils were fixed and dilated and the only sign of brain function that we were able to determine at that time was an occasional gasping respiration, a gasping breath," Holman testified.

I had always wondered what happened to Natalie at the hospital, and now it was being laid out before me. Dr. Holman said he realized Natalie had no signs of higher brain function that he could detect, and that all lower brain function was also gone, except for feeble attempts to breathe. When they administered oxygen through a breathing tube, along with a ventilator, her vital signs were restored to normal.

The first signs of chaos inside Natalie's tiny head appeared when Dr. Holman had peered into her brown eyes with an ophthalmoscope.

"I noticed there was blood in the back of her eyes, something we term 'retinal hemorrhages,'" he explained. At that point, he had rushed her in for a CAT scan to check for brain injuries. The scan showed that Natalie had been bleeding in and around her brain. It also showed bleeding just below the membrane that surrounds the brain, called a "subdural hematoma."

"She also had evidence of severe swelling of her brain cells. This was consistent with her brain being badly injured."

Dr. Holman testified that a respirator and heart medicine supported Natalie's life the rest of the day and into the evening. Holman called in a neurologist and in the early evening a cerebral flow study was ordered to test the blood flow to the brain.

"It showed no blood flow and was diagnosed as brain death,"

Dr. Holman said. The doctors talked with Tom and Cindy Beard and they agreed to take Natalie off life support. She died at nine o'clock that evening.

Assistant District Attorney Gretchen Hayward prosecuted my case. She was an imposing woman in her early-50s, and I was afraid of her from the start. Her voice and demeanor were cold and harsh; she made me feel guilty with almost every question or statement. Obviously, she was trying to convict me. I had never attended a trial before, but I'd watched them on television or in the movies. Now I was feeling the full brunt power of a damning prosecutor.

"What caused Natalie's death?" she demanded of Dr. Holman.

He replied that he was amazed by how quickly Natalie had progressed to brain death, which implied that Natalie had suffered a devastating injury.

"The injuries, retinal bleeding, severe brain swelling and bleeding in the brain are all consistent with what we would determine as high acceleration/deceleration forces applied to her."

He explained that this type of injury was common in high-speed vehicle crashes, and is also commonly seen in children who are shaken.

"Since Natalie was not in a car accident, it is your opinion that this is 'Shaken Baby Syndrome?'" Hayward asked carefully.

"Yes, "Shaken Baby Syndrome" is an injury that occurs to children usually less than six or seven months old. A child is held by the sides of the chest and shaken vigorously. Children this age have weak neck muscles. The head rolls back and forth, which tears blood vessels on the brain surface, called subdural hematomas."

Dr. Holman testified it would require an extremely high force, a very dramatic shaking to generate the injuries Natalie had incurred. He went on to say that the baby would not appear normal or make eye contact after such a severe shaking. In fact, she would not be aware of, or be able to respond to her environment at all. And she could not suck formula.

"I am certain it was "Shaken Baby Syndrome" and Dr. Robert Huntington (coroner) confirmed that in his autopsy report."

I was absolutely stunned at Dr. Holman's testimony. Extreme force shaking? My mind couldn't grasp the implications of his statement. How had Natalie received such extensive brain damage? It just made no sense, given the brief time I had shared with her that morning.

Then, the prosecutor asked the doctor about his call to me that morning. "Did Mrs. Edmunds tell you whether or not the child appeared normal when she arrived at her home that day?"

"She stated the child appeared to be in her normal state of health upon arrival," he responded.

I was relieved when Steve questioned Dr. Holman and quoted Dr. Huntington's preliminary autopsy report. The coroner had stated in his summary, "She died with signs of brain injury. The relatively confined areas of bleeding argue *against shaking*. This brain must be carefully studied before the case is signed out."

Wow! This seemed like a huge contradiction. Unfortunately, it was soon knocked down when we read the final autopsy report, in which the coroner changed his tune and decided to go along with the doctors' opinions. The final autopsy report stated that Natalie's injuries were consistent with "Shaken Baby Syndrome". As the doctors presented what they considered the *facts*, the medical evidence did indeed seem to stack up against me into an alarming heap.

It was I, Audrey Edmunds, mother of three, versus skilled doctors and a powerful police force. Detectives interviewed my four-year-old daughter, Carrie, who confirmed that she did not see Mommy hurt the tiny baby. Nobody, besides young children, was with me during the critical hour that Natalie was at my house. I was the only person on the earth who *knew* I had not shaken or injured that child. But was my word alone enough to save me? After the astonishing preliminary hearing, I wasn't so certain.

CHAPTER FIVE

Although I had strong support from friends and former neighbors in Waunakee, I was relieved to be back home, five hours away from the accusers. I could breathe easier and carry on my daily life without worrying that someone at Carrie's preschool or the grocery store was judging me.

It was impossible for Dave and me to explain to our small daughters exactly what we were facing, so we focused on maintaining our regular routine to keep them secure and stable. At the end of April, we celebrated Allie's second birthday. I put together a family party and baked a cake. The girls squealed with delight over the presents and revelry. It was my birthday, too, but I didn't feel much like celebrating. I had turned thirty-five, entering what should have been the prime of my life, with a wonderful husband, children, health, and a beautiful home. As I blew out the one candle on Allie's cake that was meant for me, all I could wish for was that this terrible nightmare would soon come to an end.

Unfortunately, my birthday wish did not come true. Instead, I actually plunged deeper into darkness. A few short weeks after our birthdays, Assistant District Attorney Gretchen Hayward dropped a new bomb: she motioned for a new bail hearing. My attorney called me to report that a woman named Johanna Evanoff had read about the charges against me in a newspaper and called the sheriff's department. She was now accusing me of hitting another toddler.

I was stunned at both the accusation and Hayward's motion. The motion stated that since the last bail hearing, Mrs. Evanoff had called authorities and said she "observed the defendant abuse a child who appeared to be two years old at the Waunakee Public Library during the winter of 1994 and 1995. She observed the defendant deliberately and forcefully hit the young child on the head with an approximately eight-by-eleven inch hardbound book. The child appeared stunned and began to cry. The defendant noticed she was being observed and acted like nothing happened and said something to the effect of, 'Let's keep that little shoe on' to the child," the prosecution motion stated.

I was absolutely staggered at the false allegation. Why on earth would this woman conjure up such a lie?

I vaguely knew her from seeing her about town and at the library, and we were always friendly and said hello to each other. She often brought her swarm of day care children and I gathered mine for story hour. My kids loved listening to the librarian read them a book. It was an organized event which was held in the basement of the library.

But clobbering a two-year-old over the head with a book? What on earth was she talking about? The only two-year-old in my care had been Jessica, and I would never hit a child in the head with a book "deliberately and forcefully" in front of so many people at the library's story hour? Had anyone else seen this happen? And if indeed I'd done this bizarre act, why hadn't she confronted me? Not only was her accusation absurd beyond belief, but now it was being used against me in a court of law!

Another mortar shell in the motion was a statement from my ex-husband, Pete, whom I'd married at the age of twenty-two. He told authorities that I physically and verbally abused him and had a "bad and violent temper." The motion quoted him as saying, "She looks nice and polished on the outside and has a good image and can be thoughtful and considerate. However, she has a private side where she can instantly snap."

I was dumbfounded at his audacity. True, we'd had a bumpy relationship and we definitely shared in some angry feuds. But we were never physically abusive to each other. Pete told authorities about one incident in particular when we were driving along the highway. He said I punched him so hard on the arm that he swerved off the road and feared we would crash--all this while his elderly grandmother cowered in the back seat.

I don't remember this incident, yet I can imagine slapping him on the arm. But Pete was six-foot-three and two hundred-ninety pounds. Could skinny one hundred-thirty-five pound me possibly have whacked this tank of a man hard enough to crash the car? Every married couple fights, and I'm sure heated arguments with a slap on the arm occur in countless homes this very moment. Of course I get angry at times. Show me one person on earth who doesn't!

Pete and I spent a lot of time with my parents and family, and none of them ever saw violence between us; instead, they were shocked by his statement to authorities. I came from a loving, stable home and did not want a marriage riddled with tension. I suggested counseling, but Pete refused and after three years of a difficult marriage, I divorced him. He never forgave me and we never had children together.

The day our divorce case went to court, Pete's attorney did not tell him about the hearing, and when he found out, Pete called me on the phone and screamed at me, rather than at his lawyer. He was so verbally abusive, I felt physically ill.

Now, after not talking to Pete for more than ten years, memories of that miserable marriage flooded back. I was saddened to the core that he was now so mean-spirited that he would lie to add fuel to the fire already stoked against me.

My attorney considered it sour grapes and the prosecution was barred from calling Pete to testify at my trial, but his lies broke my heart and I knew I could never trust him again.

Armed with these two strong "witnesses" and their allegations, Gretchen Hayward asked the judge for a new bail hearing, and moved to ban me from unsupervised contact with any children including my own daughters. Jenny was only three months old at the time and I was still breastfeeding.

Meanwhile, investigators were interviewing my friends and neighbors, who assured me that my accusers were on a witch hunt for anything negative they could find to destroy my character and credibility. Friends said one detective became frustrated when they shared only loving stories about me, and one friend told me Sheriff's Detective Dawn Johnson slapped her notebook shut and said, "I'm tired of hearing the same good things over and over about Audrey Edmunds."

They even sent detectives to Minnesota to dig up dirt about me, and my brother Wayne bristled with anger during his interrogation. Finally, he jumped to his feet and stormed out of the meeting. He drove straight to our house and sank down onto the couch in the living room.

"They tried to make me say you're a mean person, Audrey.

They aimed to shove words into my mouth. It was despicable."

My supporters stayed strong, and my attorney told me that Dino, who worked for a company that delivers quality food goods directly to the home, told Steve that he saw me many times in Waunakee and observed how caring I was with children. Dino said he often stopped by my house unannounced and never witnessed me mistreating children or looking stressed from the kids in my care.

His kindness brought tears to my eyes. To think that someone took the time to call my attorney just to say nice things about me! I was extremely grateful. I didn't realize at that time how important character witnesses would become. Though Dino did not testify at my trial, his support was consistent with that of all the others who had interacted with me daily and knew my true character. The person the prosecution was trying to create just did not exist.

Yet, detectives tried everything to fashion me into some kind of angry ogre. When they interviewed my four-year-old daughter, Carrie, they asked her, "What does your Mommy do when she gets frustrated?"

Carrie said I spanked her with my hand. She had always been a strong-willed child, but I considered her delightful and high spirited. I was consistent with discipline and, yes, Carrie got a few swats on the bottom, but not often. It was a far cry from child abuse.

I was starting to understand the judicial system. Doctors find brain injuries and eye bleeding in a baby who eventually dies. They theorize it is "Shaken Baby Syndrome". If this is true, somebody had to shake the baby. Since the baby, who was at my house for less than one hour, fell ill in my care, they concluded that I had shaken the baby.

They had no witnesses or physical evidence that I shook her, and she had no finger marks or bruises on her arms or torso, no broken bones (especially ribs) where I would have grabbed her so forcefully and shaken her with such violence that it would be equivalent to dropping her from a two to four-story building. She had no neck injuries from this alleged brutal shaking, and I had firmly and repeatedly told them that I had not shaken the baby.

But the prosecution had pointed an accusing finger at me, and now they needed to come up with some kind of damning evidence that would convince a jury that I was a violent woman who could snap in an instant.

First degree reckless homicide is so heinous a charge that the prosecution must prove beyond a reasonable doubt that: 1. I shook Natalie so violently it could cause death. 2. I knew my violent actions could cause death. 3. I had utter disregard or extreme indifference to the value of Natalie's life.

If this could be proven, I would face up to forty years in prison.

This was clearly why my accusers had stacked up fifteen years of alleged violent behavior and laid it at my doorstep. Here's the list:

I *allegedly* clobbered a kid with a book.

My vengeful ex-husband *alleged* that I was a horrid wife.

I spanked my child.

It certainly didn't seem enough to convince a jury beyond a reasonable doubt that I was a vicious, disgusting person capable of murdering an innocent baby with no care or regard for her life.

A hearing was set for May 30, 1996. Fortunately, my attorney was able to weaken the accusations considerably. In a sworn affidavit, Jessica's mother, Chris Henning, described an interview with a detective after Mrs. Evanoff alleged I had hit Jessica in the library. Chris firmly stated, "I have trusted and would still trust Audrey Edmunds to care for my children." She even took Jessica to a pediatrician, who confirmed there was no evidence of child abuse.

Nobody ever asked Jessica if I hit her because she was only two years old at the time of the alleged incident and Chris has absolutely no memory of Jessica ever being upset in my care.

Even more shocking, Evanoff actually recanted her statement. Now she said she'd been helping children into their coats that day at the library when she heard a loud boom. She looked up and saw me holding a book above Jessica's head, but she admitted that she never actually saw me hit Jessica. She just surmised that I did because she heard a boom!

Mrs. Evanoff told authorities in court documents she was miffed that I was being kind to the child after she thought I had struck the toddler hard, and was shocked that I was so friendly on the elevator ride up from the library basement.

I'd been kind and friendly because I had not bashed a two-year-old girl on the head with a book! I had no idea she'd even suspected me of something so deplorable.

At the May hearing, I was relieved that the judge did not increase my bail or order only supervised visits with my children. But he did impose a new constraint. To prevent any possibility that I could "snap" again, he insisted that I take an hour's break from my children if Dave was not home during the day.

Of course, Dave was away every weekday, so instead of relieving stress, it compounded it for me. Now, I had to impose on friends and neighbors to watch the girls for that hour while I left the house, drove around, shopped a bit, and found other things to do. I really wanted to be at home, supervising naps and starting dinner, and on some days I drove to Hudson so my parents could help.

It was extremely humiliating and demanding of all of us, but of course I complied completely. Every day I juggled my "hour off", filled out a form confirming that I'd done so, and mailed it once a week to the Dane County Courthouse.

Summer was a tumult of emotions. I tried to stay faithful to God and trust that soon the truth would prevail and that a jury would find me innocent. First degree reckless homicide would probably mean a maximum security prison and I couldn't picture myself behind bars in a tiny cell.

I had never even dreamed that this nightmare would drag me so far from my family, but my attorney warned me that juries are unpredictable and I had to face up to the possibility that I could actually lose the case.

These thoughts scourged me that summer as I tried to create an atmosphere of happiness and normalcy for the girls. I continued to decorate our new house, adding a window treatment in the kitchen and accessories here and there. By doing so, I was reinforcing my prayers that I would be there to enjoy our beautiful home with my family.

My travel was not restricted, so for Labor Day weekend we drove through Wisconsin and Upper Michigan down to Saginaw, Michigan to visit our dear friends, Mark and Jill. Dave and Mark had been best buddies since college. Mark met Jill, and Dave met me, around the same time in the late 1980s, and although we lived far apart, we got together when we could for enjoyable double dates. Dave was the best man at their wedding in May, 1988, and three weeks later, on June 3rd, Mark stood up for Dave in our wedding. We were living parallel lives and even had our children about the same time.

After Dave and I moved to Toledo, we were only a two-and-a-half hour drive from Mark and Jill, and we burned up the highway back and forth for barbecues and weekends together. Our favorite tradition was Labor Day at Mark and Jill's. When we started this custom, we had four children between us under the age of three. Jill and I loved caring for the toddlers and infants while Dave and Mark played golf.

Then, the men would take over so Jill and I could shop at their local outlet stores, where we'd buy matching outfits for Carrie and Lindsay, Jill's daughter. I have so many wonderful memories of taking the kids to the farm market to ogle pumpkins, watermelons and fall flowers. We always served corn-on-the-cob and as the kids got older, they had shucking duty. We took lots of pictures.

I was excited to continue our tradition that difficult year and Jill hugged me with concern. She was a TV news reporter and had covered many trials in her journalism career under the name, Jill Wellington. She was a perfect sounding board for my situation. Although she wished she could use her journalistic skills to help me, she was too far away. However, her writing ability would become very important later on.

I tried to keep things light and positive over that Labor Day weekend, but the trial was looming closer. Jenny was six months old and I hugged her constantly, not wanting to miss a moment of her sweetness. The pictures taken of me that weekend show me as a stressed mother with a drawn face and dark circles under my eyes.

We hugged Jill and Mark goodbye at the end of the holiday and headed back home. I was exhausted when we finally arrived, and Dave and I tucked the girls into bed, knowing that tomorrow would be a special day: Carrie's first day of kindergarten.

I have a vivid memory of that next morning, which should have been an exciting and happy milestone for my first child. Instead, it was filled with heartache for me. After I hugged and kissed her goodbye, I watched Carrie run down the hill in our front yard to hop on the school bus. I was wearing dark sunglasses to hide the tears that flooded my eyes. How could a little five-year-old lose her mother? I would have perished if I'd lost mine at that age.

Carrie needed me so much, and I couldn't imagine missing the day my other two daughters hopped on the school bus for the first time. And I was going through this hell because a prosecutor wanted to win a case on my back, thus neatly putting a child's mysterious death into the "Case Closed" file!

Yet, no one seemed to be doing exactly that: finding out what had actually killed Natalie.

CHAPTER SIX

That fall, Allie and I waited excitedly for Carrie to leap off the school bus each day. She adored being the star as we welcomed her home with hugs and kisses. Some days she stayed home and played with us, but other times she scooted off for fun with the neighbor kids. She was growing more independent and learning a lot at school, but everyone knows an emerging blossom needs sturdy roots. Carrie needed her mother in every way.

I enjoyed helping out in Carrie's classroom, reading stories to the children. I had always dreamed of my daughters entering school and me assisting in their classrooms.

At Carrie's first parent-teacher conference, I confided in her teacher, Mrs. McGlade, about my circumstances. I wanted her to understand my family's situation so she could support Carrie if the time came. She told me she had worked in a hospital before she became a teacher and knew a little about "Shaken Baby Syndrome". To my relief, Mrs. McGlade was kind and compassionate and welcomed me as a contributing parent in Carrie's class at any time.

One of my favorite activities was baking and decorating cookies with my daughters. They created a cheerful mess as they helped roll out the dough on the kitchen table and stamp out various shapes. After baking, Carrie and Allie smeared them with colorful icing and dotted them with sprinkles. Jenny was now seven months old, and happily sat in her high chair playing with plastic cookie-cutters. The girls often begged me to bake cookies, and each time they did, my heart ached, wondering if these special bonding moments would soon come to an end.

The burden I was carrying went beyond my emotional fragility; in addition, my legal bills were steadily mounting. The cost to hire Steve Hurley to defend me was fifty thousand dollars, far beyond our means. Dave's employer was wonderfully supportive and generously loaned us the money. I was deeply touched and appreciative when friends, relatives and people we didn't even know sent contributions to help cover our legal and travel costs. Dave was blessedly supportive, saying he didn't care how long it took to pay off the loan because getting me vindicated was priceless.

Twice before the trial, the prosecution offered me plea bargains. Steve Hurley explained the process to me. "You can enter a plea of 'no contest'," he said. "This means you are not declaring guilt or innocence."

I discussed each of the plea offers with Dave, but they never specifically stated the length of the prison term. Steve explained the offers and told me possible consequences if I did or did not take the pleas. Unfortunately, he could not give me a clear picture of what would actually happen. My attorney neither encouraged nor discouraged me from any decision, saying the choice was mine.

Because I knew I did not shake or injure Natalie, I couldn't now lie and offer even a hint that I might have abused that baby. I was profoundly frightened of spending any time in prison, but both Dave and I believed there was no valid evidence to convict me. To uphold my honesty and integrity, I firmly rejected both plea bargains. I chose to go before a jury of my peers, feeling strongly that they would discern the truth and that I would be freed to go back to the life I loved.

One obvious question arose during those months leading up to the trial, and I learned that others were wondering the same thing. The prosecution's defining case against me was a specific set of catastrophic brain injuries that they declared, "Shaken Baby Syndrome". The name itself implies that someone shook the baby.

Since I was certain I was not the monster who had flown into a rage and shook that baby with as much force as a car crash, the glaring question was: Who did? The only other possible shakers with access to Natalie before she was dropped off at my house the day she died were her parents, Tom and Cindy Beard.

My supporters and I were outraged that investigators never seemed to have considered the possibility that Natalie's parents could have shaken the baby, rather than me.

The Sheriff's detectives quickly latched onto the doctors' "Shaken Baby" label and theorized that if Natalie had been violently shaken, she would have fallen limp immediately. Even though the Beards had Natalie for four days before Cindy dropped her off at my house, and the baby was with me for less than one hour, the doctors were adamant that her injuries had to occur in my care, because that's where the baby fell unconscious.

I was still thoroughly confused about the "Shaken Baby" diagnosis. Since I knew I had not shaken her, I began to analyze Tom and Cindy Beard as possible suspects, looking for any evidence that they could indeed have shaken Natalie.

I started with the morning Natalie fell limp. Cindy told me she had been up with her two times the night before and that she would not feed well. She also refused her morning bottle, and when she arrived at my home she was inconsolable and continued to cry after Cindy left. I didn't think much of her crying that morning because Natalie was often fussy. I even told Dr. Holman when he called that day that she was normal when she arrived. *Normal* for Natalie was crying.

But thinking back and studying that morning carefully in my mind, the scenario certainly made it possible that Natalie had been injured *before* she was brought to my house. Why didn't detectives investigate that possibility?

My friends and neighbors were abuzz with this type of analysis. My dear neighbor Patti Larson used to walk with me at five-thirty in the morning before our husbands left for work. Her daughters, Alyssa and Erin, are the same ages as Carrie and Allison, and Patti also babysat other children in her home. We walked Alyssa and Carrie to preschool each morning and were often together with our daycare broods.

I remember Patti telling me that Natalie was overly fussy. A few times, she offered to hold Natalie and try to comfort the crying baby. Patti pointed out to me that Natalie's motor skills were delayed and abnormal, and said she never saw Natalie roll over on her own. She'd always thought it was overly solicitous of me to pad the stroller and be careful of bumps when we took walks together. I knew if I didn't, that Natalie would start to scream.

"She's a very delicate child," Patti said "I have never seen you handle her with anything but patience and care. Why aren't they investigating the parents or grandparents?"

Natalie's father Tom was about six feet tall and lanky. His day job was with CUNA Mutual Insurance, but his passion was music and he played keyboard and guitar in a local band with some buddies.

Tom was friendly to me the few times he came to my house. He'd dropped off Natalie only twice, and the second time was the morning after Cindy was out of town overnight for work. He'd called me before seven o'clock in the morning asking if he could bring Natalie early so I could feed her the bottle and I had agreed.

After Natalie died, I learned that the night before this incident, Tom was home alone with the baby. He called the hospital shortly before ten o'clock saying he was having a difficult time dealing with Natalie's crying and was desperate for help getting her to sleep.

The hospital staff advised him to leave the house for a few minutes so he could calm down and relax. This call is documented in Natalie's medical records.

Another time, Tom picked up Natalie at my house after work. She was in the kitchen propped in her walker with blankets because she couldn't hold herself upright yet at the age of six months.

Tom walked towards her and then stopped. "How do I pick her up from that?" he asked, looking confused.

I reached down, lifted her out and handed Natalie to Tom, surprised at how little understanding Tom had of his own baby.

Vague comments about Tom filtered down to me in the neighborhood. I had no idea if they were true, but wished that police would investigate the possibility that someone else shook baby Natalie.

More damning information about Tom came when Natalie was in the hospital. Medflight pilot Scott Tish, who flew a dying Natalie to the hospital, saw Tom arrive at the emergency room parking lot. He observed that Tom did not appear distraught and walked at a normal pace, rather than rushing. Tish said Tom displayed an odd lack of panic, and inside the emergency room, Tish had heard Tom talking to Cindy. He noted that neither parent sounded at all alarmed.

Tish felt their behavior was abnormal, in view of their daughter's serious condition.

The hospital chaplain, John Emmart, said in a statement that, both Tom and Cindy had been "highly guarded" at the hospital, barely expressing grief. The chaplain said while their daughter lay dying, Tom Beard appeared afraid to enter Natalie's room. Once inside, neither parent's demeanor changed. According to the chaplain, the father stood three feet behind the mother with his hands stuffed into his pockets, rather than touching his daughter. A nurse on duty told my attorney that the first time she saw Cindy cry was with me. Waunakee Police Sergeant Kevin Pendl later stated that Tom Beard was nervous, fidgety and under great duress when he met with the police at six that evening, just hours before his daughter died. Of course, that could be explained by the terrifying situation, but Sergeant Pendl did make this observation.

These are all observations written in court documents, but I have no idea if the parents were really just in shock.

I recalled that on my own visit to the hospital the afternoon Natalie fell ill, Tom never left his parents to ask me any questions, or to talk with Dave and me.

Cindy was tall and slender and I had always considered her quite meek. She was very soft-spoken. Even though she had an excellent job as a designer for American Family Insurance in Madison, I felt she carried the burden of caring for their daughter.

Two months after Natalie died, Tom and Cindy quietly moved to another town. There was never a *For Sale* sign in their yard, but one day a moving van showed up and they were gone. They never contacted me again.

I was quite saddened and bewildered by the many statements against Tom Beard but had to ask myself, were these parents trying to hide something? Even worse, if they had done something to injure Natalie and cause her death, how could they let me take the blame? Surely they knew the hell I was going through, and the fact that I could be locked in a state prison for forty years! Who, with any conscience, could take a mother away from her three little girls to save their own hides?

With the frightening medical "proof" of "Shaken Baby Syndrome", I was obviously trying to figure out WHO SHOOK THE BABY. But just like the accusations against me, mine against the Beards' were just as faulty.

Meanwhile, my trial was scheduled to begin on Monday, November 18, 1996, just ten days before Thanksgiving. I was anxious to get the trial over with to get that massive burden off my shoulders--I was still hopeful that the truth would set me free.

Steve instructed me before the trial not to let negative or false implications distract me, but when I agreed, I actually had no idea how difficult this request would become during the trial.

We arranged to stay with friends in Waunakee for what we presumed would be a week-long trial.

The night before we left for Wisconsin, I lay in bed and sent up a heartfelt plea to God: "Please let the truth prevail." I hoped and prayed that He was listening.

CHAPTER SEVEN

Monday morning, the first day of the trial, I awoke with a sense of relief that the end of this nightmare was probably in sight. Of course, I had no idea what would confront me as I sat at the defense table. Newspaper headlines declared this a major trial, and I was accused of murdering a baby. I knew I was innocent so I never took that ugly charge to heart. I felt that my integrity would keep me strong.

I am still grateful to our friends, John and Barb Rowe, for opening their home to us. John is a doctor and pilots his own plane. Their lovely, spacious house was built on the Waunakee airport runway, and it would become headquarters for my family and our supporters during the trial.

That morning, I donned a blue dress, but in my fearful state, I could barely lift my arm to brush my hair. As Dave and I kissed our three little girls goodbye, they had no idea they could possibly lose their mother

At eight o'clock in the morning, I sat at the defense table with my attorney, Steve Hurley. I felt awkward with news cameras pointed at me and reporters poised with pens and notebooks. Jury selection began and proceeded smoothly, but I did not understand all the attorneys' questions for the jury candidates. When that lengthy process was completed, Judge Moeser intimidated me by reading a list of one hundred possible witnesses for my trial. Obviously, it was going to be bigger than I had imagined!

Later that afternoon, the courtroom bustled as Judge Moeser reserved extra seating for my large faction of about sixty relatives, friends and church members, all clamoring for a good view of the opening arguments. I was thankful to all of them and felt a fiery sense of support when they greeted me with hugs and best wishes.

The warm feeling cooled abruptly, however, when the newly seated jury filed in, the judge slammed down his gavel, and the trial that would determine my fate began. First at the podium was my nemesis, prosecutor Gretchen Hayward, and I braced myself for her opening statement.

Ms. Hayward began by taking the jury on a moment-by-moment account of Cindy's morning the day Natalie died. The prosecutor said the baby seemed normal and "evidence will show she took an alert, beautiful child" to my house.

I was taken aback when Hayward said the Beards were concerned about what level of care I was giving Natalie. She claimed that from the time they had brought her to my home, Natalie's fussiness had increased. When Cindy had dropped the baby off in the morning, it wasn't unusual for Natalie to cry, she added. She didn't mention that the Beards knew Natalie was colicky. No, the baby was supposedly unhappy because of me.

"It became a real concern," Hayward said to the jury. "The baby had never cried like that before."

Hayward theorized that I was highly stressed from trying to handle my own kids and dealing with the pressure of an unplanned pregnancy. I hated hearing that term "unplanned pregnancy," since all three of our children were meant to be and welcomed with love into our family. In addition, my husband's employer had transferred him and he now worked out of town. To top it off, she concluded, I was also caring for another neighborhood child.

Hayward's theory was that I had cracked under the additional tension of Natalie's fussiness and lack of feeding that morning. Then, in a dramatic gesture, Hayward shook her fist at the jury and told the panel that I had I shaken Natalie in a fit of fury and frustration, making the baby's brain "slosh back and forth within her skull."

Hayward firmly stated Natalie died of "Shaken Baby Syndrome" caused by an enraged adult...me! "Doctors can't tell you when it occurred, but they can tell you when it didn't occur," she proclaimed. "It didn't occur before Natalie was handed over to the defendant, because if it had, she would not have been handed over as a normal infant. She would have been a lifeless little baby."

Hayward's rendition certainly bore no resemblance to the actual events in my home that morning. In fact, her scenario was a blatant falsehood the state had fabricated to blame me, the designated perpetrator. It wasn't based on the truth in any way, shape or form. What the prosecution said happened at my house...did not happen!

How I wanted to leap to my feet and shout to the jury, "She's lying!" Instead, I sat there as *composed* as I could pretend to be, feeling my heart sink like a stone. If the jury was going to believe these lies, I *was* in trouble. I was relieved when Gretchen Hayward finally finished.

Steve then rose and grasped my hand in his. "This is Audrey Edmunds. She is a good and patient woman."

I had to suppress tears. I needed this man to defend me and state the truth. It was a relief to hear his words, revealing the facts of the case, not the prosecutor's fantasies.

"No one will ever say they saw Audrey Edmunds do anything as dramatic as what the state just described to you," he told the jury. "She did not care for extra children in her home because she lacked money. She was only paid $2.50 an hour. She did it because she loves children and has been babysitting since she was nine years old."

Steve stated that doctors disagree about how long it takes to see the effects of "Shaken Baby Syndrome", and suggested someone else could have shaken Natalie before she arrived at my house. He ended his opening statement with these words, "No one will say Audrey mistreated Natalie that day or any other day. Instead, the state will show you evidence that is nothing more than their opinions of what happened."

Steve's eloquent closing line left me peaceful as we left the courthouse on that frightening opening day of my trial.

***

The next morning I was back at the defense table with Steve. Before the jury was seated, Judge Moeser ran through some motions. Once again, I was confused about the court proceedings as the two sides sparred about admitting pictures of a supposedly healthy and happy Natalie taken two days before she died. Steve protested, saying they would needlessly prejudice the jury. Judge Moeser declined to rule on it.

Just before nine o'clock, the jury filed in and the judge read through his instructions for the panel. I was heartened when he said, "While it is your duty to give the defendant the benefit of every reasonable doubt, you are not to search for doubt. You are to search for the truth."

The jury *had* to see the truth. That was my greatest hope.

First on the stand was Natalie's mother, thirty-four-year-old

Cindy Beard. She talked about Natalie being a fussy baby from birth when she had difficulty breastfeeding, and admitted that the infant was hungry and cried all the time.

The baby improved after switching to formula, however, and Cindy returned to work leaving Natalie with Kay Hinck, another day care provider in Waunakee. Cindy testified that Natalie was happy at Kay's house, but she cried at home in the evenings. Cindy suspected she had colic.

She then spoke of how she took primary care of Natalie, including feedings, baths and getting up with her at night. "I didn't mind, I enjoyed it," she said. "Tom did all the other things around the house." She described a lively rapport between Daddy and baby, with Tom cooing and playing with Natalie.

Cindy testified that Kay could not watch Natalie starting in September, so Cindy began looking for a new daycare and heard about me. She described her visit to my home and how she'd interviewed me.

"I asked Audrey how she felt about corporal punishment and she said she didn't believe in it. I was glad, because I don't either."

I frowned. I didn't remember discussing corporal punishment with Cindy at all. Natalie was only five months old at the time, so it was not an issue.

Natalie first came to my house on September 6, 1995. Cindy said she immediately noticed that the baby cried when she handed her over to me before work and wailed when she picked her up in the evening.

She testified that on the second day Natalie was in my care, she noticed a rash on the baby's head and asked me about it.

"Audrey said, 'I probably should have told you. Natalie got hit in the head with a piano toy in the same location as the rash.' I looked, but there wasn't any lump or bruise. It was a rash."

I remembered Cindy asking me about the rash, but didn't recall seeing it myself. I told Cindy that Natalie got bumped in the head that day with a small wobble toy; it was certainly not a toy piano. Two-year-old Jessica had the toy in her hand and walked over by Natalie and plopped it on her forehead. I saw this happen and picked up Natalie, took her into the kitchen and held her closely.

After a few minutes she stopped crying. This left a small pink mark on Natalie's head. It was a minor incident, but I was honest with Cindy and told her about it when she picked Natalie up that afternoon. She did not say she was concerned at the time.

Then Cindy said she noticed a quarter-size bruise on Natalie's right temple after the baby's fourth day with me. She showed the jury a picture of Natalie with this bruise.

"I took the picture a few days later because we dressed Natalie up in a Badger outfit. We were going to a friend's house to watch the Badger game." Cindy explained that she'd taken the picture to show the outfit, not the bruise.

I was uncomfortable when Cindy talked about other marks she noticed on Natalie the first week of October. I had never seen them and Cindy never mentioned them to me.

"There were some small spots on her bicep that looked like little pinch marks. They weren't a bruise or a scratch. Almost like bleeding under the skin...really small little marks."

"Did you notice anything else?" Hayward asked.

"I noticed a scratch underneath her jaw line. It looked like a fingernail could have scratched her. It was small."

I squirmed inside listening to her describe minor, common injuries. Nobody breezes through childhood without mundane bumps and bruises. Now they were shining a glaring spotlight on Natalie's. I couldn't figure out why Cindy was putting so much emphasis on this now, yet had never discussed them with me. I cringed as Cindy elaborated on minute issues as the jury drank it all in.

I was decidedly annoyed when Cindy testified that Natalie usually wept when she dropped her off at my house, which she hadn't done with Kay. With the minor injuries and crying, Cindy said she worried that I was not properly supervising their daughter. She told the jury that she talked to Tom about quitting her job, taking Natalie out of my care, and staying home with her.

"We were short-staffed at work," Cindy said. "So I told my supervisor I would gradually cut back my hours until I was working only mornings in December."

Cindy testified she called Kay, hoping she would baby-sit for Natalie again, and Kay had agreed to take Natalie starting at the end of October.

It was hard to sit and listen to this testimony, since Cindy had never told me she was unhappy or concerned about my care of Natalie. As a parent myself, if I felt uncomfortable with a daycare provider, I would certainly share it with the caregiver. And in Cindy's case, she was well aware of Natalie's neediness and had told me she often pushed Natalie around her house in a stroller, trying to calm her.

Cindy knew the truth about Natalie's crying because it had happened in her own home. Several times, Cindy had arrived to pick her up at my house to find Natalie sleeping in her car seat. As Cindy lifted the infant carrier, Natalie would startle and let out a yell.

The reason Cindy had called Kay was actually because I'd informed her that I was moving and that she needed to make other child care arrangements. But the jury didn't hear that. The jury only heard Cindy chatting about how she and Tom adored their baby and enjoyed watching her grow and thrive. The jury members also watched the home video she'd shot of Natalie two days before she died. My heart ached as I watched the baby on that tape. The jury was very attentive during the four minutes they watched Natalie lying on her back wiggling her feet at a mobile of animals hanging above her, cooing and giggling. I was heartsick at the loss of Natalie.

Yet, I thought it was highly prejudicial to show pictures and videos of a smiling Natalie to the jury. Of course, her parents had taken photos of her when she was happy. What kind of parent snaps a picture of a crying baby? The photographs and video didn't show that Natalie was more frequently fussy than she was happy. Instead, the prosecution and Cindy were painting an inaccurate picture of Natalie's ongoing colic problem.

It was while I watched that video that fear stabbed me, hard. Perhaps the truth I desperately wanted the jury to consider would not be the *truth* I knew was accurate. The prosecution was arming itself to create a very different *truth* about Audrey Edmunds. When the judge called for a break around ten-thirty, I was frightened to my core--and the trial was only beginning.

***

After the break and before the jury was called back, the judge and lawyers began to discuss the issue of the 9-1-1 tape. The prosecution wanted to play it for the jury, claiming the tape clearly showed how upset I was, as well as the fact that Natalie's condition was deteriorating quickly.

Steve argued it would prejudice the jury and he thought the state wanted to play it for very different reasons.

"I would expect the state will bring up the 9-1-1 tape in closing arguments and infer guilt on Audrey for her emotional reaction and the quality of her child care," Hurley said.

Hayward responded, "It's the best evidence of how this child appeared at the time and how the defendant was relating to this child under a charge of recklessness, which is what the charge is."

This statement shocked me. The prosecution was concocting the charge of recklessness; and yes, of course I was screaming with fear on that tape. A baby's life was in my hands and I was not medically trained to help her. Wouldn't this confirm the fact that I did possess human compassion and had made a valiant effort to save her?

However, Assistant Prosecutor Hayward was saying I was terrified because "I had just severely shaken baby Natalie."

Judge Moeser considered both sides' arguments and decided to allow the prosecution to play the 9-1-1 tape. My attorney asked the judge to ban the state from ever suggesting that my hysteria implied guilt.

Hayward immediately objected and the judge ruled he would consider my attorney's motion before closing arguments. Now I had another damaging statement hanging over me for the rest of the trial.

Steve approached the judge privately and asked, without the jury present, why the judge had barred him from bringing up Tom and Cindy's limited reactions at the hospital that night. Steve had lined up witnesses to testify that the parents were oddly calm when they saw their dying daughter. Wasn't it only fair that, if the jury got to examine my hysteria, Natalie's parents' strangely guarded demeanor was worth exploring?

However, the judge said the parents' behavior was unrelated to my own, since it occurred after Natalie had been stabilized in the hospital. He also barred Steve from presenting these witnesses to their odd behavior, which made no sense to me. Why would the judge forbid the jury from hearing all angles of this story? Once again, it felt like statements that would help my case were being withheld from the jury.

With the jury back in the box, Cindy resumed her testimony, describing the morning of Natalie's death and how the baby had cried three times the night before and wouldn't eat. The next morning, Natalie still would not feed well and when they arrived at my doorstep, the baby began to cry.

I didn't know if I was the only one who caught it, but Cindy's description did not mesh with Hayward's assertion that Cindy had brought a normal child to my home that morning. Cindy's account of Natalie howling that morning was pretty much what I remembered, too.

Finally, Steve got his chance to cross-examine Cindy. We quickly learned that all was not serene in the Beard home. Steve honed in on Cindy's primary care of the baby while Tom took care of the house.

"You also had cleaning people in your home and a lawn service?"

"Yeah, we had cleaning help and two neighbor boys came over and clipped the lawn."

"And Natalie would stress out Tom?"

"Yeah, I guess you could describe it as that," Cindy testified.

Cindy also confirmed she was so concerned about Tom's tension around Natalie that she questioned having another baby. She also revealed that Tom suffered from migraine headaches and was often away from home with his rock band, his friends or was watching sports.

Once Cindy worked late, and Tom had wanted to watch a football game, so she hired a babysitter to watch Natalie. I was glad the jury got to hear a bit about Tom Beard's attitudes from his own wife.

I was also happy when Steve asked Cindy about Natalie's trivial scratches and bruises.

"You have had minor mishaps with Natalie, too," Steve stated.

"Yes," Cindy answered. She told about a time at home when Natalie struck her head on a toy gym, and another time Cindy had lost her grip and Natalie slipped in the bathtub, grazing the side of her head on the porcelain.

"Do you remember informing Audrey one day after you took her there that Natalie was going through a phase of aggressively shaking objects and hitting herself?"

"Yes."

"So you recommended that Audrey give her soft toys?"

"That's correct."

I was beginning to understand how this trial was going to play out for me. When the assistant prosecutor questioned the witness, I would be shocked, angry and frightened. Then Steve would share the truth with the jury and calm me down. This pattern wove in and out during the trial.

I must say this about Cindy Beard on the witness stand. As a fellow mother, I felt deep compassion for her. I thought she held up well. My heart almost broke when Hayward asked her to hold and describe Natalie's soiled outfit—the one she'd worn the day she died. Paramedics had slashed her tiny shirt down the front in an effort to save her. No mother should have to endure such sorrow.

As the jury broke for lunch around noon, the attorneys, the judge and I stayed in the courtroom for a special hearing to determine if Johanna Evanoff would be allowed to testify against me about the alleged library incident.

Mrs. Evanoff, with her short, sandy-colored hair, took the witness stand and told the judge about a morning at the Waunakee Public Library in the winter of 1994-95. Well, actually, she couldn't remember if it was that winter or the year before. She testified she'd been caring for seven children between the ages of one and five, helping them into coats and shoes.

Suddenly, she recalled, she heard a "huge boom," looked up, and saw me with a book held flat over the head of a two-year-old. The only two-year-old with me was Jessica. Mrs. Evanoff said I had the hardbound book firmly in my hand and was lifting the book up. It was obvious to her I had just struck this child.

"What did the little girl do after she was struck in the head?" the prosecution asked.

"It was like a little quiver of her head...just a little bit... then she looked kind of stunned, then she cried."

"Did she appear injured?"

"No. Hmm-mm, no. But I worried that her neck could have been smashed."

I was stunned at Johanna's speculation about this incident. I had to really think back on the time I saw Mrs. Evanoff in the library at story hour. I do remember seeing her, but since I had never struck a child with a book, I didn't know what she was talking about.

She testified she did not actually see it happen, and I stared Joanna in the eye, willing her to tell the story accurately, but she avoided looking at me. The only thing I can think happened is that I was holding a book, and that hand was over Jessica's head. Two-year-olds cry for many minor reasons. She could have been tired, or not wanting to leave the library. I don't even remember her crying.

She went on to say she was upset about the incident and told her husband that evening, speculating that a doctor should check the little girl for neck injuries. She claimed on the stand that the worry actually kept her awake at night.

Johanna Evanoff was a former teacher. If she was truly concerned that I'd abused a child right in front of her and the librarians, why hadn't she said anything to me or another authority who could have stepped in and helped Jessica?

I was even more appalled when the judge ruled that Mrs. Evanoff could testify. I knew her dramatic story, another false ploy the DA used to try to make me appear hostile, would be a huge blow to my case.

I had no idea how right I was.....

CHAPTER EIGHT

After the break, Jessica's dad, Jim Henning, took the witness stand. He testified that when he'd arrived that morning with his daughter, Natalie was crying in her car seat on the kitchen table. He hadn't seen her; he just heard her.

"Was that abnormal?" Hayward asked.

"No. Every day that I can remember taking Jess to Audrey's, if Natalie was there, she was crying."

"Do you recall what kind of cry it was that day?"

"The kind of cry where the child's feelings are hurt, as opposed to crying out of pain."

He also testified that I showed "terrific patience" with Natalie, and his own three kids "loved me to death."

I was a bit reassured after Jim testified, but a new drama exploded after his turn on the witness stand. The 9-1-1 tape of my call for help was played for the jury. The moment I heard my own hysteria, my mind shot back in time to those terrifying moments.

Me: "I can't get any life out of her…she's warm, but she's lifeless," I screamed into the phone. "Please, God, please, God! Oh, pleeeeease!"

Dispatcher: "Calm down and help her. Is there anything in her mouth?"

Me: "Milk is coming out of her mouth."

Dispatcher: "Is she breathing?"

Me: "Oh, oh, my God! I don't know! I don't know!"

Dispatcher: "Take a deep breath, take a deep breath. You need to help her."

I sat in my seat and wept as I relived the horror of trying to perform CPR on a lifeless infant. The 9-1-1 tape cut to the core of my being. How could Gretchen Hayward dare say I had utter disregard for Natalie's life? This tape proved that I'd been overcome with concern, and that I'd made gallant efforts to save that baby girl.

I noticed some of the jury members crying, too. The 9-1-1 tape was honest, but I also knew Hayward could, and would, twist my words.

After the court heard the 9-1-1 tape, Waunakee Police Chief Robert Roberts and Sergeant Kevin Plendl testified they arrived within minutes of my call. Their statements were similar to those given at the preliminary hearing about finding Natalie with dilated pupils and a fixed stare. Roberts called Natalie's shallow breaths "death gasps."

"What was Ms. Edmunds condition when you walked in there?" Hayward questioned her witness, staring him down.

"She was talking on the phone crying, speaking very loud… seemed hysterical."

"Did she tell you what was wrong with the baby?"

"She said she'd propped the bottle and believed the baby choked." Roberts also repeated what he'd said in the preliminary hearing: When he turned Natalie on her side, formula had leaked out of her mouth.

My fear from the beginning had been that Natalie had choked on the formula. But once doctors discovered the brain and eye bleeding and surmised it was "Shaken Baby Syndrome", the prosecutors felt they had to prove Natalie died from having been shaken. Yet here was the police chief testifying he had witnessed formula coming out of Natalie's mouth.

It clearly alarmed Hayward when Steve questioned paramedic Jaime Kessenich on the witness stand. "Do you recall hearing fluids in her chest area when you attempted ventilation?"

"Yes."

When it was her turn to interview the paramedic, Hayward pounced on that and asked, "Do you recall Dr. Mysore, the Med-Flight doctor, indicating there were no fluids beyond the windpipe?"

"No."

"You don't recall him saying that?"

"No."

"No further questions."

That ended testimony for the first day. I felt the statements about fluid spewing from Natalie's mouth and heard in the lungs were crucial to my belief that Natalie choked. I would always feel guilty about propping up her bottle, but that didn't mean I had committed first degree reckless homicide.

I was grateful to stretch my limbs after the grueling day

of sitting. Dave and I, along with friends and family, returned to the Rowes' house. Once we'd arrived, I felt a deep longing to see my daughters; I missed them so much and couldn't wait to hold them close and tend to them. We were used to spending all our time together, and it was difficult to be away from them during my long hours in court.

Members of Crossroads Church came to the Rowes' house bearing hot and cold dishes to feed us, and soon this welcoming home became our gathering spot each day after court. The continuing love, care and support was beyond heartwarming--it sustained me through the painful trial. That night, exhausted, I fell into a fitful sleep.

***

Day Two of testimony launched a parade of Hayward's medical experts. Today, I know that I was a victim of the time of my trial. Back in 1972, radiologist Dr. John Caffey and neurosurgeon Dr. Norman Guthkelch had coined the term, *"Shaken Baby Syndrome"*. They declared the two tell-tale signs of the syndrome are subdural hematomas (blood pooling under the outer membrane of the brain), and retinal or eye bleeding. The two medical experts considered the markers almost exclusive to babies who had been shaken. Note the term was *"almost* exclusive."

The medical community was quick to grab onto this new, tantalizing syndrome and cases soon popped up with regularity in the media. Babies diagnosed with these injuries were immediately considered "shaken babies," and over the next thirty years, hundreds of parents and caregivers around the world were wrongly accused and convicted of shaking babies to death, despite declaring their innocence and citing other probable causes.

In fact, two other cases went to trial in Wisconsin the same time as mine. The other two, however, were acquitted.

Dr. William Perloff, head of the University of Wisconsin-Madison Pediatric Intensive Care Unit, was first on the witness stand that day. He called himself an expert on "Shaken Baby Syndrome", saying he had dealt with at least forty cases of the condition.

"Last year we had an epidemic," Dr. Perloff testified. "We had six cases in probably three months. Typically it's about four."

That should have ignited a warning flare. How could Dane County have six cases of "Shaken Baby Syndrome" in just three months? It sounded more like an epidemic of over-zealous diagnoses rather than a series of over-stressed parents shaking their kids.

But back in 1996, Dr. Perloff told the jury that he was an expert on the syndrome, and the jury believed him.

Dr. Perloff said he was trained in identifying "Shaken Baby Syndrome" and was actually teaching classes on the subject. He also proudly stated that the court had certified him as an expert to testify in trials about the disorder. And God help me, this highly regarded expert on "Shaken Baby Syndrome" was now on the stand testifying against me!

The doctor was adamant about Natalie's subdural hematomas and retinal bleed, and he downplayed the possibility that she had choked on formula. He agreed that the paramedic had noted a milky material that appeared to be formula in the back of her throat the day they tried to save her.

"But when the paramedic looked down the airway through the vocal cords, there was no milky material that was actually in the airway at the time," he assured the court.

Hayward asked him, "Did you reach an opinion to a reasonable degree of medical certainty whether Natalie's condition was caused by aspirating or choking on formula?

"Aspirating or choking on formula were not a cause of her cardiopulmonary arrest and death," He assured the hushed courtroom, explaining that there was no material found in her airway at the time they inserted the breathing tube; the major brain injuries, he felt, were sufficient explanation for Natalie's death.

I was still highly perplexed about those brain injuries and was still sure that Natalie choked on formula. Police Chief Robert Roberts had testified just yesterday that formula came out of Natalie's mouth, and I had screamed on the 9-1-1 tape that milk was spilling from her mouth. Then, too, there had been a chest x-ray done on the morning Natalie died, and it showed aspiration pneumonia caused by a liquid in her lungs. I told authorities the moment I found Natalie limp that she had formula in her airways, which had trickled out of her nose and mouth. I just could not understand why doctors ignored these facts and had hopped on the "Shaken Baby Syndrome" train.

But the "Shaken Baby Syndrome" expert continued his testimony, explaining that Natalie's brain was "like fresh Jello that sloshed back and forth banging against the skull."

However, he admitted that he couldn't be sure that shaking alone caused her death. Instead, he was now calling the cause of Natalie's demise, "Shaken Impact Infant Syndrome."

What impact? I wondered, mystified. This was new to me. Now I had not only shaken Natalie, but I'd also slammed her head on something, too?

"She had bleeding under the scalp at the back of her head, where presumably the impact occurred," Dr. Perloff testified. "Her loss of consciousness, retinal hemorrhages, characteristic type of subdural bleeding, profound brain injury and bleeding beneath the scalp are all signs and symptoms of "Shaken Impact Syndrome", a new syndrome discovered back in the 1980s.

Prosecutor Hayward asked him if these symptoms could occur from sources other than "Shaken Impact" or "Shaken Baby Syndrome" and Perloff said, "Certainly." But doctors had no evidence of any other trauma, such as a car accident or a high fall that could have caused Natalie's injuries, so they surmised it was "Shaken Baby" or "Shaken Impact Syndrome."

At this point, all I wanted to do was to scream out that they were wrong. Now, my attorney asked Dr. Perloff if he had considered my statements to police that I did not abuse Natalie. He admitted that no, he did not.

Doctors and the pathologist failed to find a single mark or injury on Natalie that proved I had grabbed the child to shake her. So why didn't they believe me, or at the very least, consider other possible scenarios?

"Do you always see external bruises in 'Shaken Baby' cases?" Hayward asked.

"No," Dr. Perloff replied. "I would say, in my personal experience, in the minority of cases I have seen external bruises where the child is grabbed or shaken."

I was flabbergasted at this testimony. I'm no doctor, but it would be impossible to shake a baby so hard that the force was equal to a car crash and *not* leave a single mark! Impossible!

Dr. Perloff was trying to convince a jury with a reasonable

degree of medical certainty that I had shaken Natalie to death, while I knew with *absolute* certainty that I had not. Would this expert's word hold more weight than mine?

As Dr. Perloff's testimony droned on, the medical statements became confusing and I noticed that the jury was losing interest. One man even sat there with his eyes closed. I was desperate for the jury members to listen carefully but even I was puzzled about talk of subdural hematomas, duras and meninges. The doctor showed slides and explained the various parts of the brain, but it was highly bewildering to anyone not an expert.

A new term Dr. Perloff threw out was *diffuse axonal injury*. He explained that each of our billions of brain cells looks like a round button with a long thread attached to it. The button is the cell body, and the thread is called the axon which transmits the signals from one button to another until it reaches our spinal cord.

If the brain is shaken, those axons get stretched and torn, which disrupts the brain signals. It is very difficult to see these injured axons under a microscope. With the limited technology in 1995, it took three days or more after the injury occurred for the silver stains to show axonal damage. If the person died sooner than three days after the injury, the silver stain could not provide the information.

The autopsy report stated there was no massive axon damage three days before her death, but that could have been because the testing back then could not detect it.

So how did this esteemed doctor know that Natalie had axonal injuries caused by shaking? He testified that she had all the other characteristics of shaking, such as the bleeding below the dura, retinal hemorrhages, and her deeply comatose lack of responsiveness, with rapid brain swelling and brain death like other patients with proven axonal injury.

"The fact that we didn't see it on the pathology (the silver stain tests) is only because she didn't live long enough to show it to us," Dr. Perloff explained reasonably.

Thanks to an imperfect testing method, the doctors back then presumed incorrectly what had happened to Natalie--and I had to sit in that courtroom and listen to assumptions that were adding up to a long conviction for a crime I had not committed.

***

Dr. Monte Mills, a pediatric ophthalmologist, took the stand that afternoon and showed slides of Natalie's eyes after the autopsy. He found extensive hemorrhages in both eyes and testified that the retinas were folded in half.

"In this setting, when we see a very young child with no history or other evidence of severe head trauma, it's diagnostic of what we call '"Shaken Baby Syndrome"'," Mills testified. "In my opinion, there's nothing else that could have caused this."

Then, Patrick Turski took the stand. He was a staff radiologist at the hospital and had performed the CAT scan on Natalie the afternoon before she died. He found two separate hemorrhages on the frontal lobes of Natalie's brain. The first was a newer injury on the right side that Turski testified was less than twenty-four hours old. The other was an old collection of blood on the left side he figured to be at least a week old.

"There have to have been two separate traumatic episodes," Turski said.

I found it interesting that these bleeds were in the front forehead area. If that were the case, how could I have severely shaken Natalie *and* banged the *front* of her head on something? That would mean I had to violently shake her, turn her body over, then slam her forehead into something without leaving any marks on her body. It made no sense. *Did anyone else pick up on this,* I wondered?

Another remarkable testimony was Dr. Perloff's earlier statement that brain bleeding could cause headaches, sleeplessness, fussiness and feeding problems. The baby's own mother had told the jury that Natalie had all these symptoms the night before she was brought to my house. Had Natalie been reacting to a prior brain injury?

This area of testimony seemed strong and I could see more than enough reasonable doubt in my case to set me free.

But after the confusing day of testimonies, I had no idea if the jury had picked up on these discrepancies, or not.

CHAPTER NINE

The fourth day of my trial began with a juror problem. Without the jury present, the judge questioned Bailiff Jan Blackmon about the strange happenings. Blackmon said the jury had been lined up and was walking back into the courtroom when a juror named Bruce Oradei asked if the jury team had to walk past the evidence table every time they came and left.

He was referring to a large conference table that butted up to the side of the jury box. It was covered with the state's evidence, including a car seat and Natalie's soiled clothing.

"Mr. Oradei made the comment, 'I know a conspiracy when I see one.'" Blackmon said.

Earlier, the panel had been standing by the door when Mr. Oradei asked if it was legal for expert medical witnesses to sit in the courtroom and pass notes to the prosecution.

Blackmon said Oradei made another strange comment as the panel had lined up for lunch the day before: "You're going to have a mutiny on this jury." Blackmon had asked him to explain and was told, "I don't tell my secrets until they happen."

Hayward seemingly believed Oradei was taking my side and that his comments were extremely inappropriate, especially since he made them within earshot of other jurors. She asked the judge to remove him from the jury.

Hurley countered that Oradei was simply keeping an open mind and asking questions. Obviously. we wanted to keep this juror and Hayward did not.

"I'm going to strike Mr. Oradei from the panel," Judge Moeser ruled, and Oredei was called in and released..

Steve and I were very disappointed. This juror clearly realized that the state was creating a conspiracy against me. It's too bad he said it aloud. The perceptive Mr. Oradei would no longer be able to help decide my fate.

Eleven years later, we contacted Bruce Oradei while writing this book to find out his true feelings about my case. Oradei said he had been a sixty-one year old lobbyist for the Wisconsin Education Association Council when he was appointed to my jury. For many years he was a union representative and negotiator, and was highly trained to observe and consider both sides of an issue. He took this first encounter with jury duty seriously and studied the body language of all involved, including Cindy and Tom Beard.

He believed the evidence table shoved up next to the jury box was highly prejudicial and had taken Blackmon aside to tell her so.

He was further disturbed when Dr. Perloff, the "Shaken Baby Syndrome" expert, approached Hayward as she took a break from questioning another doctor. He whispered something into her ear, and it was clear to Oradei that Hayward had changed the line of questioning after his input.

"It was at that moment the doctor crossed a bridge," Oradei told us. "He went from being an expert witness to an advocate of the state's case." In other words, the doctor's role as an expert witness was to allow the jury to hear all the evidence and then decide the case. But now the doctor was promoting the state's side, which seemed highly biased, especially if the jury could see it happening.

What Oradei didn't know was that Judge Moeser had ruled earlier that the doctors could sit near the prosecutor's table and provide input. This seemed wrong to Oradei, but actually happens legally in other courtrooms.

Oradei denies the bailiff's specific comments about a conspiracy or mutiny; instead, he said he took Blackmon aside to tell her his concerns. When the judge removed him from the jury, he had to find his own ride home to Sun Prairie, Wisconsin, a sixteen-mile drive from Madison.

Oradei said he had not formed an opinion about my guilt or innocence when he was released, but he did keep an open mind. So we will never know if Bruce Oradei would have changed the outcome of my trial.

The pediatric ICU physician, Dr. Gregory Holman, was up next, sharing Dr. Perloff's opinions. He testified for an interminably long hour about "Shaken Baby Syndrome" all over again.

After a break, Dr. Robert Huntington, the pathologist who had performed Natalie's autopsy, took the stand. He was an affable character with thick white hair and a Santa beard. Steve thought he looked like the wild scientist in the *Back to the Future* movie. Indeed, he offered amusing explanations, but I wasn't laughing as he presented more damning evidence against me.

"Approximately how many times have you testified as a pathologist?" Hayward asked.

"Oh, just a few hundred times by now. I don't really keep count."

He testified about two old bruises that he had confirmed under the microscope; the one in front, and now, we learned, there was an old bruise on the back of Natalie's head.

"These are deep in the scalp outside the skull, but not where you'd see them from the outside. In other words, ladies and gentlemen, this baby was injured several times before," Huntington said.

He also talked about fresh areas of subdural bleeding.

"How much blood was there?" Hayward asked.

"Not a whole big bunch. Maybe a little over a teaspoon in the whole of these bruises. That shows at some point that the kid's head collided with something."

Huntington went on to say that besides a direct collision, there is only one other way one can receive these deeper hemorrhages-- when the brain is moved in opposition to the skull as in shaking, which he called "shearing force."

As I listened, I found the most important part of the pathologist's testimony to be his estimated times of injury. He said that the newer bleed injury could have happened anywhere from two to twenty-four hours before the child died. That meant someone could definitely have wounded Natalie before she arrived at my house.

Huntington also stated that the older bruise could have occurred as early as two days before Natalie died. Tom and Cindy had her with them for the four days before her death.

To me, this was testimony that should be seriously considered, and I was momentarily buoyed by the pathologist's words. However, surrounding this statement were confusing medical explanations, which made me wonder whether the jury really grasped the significance of his time frame estimates.

That afternoon, Natalie's father, Tom, testified but offered nothing new. I found myself becoming angry when he talked about picking Natalie up from my house. He told the court that he'd thought my home environment was hectic, and he wanted to get Natalie out of there and take her home as quickly as possible.

"Audrey's oldest daughter, Carrie, from time to time, would sort of be in Natalie's face," Tom said. "It seemed as if Natalie didn't really appreciate all the attention she was getting." Certainly, Carrie's interest could be interpreted in many ways—why would he assign such a troubling interpretation to it?

After Tom's testimony, Hayward presented a pageant of the Beard family's friends and relatives to testify to Natalie's happy home life. It was a repeat of what Cindy had described when she was on the stand. Now on this fourth day of the trial, the testimony was becoming repetitive and tiresome. I longed to take a brisk walk outside in the November air.

Instead, I was a hostage in a sweltering courtroom. Even the judge apologized for the overheating problem.

Late that afternoon, another round of medical testimony began. This time the hospital's pediatric neurologist, Dr. Robert Rust, took the stand. I braced myself for the repeated barrage of alleged "Shaken Baby" symptoms, and was numbed once again by his testimony. However, I snapped out of my tedium when Dr. Rust added a new possible cause of Natalie's death: now, he was suggesting "a shaking with asphyxiation." In other words, something had blocked her breathing so oxygen could not enter her brain.

I was immediately reminded of my suspicions that Natalie had choked on formula, but Dr. Rust said they had no evidence of formula having blocked the airway. I had told authorities and so had the paramedics that formula came out of Natalie's mouth and nose. Why did was the doctor denying this evidence? Instead, Dr. Rust suggested that Natalie could have been strangled or smothered by a pillow after she was shaken.

It was beyond upsetting to sit at that table and not react to such repulsive testimony against me. I was relieved when Steve immediately jumped on this theory, asking if any external neck injuries had been found that would prove strangulation.

"There are no marks on the throat," Rust admitted.

"Were there any fibers found in the child's lungs or nose?" Steve asked.

"I'm not aware of any found."

"Did you know that the police did not note any pillow being out of place in the bedroom?"

I couldn't believe that Judge Moeser was allowing Rust to offer such nonsense to the jury? How could they possibly wade through the complicated medical testimony to weed out the fabrications? At the end of the day, I was totally exhausted.

I was deeply depressed when we returned to the Rowe's house where my only solace was hugging my dear children.

***

Friday morning, the fifth day of the trial, brought me some relief. Hayward announced she would rest her case about noon, and finally, it was time for Steve to begin my defense.

Last on the stand for the state was Johanna Evanoff with her library-book-bashing story. I still don't understand why the judge allowed her testimony when it was clear that she never saw this actually occur. Fortunately, the assistant librarian, Karla Stafford, testified that she managed story hour at the library. She and another librarian always remained in the area until every participant had gone, and they never witnessed me striking a child over the head with a book.

I wondered why the judge didn't bar Mrs. Evanoff's untrue testimony, but was at least thankful that Hayward finally rested her case before noon.

The jury filed out for lunch, but the attorneys and I stayed in the courtroom as the judge listed all the evidence the defense planned to present. I was stunned when Judge Moeser allowed all of Natalie's medical record except for the last two very crucial pages.

"The portion of those two pages that deals with the parents' need for counseling is not being received, but everything else that applies to Natalie is being received," Moeser said.

Once again the judge barred us from telling the full story, so the jury could accurately decide if I really murdered a baby. My entire life was at stake along with my family's lives. We had just heard Natalie's pediatrician, a prosecution witness, testify that the Beards had called the clinic twenty-five times in the six months since her birth with concerns about Natalie's health. Steve suggested that this was an excessive number of calls, and if a doctor had written in Natalie's medical reports that the parents needed counseling, I strongly felt the jury should hear this information. Once again, however, Judge Moeser robbed me of revealing the complete, true story to the jury.

Those two pages would have boosted our first defense witness. Steve had scoured the country but could not locate a single doctor who would testify that this was not a case of "Shaken Baby Syndrome". Steve called "Shaken Baby" a belief that was "in vogue" among the medical community. He did hire Dr. Mary Dominski, a pediatric neurologist at the Dean Clinic in Madison, Wisconsin, to examine the case and form an opinion. She, too, believed Natalie was a shaken baby, but she was not tainted by the prevailing attitude towards me from the University of Wisconsin Children's Hospital.

Steve gave her all the reports including the autopsy, eye pathology, Natalie's medical records from the day she died, her medical documents from her pediatrician, the complete set of X-rays and CAT scans. He also included the written statements and opinions of the physicians who treated her, plus police and sheriff investigation reports, including interviews with Tom, Cindy and me. Dr. Dominski got to see *all* the evidence, including the last two pages about the Beards' need for counseling.

"I think that to a degree of medical certainty, it is probable the injury occurred *before* this child arrived at Audrey Edmunds' house that day," Dominski firmly stated on the witness stand. At last, somebody was considering the entire picture. I was elated!

Dr. Dominski testified that she did believe somebody shook the baby because Natalie's brain had the two hallmarks of "Shaken Baby Syndrome": brain bleeding and retinal damage.

I didn't realize until much later how that man-made invention, "Shaken Baby Syndrome", had damaged so many lives. It was even making me believe that Cindy or Tom Beard could have shaken Natalie. I wondered, if I didn't shake her...who did? But doctors still embraced these assumptions during the era of my trial, and Dr. Dominski believed them, too.

Based on all the reports, Dominski estimated the injury occurred sometime less than twelve hours before her death, but before Natalie arrived at my house.

"Why do you think that?" Steve questioned.

"I was very concerned upon reading the reports that Natalie was an extremely irritable baby that day. She was crying inconsolably. She wasn't eating well. She hadn't finished her bottle, which is a remarkable occurrence."

Dominski said this was consistent with a child who is in pain or intense discomfort. A subdural or a subarachnoid hemorrhage can cause this irritation.

"Subarachnoid blood hurts," she testified. "It's very painful. So looking at this inconsolable crying, poor feeding and easy irritability, it is medically probable she already had the subarachnoid hemorrhage from being shaken before she arrived."

I clung to every word Dr. Dominski uttered. Her testimony resonated with my own experience that fateful morning. "I think Natalie had a seizure resulting from the brain injury and the subarachnoid blood that was present before she arrived at the sitter's."

I wanted to leap into the air to emphasize this theory to the jury. Since I had not shaken Natalie, something *had* to happen before she arrived at my house. For the first time, I was listening to a scenario that was absolutely possible. Any medical evidence or opinion that I had done the shaking was a flat-out fabrication.

Now an expert was telling the jury what finally made sense to me. Dominski explained that a shaking can cause a subarachnoid or subdural hemorrhage or bleeding in the brain.

"The outer brain membrane is rich in pain receiving fibers. If an adult has even a small subarachnoid bleed, they will tell you, 'This is the worst headache of my life.' A baby can't tell you that in words, but will cry and not eat and be very irritable."

Dr. Dominski testified that the brain bleeding caused a seizure that nobody had witnessed. It certainly could have happened while I was out in the garage getting the stroller ready to bring Carrie to school that morning.

"A seizure can impact the primitive part of the brain--the

part that affects swallowing, breathing, heart rate, eye movement and consciousness," the doctor explained. "When the brain doesn't get enough oxygen, swelling and the muddle of characteristics you saw on the brain scans can occur."

That would certainly explain why I found Natalie limp. It was wonderful to finally hear a *logical* possible cause of Natalie's sudden collapse and ultimate death.

Dr. Dominski went on to dispute the other doctor's opinion that Natalie died of massive axonal injury. She said that would require a rage-filled force with a lot of movement and possible impact. If that were the case, the brain scans would show more than the small subdurals.

"I would expect to see evidence of bruising of the brain matter itself, bigger bleeding where the hit actually occurred and more bleeding where the brain moved along the surface under the skull. It wasn't there."

Doctor Dominski tossed away possibilities of smothering or strangulation, saying there was no external evidence.

"What about Dr. Perloff's opinion that Natalie Beard had bleeding in the back of the head?" Steve asked.

"There was an old hematoma in the back, but I wasn't sure when reading Dr. Perloff's testimony which hemorrhage he was referring to."

I felt that Dr. Dominski had based her testimony on the reality I'd experienced on the dark day Natalie died. She was the only person who looked at every possible angle and made her conclusion based on facts. She did not look at the symptoms and concoct a possible scenario to fit it.

Next, Steve called Dr. Susan Padberg, Natalie's pediatrician, to the stand. Dr. Padberg testified that she saw Natalie on September 6, 1995 and noticed the bruise on Natalie's forehead that Cindy Beard had referred to on the stand. Cindy had said she noticed the bruise four days after she started bringing Natalie to my house. She also showed the jury a picture of Natalie with this bruise.

Dr. Padberg testified that when she examined the injury on September 6th, the bruise was yellow,

"That indicated the bruise had been there for some time," Dr. Padberg testified.

"So if you saw the bruise on September 6th, and the bruise was yellow, is it your opinion to a reasonable degree of medical probability that the injury causing the bruise happened prior to September 6th?" Steve asked.

"Yes."

September 6th was the first day Cindy Beard had brought Natalie to my daycare. I was glad to clear up the bruise incident, but also miffed that it had been introduced in the first place, complete with a picture of a bruised Natalie. Clearly, this injury had not occurred at my house. The photo was highly prejudicial and should not have been shown.

Despite the logical testimony from our defense witnesses, my future was still uncertain. Ultimately, it was up to the jury to decide which doctors they would believe.

CHAPTER TEN

Friday ended with my dear neighborhood friend, Patti Larson, taking the stand. My trial was traumatic for all my friends who were walking along this frightening path with me. Patti was especially upset about testifying as a character witness. She barely slept the first week of the trial and was barred from sitting in on the proceedings because she had not yet testified.

Patti was most concerned because she once told investigators she saw me spank Carrie. She had talked to my attorney about this before the trial because she knew the state would ask her about it and she did not want Hayward to twist this minor incident into a violent act.

Steve advised her to be honest, but Patti was still afraid to give her testimony; what should have been a glowing testament to my character would hurt me in the end. On the stand, Patti was shaky, but Steve purposely brought up the spanking incident in such a way that she could explain it.

"How many times did you see Audrey spank Carrie?" Steve asked.

"Once."

"What did Carrie do?"

"She was just irritating the other children. Audrey asked her several times to share with the other kids, but she wouldn't listen. Audrey spanked her and sent her to her room for a few minutes."

"Did Audrey lose her temper?"

"No."

I felt badly that Patti had to testify against me, and I was angry that a mild spanking was even an issue. Surely the jury would distinguish my responsible parental discipline from child abuse! Patti described how I handled Natalie when she was fussy.

"Audrey always seemed to find a way to soothe her. She had tremendous patience," Patti said. "I have seen other adults struggle to calm infants, but Audrey was always more than willing to put up with the crying and do whatever she had to do to make Natalie happy."

After the testimony ended for the day, Judge Moeser decided to continue the trial on Saturday because everyone was eager to finish the trial before Thanksgiving.

At the end of that wearing day, my supporters were encouraged by the defense witnesses. *The Capital Times* reported that my mother smiled and sighed with relief as she left the courtroom, and my dad winked at a reporter. "It's looking up," one of my supporters supposedly said as he slapped the backs of other allies in the hallway.

However, I could not share this elation because after the jury filed out, the proceedings droned on for me and the attorneys.

Prosecutor Hayward claimed that my attorney had opened the area describing my level of frustration, violence and patience in specific instances. Now, she wanted to introduce my former husband and the abuse he alleged I'd given him.

Oh, no! I cried inwardly, knowing my ex-husband and realizing his words would be like dropping a small atom bomb into my trial. I was greatly relieved when Judge Moeser ruled that my exes' statements would be highly prejudicial, since they were from twelve years earlier and were made while our marriage was breaking up. The judge ruled that my ex-husband's allegations would be excluded from my trial.

I left court on a high note, thanks to the judge's ruling. But I was far from relaxed. Steve had scheduled me first on the witness stand the next day.

***

Taking the stand in my own defense was a huge decision, and Steve talked to me ahead of the trial. He suggested I testify to show I was not a cold-blooded killer. I still wasn't sure, so we had long discussions about this decision, and Steve's friend and legal counsel, Hal Harlowe, conferred with me as well. Hal practiced cross-examining me, and both he and Steve felt I was prepared.

Although I was petrified at the prospect of testifying, both attorneys advised me to answer each question honestly and share what I could remember. Because I had nothing to hide, telling the truth should not be difficult.

I wasn't worried about Steve's questions, but I was terrified to face Gretchen Hayward. I was already disgusted by her cold, harsh tone throughout the trial. She was a masterful storyteller, inventing tales about my life and Natalie's death that just hadn't happened, and thus could never be proven. Every word she uttered was aimed at intimidating both the jury and me. As Steve told me, she was doing her job well.

As I took the stand in my own defense, my fears melted away as Steve opened my testimony with friendly chatter about my background. I briefly told about my childhood and how I got into babysitting. He asked how I met Dave and I talked about my enjoyable pregnancies, easy deliveries and happy home life with Dave and our daughters. Then, he moved me forward and let me share my rich faith in God and my involvement at church. I began to relax and spoke with clarity and growing ease.

Then, Steve asked me about caring for Natalie at my day care home and questioned me about the baby bumping her head on the toy piano. Why did everyone continue to call this a piano, which sounded so heavy and ominous. The toy was actually small, in the shape of a duck that chimed when wobbled. This slight knock from the toy was not serious at the time, and Natalie's own pediatrician had already testified that the bruise on Natalie's forehead occurred before this toy incident at my house. But Natalie did cry when the toy bumped her in the head. Steve asked what I did for Natalie after the incident.

I told him I took her from the car seat into the kitchen and spent time holding her and calmed her. He continued to push for more information but I could not figure out why he was pressing me about it. Later, he told me he was trying to show the jury that when Natalie was hurt, I was able to calm her down. Steve also brought out the fact that Natalie's parents did not know how to pacify their own baby and had called the doctor twenty-five times for help.

After lunch, I felt as if I were walking the gangplank as I took the witness stand to face the prosecutor's cross-examination. I wiped my sweaty palms on my skirt and worried that my voice would tremble—and it did. I knew Hayward would try to manipulate truth with her questions.

Sure enough, she stated that my pregnancies couldn't have been "all that fine." I couldn't always have felt good, and nobody lives in Utopia all the time.

Then, she moved forward to the day Natalie had died. She painted my life as chaotic the morning that Cindy dropped off a crying baby. According to Hayward, I couldn't have been as happy as I said because I was facing a move, an unplanned pregnancy and was caring for lots of children.

But *I* knew how I felt that morning and I was in high spirits for all those reasons. Also, Jim Henning, a prosecution witness, had testified that he saw me that morning and I was behaving normally.

I found it almost impossible to hide my extreme exasperation at the prosecutor. I knew my answers were strained and terse, but I was glad I took the stand. Gretchen Hayward had made up her own story and tried to get me to agree with her or deny it. I wanted to scream, "You are making things up that are not true and did not happen!"

The biggest stress point came when Hayward questioned me about Natalie's eyes that fateful morning.

"You told Detective Dawn Johnson that as you were carrying Natalie in her car seat to the bedroom, she was looking at your face and you were looking at her face?"

"We were face-to-face, but she was crying and her eyes were closed," I answered.

"You told Detective Johnson her eyes were tracking your movements, didn't you?"

"No, we did not discuss tracking."

Hayward was desperate to prove Natalie was alert when first dropped off at my home, which would supposedly prove I injured her. This testimony scared me because I knew what she was trying to imply, but none of it was accurate!

I was exhausted when I finally stepped down after three-and-a-half hours of difficult testimony. I worried that my fragile performance on cross-examination would not play well with the jury, and I knew I also acted defensively, which one could construe as guilt. But I was simply responding to Hayward's obvious commitment to misinterpret whatever I said.

The rest of the afternoon was filled with former neighbors and friends testifying on my behalf. I know it was agonizing for them to take the stand and I will forever be grateful to Tina Hinz, Beth Naughton, Martha Rortvedt, Jodi Siehoff, Barb Rowe and

Shari Spahn. Their support ended my brutal courtroom appearance on a lighter note.

Steve told me later he thought we'd won the case-- until I began to testify. He thought I'd done wonderfully on direct examination, but collapsed on cross. He called me "a doe-in-the-headlights." Although I was calm and articulate when we practiced, his heart sank when my nervousness overtook me on the stand. Fortunately, he didn't share those thoughts with me that day.

Dave and I returned to the Rowe's house and scooped our daughters into our arms. We tried to enjoy Sunday away from the strains of the courtroom, but I found it challenging to present a happy face for my girls. More than anything, I just wanted to fall into bed with them, hold them close and sob all day long. Instead, I had to maintain my aura of composure around our children or risk terrifying them. The weight of it all was almost unbearable.

Dave was feeling the strain, too, but hugged me often to comfort me. He never wavered in his support and I was extremely grateful to have him by my side.

***

Monday morning the state presented one rebuttal witness, Dr. Jeffrey Jentzen, the chief medical examiner in Milwaukee and yet another "Shaken Baby" expert. I was thoroughly worn out from listening to this same line of testimony. I was quite relieved when he stepped down and the evidence and testimony phase of my trial finally ended.

It was just past ten thirty Monday morning and Judge Moeser dismissed the jury for the rest of the day. He told them to rest up for a long day tomorrow and to eat a solid breakfast. Closing arguments were expected to last four to five hours.

After lunch, Dave, my attorney and I returned to the courtroom to discuss the judge's instructions to the jury. These included what he would allow or bar the lawyers from saying during closing statements.

The judge decided Hayward and Steve could interpret my hysteria on the 9-1-1 tape, which meant the prosecutor could conclude I was frantic because I had just shaken Natalie. Moeser said the jury could decide for themselves which version to believe. *Sure,* I thought bitterly.

The biggest decision made that afternoon was whether to allow the jury to consider a lesser charge of second-degree reckless homicide. Steve and I were adamant the charge be either first degree or not guilty. The difference in the two degrees was utter disregard for human life. We felt that if the jury believed I valued Natalie's life, it could not convict me of first degree reckless homicide, and I would go free.

This, of course, was what the prosecution most feared! They argued that the jury could be swayed by the 9-1-1 tape and surmise I did have concern for Natalie's welfare. They also said that the testimony of our defense witness, Dr. Dominski, who had stated she believed Natalie was injured before she arrived at my house, could provide reasonable doubt about the timing of Natalie's injury, which would define my concern for Natalie's life in the 9-1-1 tape.

The prosecution wanted the jury to have the choice to go with a lesser charge so that I would not walk free.

Steve, Dave and I felt sick when Judge Moeser decided to give the jury three choices for a verdict: guilty of first degree reckless homicide, guilty of second degree reckless homicide, or not guilty.

Steve knew that if the jury believed the medical testimony, but rejected the theory that I had disregard for human life, they could still convict me of second degree reckless homicide. The very thought of a conviction kept me awake for hours that night. What was going to become of me—and my devoted family?

***

Tuesday was a madhouse in Dane County Circuit Court. More than one hundred spectators and reporters competed for seats, so a closed circuit television monitor was set up in another courtroom to accommodate the overflow. My nerves were almost shot by this point, and all I wanted was for the trial to be over and to hear the words, "Not guilty.". Despite all that had happened in the courtroom, I still clung to faith that the jury had recognized the truth of what had happened to little Natalie.

I braced myself for Gretchen Hayward's closing statements. I felt ill just listening to her arguments, as she described how her expert medical witnesses had agreed Natalie was severely shaken and I had probably struck her head against something. Her limpness and fixed gaze would have been obvious immediately after such a brutal injury. Hayward told the jury I had lied to protect myself.

"She is not able to admit to all her supporters that she is not perfect," Hayward stated. "But there is a very imperfect side to her. A side that snapped."

Then Hayward dramatically lowered her voice as she admitted she did not know the exact time Natalie was shaken. "The key is, whenever it happened, it occurred while Natalie was in Edmunds' care," Hayward said. "There was one hour of time. During that hour something happened to make Audrey Edmunds lose her temper to such an extent that she shook the baby."

I couldn't believe that she was making all this up, and that the jury was listening to these lies intently!

"Maybe it was because the baby was crying or maybe because the baby was not taking the bottle well; maybe because the day was hectic."

Listening to Gretchen Hayward make up lies and toss them out as if they were facts both enraged and terrified me. How could that one innocent hour with Natalie have hurled me into this maelstrom of lies? I forced myself to hold it together so the jury would not see how enraged I was.

I thought Steve was eloquent as he delivered his closing statement. He asked jurors to consider that "even a parent can snap." He suggested Tom and Cindy were tired, awkward parents with a constantly crying baby.

"Who is more likely to shake little Natalie out of frustration?" Steve asked the jury. "Edmunds, who had two daughters of her own and cared for children for years? Or first-time parents who by all accounts had a needy baby?"

The humbling moment of the entire trial came when Steve held up a picture for the jury's view. He lowered his voice and said, "This is Natalie. She was a beautiful child and she is gone."

His remark reminded me that a beautiful, precious baby was no longer on this earth. Natalie was indeed dead, and suddenly I wanted to put my head down on the table and weep for her.

I still had no idea how this little girl had received such ghastly injuries. I only knew that I did not inflict them. In fact, it was I who had tried to save her!

After four hours of closing arguments, the jury recessed to begin deliberating my fate. They began at one- thirty that afternoon and as the hours crept on, I was torn between wanting to get this ordeal over with, and terror that they would find me guilty.

At one point, we were called back to meet with the judge and prosecutor. The jury wanted us to define my awareness of my actions against Natalie. In other words, did I know my actions could cause Natalie harm.? Steve later told me he was concerned because this meant the jury was considering both first and second degree reckless homicide.

I burst into horrified tears. My friend, Betsy Adams, held my arm trying to calm me and Dave looked stunned. I knew he was keeping a brave front for me, but I saw his jaw clench and realized he was petrified in fear. I wanted so badly to be with my children at that moment. What if the court hauled me away and I never got to say goodbye?

The jury deliberated for eight hours, not very long for such a complex case. We were called back to court at nine-thirty the next evening. Steve Hurley was by my side along with two of his assisting attorneys and Dave took a seat with my family in the audience.

I walked into that courtroom with as much poise as I could muster but inside, I had a feeling things were going to go badly, and I could barely stop myself from trembling.

CHAPTER ELEVEN

The courtroom was filled to the brim and overflowed into an adjacent room with closed circuit television. My heart was pounding as I watched the jury file in. I studied their faces, but saw nothing to indicate what the verdict would be. It was not written on their faces; it was written in the white envelope that one of the jurors handed to the judge.

Judge Moeser was now holding my future in his hand, and it seemed like an eternity as I watched him open the envelope, adjust his glasses and begin to read. When he was finished, his eyes did not reveal his feelings. Instead, he warned the spectators to avoid displaying emotion until the jury exited. Then, he cleared his throat and I braced myself for the verdict.

"We, the jury, find Audrey Edmunds guilty of first degree reckless homicide in the death of Natalie Beard."

I heard gasps from the audience, and then the entire courtroom dropped away as my mind tried to focus on understanding what the judge's words meant to me.

Steve leaned over and asked me to let go of him so he could speak to Judge Moeser. I hadn't even realized that my left hand was clenching his arm. I was so afraid! What would happen now? Judge Moeser's reading of the verdict will always remain the most frightening moment of my life.

After the jury filed out, the spectator area exploded with sobs and embraces. *Wisconsin State Journal* reporter Elizabeth Brixey wrote that the Beards left quickly. Their friends and family declined to comment on the verdict.

"It's been extraordinarily difficult for the family," Brixey quoted Gretchen Hayward. "Can you imagine losing your child and then having to go through this trial?" But she also quoted my friend, Betsy Adams, who said, "Justice wasn't served for Natalie, and it wasn't served for Audrey or her children."

Meanwhile, as I sat numbly trying to absorb what had just happened, I watched Steve approach the judge and speak briefly with him.

Then, Steve led me to an area right off the courtroom. Dave and I sat down while Steve and his legal team stepped aside to discuss the situation. Dave and I were both speechless, and I could no longer hold back the tears. I pulled off all my jewelry and shoved it into Dave's hands, terrified that the police were going to quickly haul me off to jail. At the time, I didn't even understand the difference between jail and prison. I just knew I would be behind bars.

And what about my babies! I needed to hold our daughters. How on earth would we tell them that Mommy wasn't coming home? We stared at each other, each thinking the same thing: how could this nightmare have happened to us?

Soon we were called back into the courtroom, where Steve asked the judge to let me remain out on bail until the sentencing. Gretchen Hayward declared I was a murderer and should not be permitted out in society.

By God's grace, Judge Moeser said he did not think I was a flight risk and allowed me to remain out on bail. He said he needed forty-five days for his pre-sentencing investigation and that the sentencing would take place in about two months. I felt some relief to know I still had two months to prepare myself and my family for my possible imprisonment.

My heart broke again when I saw my parents' tearful faces when they joined us after the proceeding. My beloved father was a junior high school teacher who had proudly taught hundreds of students about our American judicial system. Now, the system he had loved and trusted had failed his own daughter, leaving him devastated.

My precious mother looked exhausted, and I wanted to hug her close and sweep away her pain. She had already been through so much with me, especially after my premature birth, at which I suffered water on the brain. I had continued to see a neurologist until I was eighteen years old.

Now that I was a mother, I recognized all the sacrifices she had made for my well being.

Dave and I drove in silence back to the Rowe's house, holding hands and looking into the night sky for some glimmer of serenity. We still couldn't comprehend that the jury had convicted me of the more serious crime. Clearly, they had believed the prosecution's theory that I shook Natalie with complete disregard for her survival.

As we entered the Rowe's house, our friend Ilene, who had stayed home to care for our girls, hugged us. She told us that the verdict was already on the news. I trudged up the spiral staircase to the second floor and found Carrie in bed sleeping peacefully. Gazing down at my sleeping angel, I lay down next to her, wrapped her in my arms and wept.

A few friends and family stopped by the Rowe's and I joined them in the living room. We all sat and stared into the fireplace as it danced with flames. Despite the fire, I couldn't stop shivering. Was I actually going to go to prison? Surely, someone would realize that a terrible mistake had been made!

***

For years I wondered why the jury convicted me. It wasn't until much later while writing this book that we tracked down two of the jury members.

Dan Burkeland had three young daughters almost the same ages as mine when he sat on my jury. Thinking about my case so many years later brought back a flood of emotions. He said eight of the jury members immediately declared guilt within an hour of beginning deliberations.

"I was the last holdout," Dan said. "I was the very last person who did not feel comfortable with the time frame of Natalie's injuries and the time she fell ill."

In the end, Dan went with the majority, who cited the seven doctors' expert opinions. Now, his heart breaks for everybody involved.

"It was difficult beyond words and it changed my life in many ways. This was the first jury I was ever on and I couldn't communicate with my wife about it during the trial. She was reading everything in the newspaper and felt Audrey was innocent. After the guilty verdict, I tried to explain to her what we had heard in court. My biggest fear was to falsely convict her."

My case so strongly affected his relationship with his wife that they have since divorced. He was also self-employed at the time; later, his business suffered.

Terry Temple was forty-seven years old when he sat on my jury. It would be both his first and last trial. Temple agreed when the jury panel gathered in the room to begin deliberations; most of the twelve member panel thought I was guilty of shaking Natalie. Burkeland was a holdout and one woman had great empathy for me and did not want to convict.

But Temple said the long parade of state witnesses declaring the baby had to die during the one hour in my care, and the overwhelming medical evidence of "Shaken Baby Syndrome", convinced the panel beyond a reasonable doubt.

"We had no uncertainty in our minds because the medical experts were very convincing," Temple explained.

I was thoroughly disappointed that the jury had not seen the inconsistencies and lack of clarity in the so-called experts' testimony. It also upset me when Temple said he thought my own testimony on the stand seemed extremely rehearsed and "fake." He said because I appeared nervous and defensive during the prosecution's questioning, the jury felt that my actions were those of a guilty person. I knew I had not performed well on the stand. But the jury had no idea that Hayward was attacking me, creating fantasies about what had happened and putting words in my mouth. I wondered how the jurors would present themselves under similar circumstances!

"I thought the defense tried to cover up what happened, and did not offer anything that outweighed the prosecution's medical experts," Temple told us. "I thought Audrey's attorney and her testimony were insincere."

I couldn't seem to escape this perception, despite the fact that the prosecutors and witnesses had essentially set up a scenario that was patently false. They had jumped onto the "Shaken Baby Syndrome" bandwagon and then created a scenario to match the symptoms.

Because such violence is born of rage, they had to depict me as an angry, aggressive person. When they learned from my friends and family that I was not at all like that, the prosecution decided to go with the two-word, damning conclusion that I had "snapped!"

Temple portrayed himself as a compassionate person, and he and the other jury members felt horrible about my family situation, with three young girls losing their mother. But they based their conviction on the "medical facts" of the case.

"After all," he pointed out, "the state presented seven or eight highly skilled expert doctors who knew their stuff."

I thought my attorney had asked the prosecution witnesses excellent questions and raised considerable "reasonable doubt" with the doctors. My God, didn't the jury wonder why the baby had no external injuries? And why had the "experts" tried to downplay the formula found in Natalie's airway? The state's case didn't even make logical sense. So why did the jury believe only their "experts" and not consider all the evidence my attorney presented?

Temple said the jury briefly considered a second degree verdict, but the judge repeatedly told them to follow the definitions of the charges. By doing so, the jury followed the rules and regulations, went with the experts' opinions and felt the crime added up to "first degree reckless homicide."

I believed I had certainly shown sincere regard for human life; after all, when I discovered Natalie choking, I called for help and tried to revive her myself. I was not a brutal woman who recklessly killed a baby and then left the scene. Temple confirmed that he trusted the prosecutor over the defense attorneys, and the state's medical witnesses basically sealed my fate.

Steve told me the legal system is set up as fail-safe. It saddles the prosecution with the burden of proof beyond a reasonable doubt. He said the system is founded on the notion that some guilty people may go free in order that innocent people don't go to prison. Yet, I was an innocent person and the system failed me. Now I faced possible maximum security prison.

Meanwhile, my journalist friend, Jill Wellington, was working at a television station in Michigan the day after the verdict came in. Her hands trembled as she punched in the phone number for the Dane County Courthouse. "Hello, I'm a news reporter in Michigan, and I'd like to get the verdict in the Audrey Edmunds case."

"Well, of course, she's guilty," the woman who answered the phone replied tersely.

Jill was stunned at this abrupt, ill-considered comment. One of Jill's coworkers knew a producer at *Dateline, NBC*. Jill called him and asked if he would investigate my case. A week later, she called the producer again and was shocked at his reply.

"I talked to some of the newspaper reporters who covered Audrey's case," the producer said. "They all say she's guilty."

"They're wrong!" Jill declared. "I thought *Dateline* probed injustice like this. It truly would be an interesting case to explore." But the producer was not interested in examining my case and never called back.

Jill also realized she was guilty of making similar assumptions as a reporter. Over her eighteen year career as a journalist, she'd found that the prosecuting attorney was eager to talk. It was easy for her to pop over to the courthouse and the prosecutor would offer a quick sound bite on camera for the evening news. The prosecutors were more than willing to share all *their* details of the crime, which made up the bulk of Jill's stories.

In the course of writing her stories, Jill would match up the prosecutors' input with video from the crime scene, and tried to gather photos of the victim and video of the accused being led into court in shackles and an orange jumpsuit. It seemed like a logical way to cover a trial, and it continued throughout the entire court process because the prosecutor was always willing to share information with the public.

Just like the jury, Jill had believed that prosecutors were generally on the side of truth and justice. They are, after all, trying to keep our community safe, right? Aren't they fighting for justice? Aren't they on the side of ordinary people?

Of course Jill had contacted the defense lawyer, too, because she was an unbiased reporter passionate about telling every side of a story. Even though she tried to interview defendants, she also knew the defense rarely talked, so no matter how hard she tried, Jill was never able to interview the accused before or during a trial. In fact, it was easy to tack a standard closing at the end of the news story saying, "We contacted the defense attorney, but he declined comment. Now it's up to the jury to decide."

Jill knew other reporters acted similarly, believing that as journalists they were thus serving the public. But Jill now realized the harm she may have done in the cases of other accused who like myself had been "criminalized" by prosecutors who created scenarios to bring in a guilty verdict.

My attorney, Steve Hurley, did the same thing in my case. He was brief with reporters and instructed me to remain silent. While I wanted to share the truth with those journalists, they never got to hear it from me.

Steve, like me, was a victim of the prosecution's deceptive tactics and was as devastated as I was about the guilty verdict.

"You put your life in my hands," he said, his voice crushed with emotion. "I wish I'd prepared you better for cross examination."

But I didn't feel it was his fault. The jury was completely blind to what really happened that day at my house. I thought Steve had fought his heart out for me and I would always be grateful for his devotion.

Two days after the verdict, we arrived at my parents' home in Hudson for Thanksgiving. As we walked in the door, the delicious aroma of turkey baking in the oven wafted over us, and I almost burst into tears, knowing this could be the last time I would breathe in this fragrance for many years.

Yet, on some level, I was still hoping the judge would see the light and set me free on probation.

I was thankful for my family and for my three beautiful girls, but the holiday was simply an emotional mess. Ordinarily, it would have been joyous, with my brother Gary home on leave from the Navy. Mom and Dad were busy in the kitchen, but they rushed out when they heard us enter. Carrie and Allison jumped into their arms, while Jenny urged me to hurry up and unzip her snowsuit so she could join in the fun.

My parents, my brothers, and their families put on brave faces, but the best I could do was to try muddling through the day. I was now thoroughly exhausted from the trial and its outcome, and barely managed to enjoy my parents' delicious dinner.

Everyone relished sharing this special family time, but our hearts were heavy with the uncertainty of my upcoming sentencing.

After Thanksgiving, Steve suggested I see a psychologist. He recommended Dr. Nina Bartell as a good therapist to help me cope with my situation. He also wanted her to prepare a summary for the judge to consider as part of his pre-sentencing investigation. When we met, I felt comfortable with Dr. Bartell and we talked openly about Natalie's death and the trial. I wasn't really nervous, but I did find it extremely difficult to discuss what had happened, and what might be awaiting me in the immediate future.

Dr. Bartell and I talked a lot, and she also observed me with Carrie, Allison and Jenny in a playroom and her office. The girls were unaware of why I was visiting a psychologist--they were only interested in the terrific toys the doctor had in her office!

In her summary statement for the judge, Dr. Bartell wrote that I was much more emotionally fragile than I was willing to admit. "She is extremely worried, more so about her children than herself," Dr. Bartell wrote. "It is likely that she will decompensate dramatically if imprisoned. She is more prone to depression than anger.

"Audrey displays neither hostile nor malicious intent. She has become even more concerned about appearances and what others might think. Although somewhat unhealthy, it keeps impulses under strict control. She is somewhat suspicious and defensive. Her tendency is to have people believe that she is doing better emotionally than she actually is."

It troubled me that she focused on my obvious reaction to my situation, rather than help me cope with the staggering circumstances. I wanted so much to relieve my mental anguish, but no one had a magic wand or pill to erase a wrongful conviction.

I had a hard time pouring out my feelings to just anyone. These feelings were deep and impossible for another person to understand, yet I clung to the hope that someone would grasp how shocked and horrified I was with the entire situation—because I was innocent!

Dr. Bartell did say in her summary that I was "open to mental treatment" to handle stress and prevent a debilitating depression. Actually, to share the truth of what happened and have someone in authority believe what I said would have been the most healing mental treatment possible.

Dr. Bartell described my relationship with my daughters as "close" and said that parenting was my major source of confidence. She wrote that I was able to keep the impact of my stress apart from my parent/child relationships. She also pointed out that Carrie sensed that something was going on in the family. Her feeling was that all the girls were too young to understand why they were being separated from their mother, and would suffer severe emotional trauma. Because the girls were developing a basic child/parent bond with me, such a long-term disruption at this stage could damage that bond permanently.

Dr. Bartell also observed Dave with the girls and said he was a supportive parent, but lacked the capability to take on the role of primary parent. She wrote that Dave was under significant stress and it was questionable if the marriage would survive if I went to prison.

My reaction was anger. Of course Dave was under great stress! However, he would step up to the plate and be the parent our daughters needed. We didn't need outside shrinks to tell us we were under extreme duress and how we would act in the future. I was miffed and defensive about all this psychoanalysis when I felt I had handled this nightmare as well as any other innocent person would. I fervently wished not to be separated from my family! Dr. Bartell's report went to the judge and came back later to haunt me.

Meanwhile, I had a lengthy meeting with John Weinheimer, a probation and parole agent for the state. A simple, down-to-earth guy, he sipped coffee during our first informal interview and his tone was one of genuine interest when he asked a question. We discussed where I was born, my family, my father's job, where I attended school, where I worked, my marriages, Dave, and our family. It was all very comfortable.

I relaxed enough with John to share how horrible I felt about Natalie's death, being blamed for it, and the appalling verdict. He asked me whether Carrie could have harmed Natalie that awful day. This had also come up during the trial. Our defense witness Dr. Kaminski testified that a slight jolt to Natalie could have caused the irritation to Natalie's brain stem that led to her death.

My attorney asked me when I was on the stand if it was possible that Carrie went into the bedroom to console or feed Natalie. I told him, yes, it was possible because I didn't have Carrie in my sight at every moment that morning. The prosecution then spun my comment to accuse me of trying to blame my own four-year-old daughter for Natalie's injuries!

This accusation was, like so many other scenarios they contrived, outrageous. I never thought Carrie harmed Natalie. I always felt responsible because I had propped up her bottle and she had, it appeared, choked. I thought the prosecution was contemptible in trying to exploit my little girl so they could contrive a case against me.

I spent seven long hours with John Weinheimer and felt some relief that someone in authority was finally listening to my side of the story. Steve Hurley was surprised John had spent so long interviewing me but surmised by the questions that he had talked with the prosecutors first.

In the end, John recommended to the judge that I serve one year in prison.

The holidays were difficult, but I mustered as much enthusiasm as possible for Dave and the girls. A week before Christmas, Allison broke out with chicken pox. My poor baby, just two-and-a-half years old, was miserable and clung to me during the first few days. I felt so blessed to be able to care for her in our own loving home. Carrie continued with kindergarten until Christmas break arrived. We decorated the house and tree and I tried to tap into my children's holiday joyfulness. By Christmas Eve, Allison was feeling better so I took the girls to Carrie's performance in the children's program at our church. She was dressed as an angel and I had to hold back tears of pride.

I was riddled with anxiety the next few months and continued to pray that something would happen to keep Judge Moeser from sending me to prison.

I put together a party for Jenny's first birthday on February 18, 1997. My dear friend, Shelley Murphy, came to celebrate with my parents and other friends. Little Jenny was awed by her one-candle cake, and as I watched her gleefully enjoying herself in the spotlight, I thought back over her first year of life. How I cherished watching her grow and learn. I was so sorry that my legal problems had tainted my baby's first twelve months on this earth.

Carrie and Allie helped Jenny blow out the one candle and helped her rip open her presents. They all giggled with delight over the new clothes and toys for the birthday girl, and I desperately tried to cling to this joyous moment.

Two days after Jenny's first birthday, I was back in Madison, awaiting my sentencing with a deep sense of dread.

CHAPTER TWELVE

The day before the sentencing, Dave and I packed the girls into our van along with Shelley and made the trek back to Waunakee. We arrived mid-afternoon and our daughters buzzed around the house with Shelley's three kids. Neighbors and friends stopped by with support and caring words. As I hugged each one of them, I tried not to think about how traumatic the next day would be.

That night, I lay in bed for a long time, unable to fall asleep, a million thoughts crowding around demanding my attention, and all of them frightening. I finally dozed off only to awaken early the next morning. Soon, Allison and Jenny tumbled out of bed and wanted breakfast, so I took them downstairs to the kitchen, drinking in the happiness shining from their sparkling eyes.

I dressed in an ivory skirt and pink sweater not knowing if I would wear pretty clothes again for the next forty years. The judge had the option to sentence me to probation, so I still had a slim hope that I would not face prison. Soon it was time to depart, but Carrie was still asleep. I slipped into the bedroom and put my arms around her. Leaning forward I kissed her, my heart so heavy I thought it would explode. I had to hold back sobs when I hugged and kissed Allison and Jenny goodbye. When would I see them again?

As if the state hadn't demolished my spirit enough at the trial, it wasn't finished with me yet. Gretchen Hayward began by addressing the judge.

"Your honor, this murder is more aggravated than any other first degree reckless homicide I can think of because it's the murder of a baby. It's one of the worst crimes to occur in Dane County and one of the most violent. That's because it's a hands-on murder. Audrey Edmunds murdered Natalie Beard with her bare hands. She shook Natalie until she could feel the life leaving that little baby."

Steve protested, but Judge Moeser overruled him.

"This is a sentencing. It's pretty wide open and people can say what they want to say and we can argue the weight it should be given," the judge replied.

Hayward continued on, explaining that Natalie's only way of protecting herself was to attempt to tell her parents she was unhappy with me by crying. However, her parents didn't understand, and although they heard her cries, they couldn't act in time. Now, they would have to suffer for the rest of their lives, knowing that they left their child with her murderer, who had shown no guilt or remorse.

"Natalie did the only thing a six-month-old baby could do to protect herself. She cried when she got to the defendant's house that day," Hayward said. "Her cries were 'don't leave me here!' That only irritated the defendant more. Rather than telling Cindy 'Please don't leave Natalie with me because she's driving me nuts, take her home with you,' the defendant had to keep up her superficial act. 'I am so wonderful. Nothing fazes me.'

The defendant did not love Natalie as she loved her own children, as she testified. And if she did, God help her own children. Natalie did not like the defendant and Edmunds did not like her because of her treatment at the defendant's house. Couple that with the rest of the stresses in this defendant's life, like a marriage that, according to her own psychologist, will not withstand a separation."

There it was. Hayward had seized the psychologist's assessment and used it to her own ends, as well as tearing apart my character and my morning with Natalie.

Even in my confused state of mind, I could not understand how Hayward or Judge Moeser could measure how I loved. Love is true and genuine and cannot be measured by another. There are no love scales that calculate love percentages. The two of them took my heartfelt statement and twisted it into another atrocious lie.

"The defendant could have called Cindy or Tom that morning to say she didn't feel good and come and get your baby," Hayward continued. "They would have come in a heartbeat. She could have put the baby in a room and left her...shut the door and not listened to her irritability. But she chose to take all her frustrations out on this little infant.

She grabbed Natalie in a fury and shook that innocent little girl with an unimaginable force, then threw her...discarded her. She meant nothing to the defendant. She still means nothing to the defendant.

I'm sorry, but what the defendant did goes beyond snapping. It shows a degree of anger I cannot imagine. A degree of hatred I cannot imagine. I do not believe that any pro-social person could commit this crime—could, with her bare hands, murder a baby within one hour of that baby arriving in her home."

It was absolutely heart wrenching to sit and listen to these lies!

"How cruel you have been, Audrey Edmunds," Hayward prolonged. "And to add to the cruelty, she pointed the finger at the parents. Tom and Cindy were in mourning, yet they were slandered and scorned and made to move from their home. It is because she is a murderer, a liar and a perjurer.

The psychologist hired by the defendant found Edmunds emotionally fragile and suspicious to the point of paranoia. She has an over-controlled denial system. She's superficially charming and personally insecure.

It is a strong *circumstantial* explanation that this defendant shook Natalie before. The defendant has such a deep- seeded denial, fueled by her support system, that she does not accept responsibility and cannot offer one shred of remorse."

Hayward called me a "perfect mother who, according to her own defense expert, can only withstand moderate amounts of stress before becoming a dysfunctional parent. Are her own children really safe? Maybe prison will protect those children."

When did anyone, including my psychologist, witness me as a dysfunctional parent? Never!

Hayward finally wound down and declared I had made the choice to murder Natalie and thus was completely responsible for being separated from my own children.

"I recommend the defendant be sentenced to twenty-five years in the Wisconsin State Prison System, contribute five thousand dollars to the cost of prosecuting this case, and pay for Natalie's burial expenses and any future expenses the Beards incur as a result of her murder."

Steve did his best to temper Hayward's annihilation of my life and character.

"It is, when one is found guilty of a wrongdoing, easy to point fingers. It is easy to abuse. It is easy to view them as one-dimensional and shallow. Ms. Edmunds is not one-dimensional and shallow," Steve said. "It is not as Ms. Hayward told you that she has more to lose than most. Audrey has more to contribute than most to her family and the community. It is not speculation or hope. It is premised on a lifetime of conduct."

The Beards stood stiffly in front of the courtroom. Cindy read from a paper that she prepared beforehand. She said I was cruel to kill their daughter and not accept responsibility. She expressed grief for all they would miss watching her grow up and it was all my fault.

"Judge Moeser, show no mercy to Audrey Edmunds," Cindy said. "Not for us, but for Natalie and all the other babies and children who need protection from adults. Please sentence Audrey Edmunds to tell us all the truth."

Tom Beard didn't speak and never looked at me during the trial or sentencing. That was odd, because a couple of weeks after Natalie's death he passed me in the car and waved at me with a smile on his face. The prosecution had corrupted Tom and Cindy's minds with lies. The Beards and the jury were blinded by speculation, not truth. As a result, neither Natalie nor her parents received the justice they deserved.

Nobody spoke on my behalf, which Steve recommended, saying that at this point, no matter what positive words people might have for me, they'd be damned by the DA. He felt supporters' statements would fall on cold hearts and deaf ears. I accepted his counsel and agreed. After all, I was under vicious, unthinkable attack.

After everyone had spoken, Judge Moeser gave me the opportunity to speak. I had thought about this statement with great passion the weeks before sentencing. I'd run through many ideas, but in the last hours I decided to say something in true compassion, but not denial. I had nothing to deny. I knew the court and everyone on the prosecution side wanted an apology, but I had nothing to apologize for. I stood and spoke from the defense table.

"To Tom and Cindy, relatives and friends, I just want you to know I am terribly saddened with the death of Natalie. God bless you all."

The few words I spoke were true, heartfelt and I hoped showed my compassion.

My heart started to pummel when Judge Moeser finally spoke. My entire future and my family's were in his hands. He talked about the seventy or so letters he received from supporting family and friends. Jill told me she had color copied numerous pages from her scrapbook with pictures of all our celebrations showing me happily nurturing multiple children.

All my other friends wrote in strong support and Moeser said he was especially touched by Dave's letter, which explained just how damaging a prison term would be for our family.

"Mrs. Edmunds raised concern in the pre-sentence interview that the jury was not always attentive. But this jury was as attentive and thoughtful as any jury I have ever seen. I had the opportunity to see them and speak with them shortly after the verdict. All of them were profoundly affected. Let there be no doubt that they made the right decision.

To Tom and Cindy Beard, I hope that today helps you on your journey to recovery. The jury believed you and I believe you. I think all reasonable, open-minded members of this community believe you."

He said it so blatantly, I was stunned. Judge Moeser thought I did it, too. The juror we talked with, Terry Temple, confirmed this. He said Moeser congratulated the jury on the correct verdict. I was absolutely presumed guilty from the day Natalie died. Even the judge pegged me.

Judge Moeser continued, "A person does not have the right to get up on the witness stand and lie. A person who admits their crime, accepts responsibility for their conduct and tells the truth under oath is much further along the path of rehabilitation than someone who does not. Mrs. Edmunds has yet to accept responsibility and that says something about her character.

She needs extensive therapy and treatment to help her eventually recognize and accept the reality of the situation. The community needs protection from someone who is unable to accept responsibility."

I started to quake when Judge Moeser said probation would depreciate the seriousness of the crime. He also said he rarely has a prosecution request to pay a portion for their costs and would take it under advisement. He ordered me to pay restitution to the Beards for their expenses and imposed mandatory court costs. Dave ended up paying the Beards thirty-seven hundred dollars.

"I am recommending to the Department of Corrections and the Parole Board that Mrs. Edmunds not be released on parole, transferred to the Division of Intensive Sanctions or released from custody prior to her mandatory release date until and unless she unequivocally confesses to this crime and makes it known to the victims.

The sentence I am imposing is eighteen years in the Wisconsin State Prison System to commence forthwith. Bail is revoked. We are adjourned."

He said it so quickly it was hard to understand the full impact. I did hear eighteen years and my stomach dropped. I also heard something about having to admit guilt before I could be released on probation. Was this legal? Could a judge force an innocent person to admit guilt?

Steve told me later judges can and often do insist prisoners admit guilt. He had seen it many times. Steve thought my sentence was heart-wrenching and cruel. The judge was guaranteeing that I would not raise my children. "He knew what he was doing," Steve said. "You took this baby, and I'm going to take yours."

Two sheriff's deputies immediately handcuffed me behind my back right in the courtroom and my whole world crumbled.

As the deputy led me out, I glanced over my shoulder and caught my dad's blanched, terrified face. Tears streamed down his cheeks and I saw my sister-in-law Mary crying, too. I looked at Dave, frozen on his feet, his arms folded over his chest as if to shield himself from this horror. I'm going to prison and my girls are losing their mother, I silently screamed, as they led me out of the courtroom.

CHAPTER THIRTEEN

I couldn't stop trembling as the deputies led me to a holding cell in the basement of the courthouse. The cell was about twelve-by-sixteen feet with brick walls, a brick bench around two walls for sitting, and a metal toilet out in the open. I stared at the concrete floor, strewn with paper garbage and God knew what germs. The deputies shut the heavy metal door with a sickening clang that reverberated throughout my body.

I saw a telephone on the wall and quickly picked up the receiver. All I could think was, "I want to call someone and hear a friendly, familiar voice."

I called Shelley Murphy but nobody answered and then I realized that she was probably still upstairs in the courthouse after attending my sentencing.

Next, I called Patti Larson and her husband Jeff answered. I heard his strong voice, said hello, and then burst into tears. He was wonderful, and offered me many words of encouragement. I pictured him in their house, where I had spent many happy afternoons with Patti, and wished I could be back in my cozy home where I belonged. Instead, I was here in a cold, dank jail cell. And this was just the beginning! Many months later, Patti told me that when she returned home from the courthouse, she found her strapping husband, all six-feet-five and two-hundred-ninety pounds, crying like a baby, his heart aching for me.

I was issued a blue V-neck shirt, blue elastic waist pants, tube socks and brown plastic shower shoes along with a bag. They told me to change into these clothes and put my own outfit in the bag—and that was the last I saw of pretty clothes.

After the clothing change, I waited alone in the cold, dreary cell for hours. Finally, I was handcuffed again and led to a jail medic. I told her I had a sinus infection and was taking an antibiotic.

"You can continue the prescription," she said, "But we will issue new pills. Some inmates tamper with their own medications and try to smuggle in mind-altering drugs."

I had no idea people did this sort of thing! I was definitely entering a world totally foreign to me.

The medic checked my vital signs and asked if I had problems with depression. Although I told her "no," I was totally numb from the court procedure and its outcome. I was still disbelieving that Judge Moeser had completely ignored the state's own probation/parole agent's recommendations that I serve only one year. Nor did they offer me any medicine or counseling for my fear and shock.

The booking process was humiliating and felt like a bad scene from a movie. But this was real life for me with fingerprinting, mug shots and paperwork. Worst of all was the dreaded strip search. It had been one of my biggest fears entering prison, and afterwards I had definitely been stripped of all dignity.

I was then given a worn brown blanket and taken to a regular jail cell. I swear the metal door weighed ten tons as the guard with the keys clanked it open and I stepped inside the stuffy space. He removed my handcuffs and left me in the sparse room. Looking around, I saw a table in the middle, a metal toilet and shower to the right, and metal bunk beds lining the other three walls.

As my eyes slowly scanned my new living facility, I finally noticed I was not alone. In fact, there were several women sitting on the bunks. Two were sleeping while two others said "Hello." I was very nervous at the thought of being alone with these women. Were these my permanent roommates? I couldn't imagine using the toilet or shower with no curtain for privacy!

I tentatively took a seat on one of the bunks. The mattress was only about two inches thick and covered with heavy royal blue plastic. The head of the mattress was angled with a pillow enclosed within it, sort of a one-piece sleeping pad.

Soon, food was delivered on a plastic tray. I couldn't even identify it, and my stomach was too upset to eat. All I could think about was my girls. I wondered what they would think when Mommy didn't come home. How would Dave ever explain to these precious children what had happened to their mother?

The other women weren't mean, but they weren't compassionate, either. Some were making a return trip to prison and knew the ropes. For them, jail was a safe house with a bed and meals. Others were withdrawing from drugs and acting crazy.

I was cautious of them all, but they told me I would be okay. However, I didn't believe them. How could I relate to these women or to prison in any way?

Early in the evening, a guard came to get me. I had visitors! I was shocked, but also thrilled at the prospect of seeing familiar faces.

I was taken to a room with three telephones, and on the other side of the plexi-glass window, I saw Dave, my parents, friends and neighbors. I was most anxious to talk with Dave to find out how he had handled the girls.

"I told Carrie that Mommy was going away for a little while," Dave said, trying to reassure me." I told her Mommy will call her and soon be able to see her again."

My heart broke when he told me Carrie had cried at these words, followed by Allison, who burst into tears as well.

I was relieved to learn that my Mom and Dad were moving in with Dave to help with the children. Although they would keep their home in Hudson, they would live with Dave from Monday to Friday to provide loving care and support and help clean and cook. I knew this was good for everyone concerned.

Other family and friends took turns talking with me by telephone. We fumbled for words but it was wonderful to see them, and we shared our pain and shock, each handling it in our own way.

Some of my friends flattened their hands against the thick plastic and I placed mine against theirs. We felt love and hope through all the madness. After a couple of hours, visiting time was over and the people I loved so much had to leave in their pretty clothes to return to warm, loving homes.

I was left behind, alone, cold and frightened. They took me back to the cell, where I flopped onto the hard bed and stared at the wall. I was so overwrought, I buried my head under the thin blanket and wept, my heart shattered into a million pieces. A light above my bed glared less than two feet from my head, which I couldn't turn off because it was controlled outside my cell. Finally, at eleven p.m., it went off and I gratefully fell asleep, through my dreams finally able to escape my imprisonment for a few short hours.

A jail officer awakened me about four o'clock the next morning and put me into another tiny cell with two other women. I had no idea what was going on and I was afraid. One of the women had already been to the state pen and knew the routine. I was so frightened! We were given a plastic tray with two pieces of soggy toast, cold cereal and a cup of milk with a spoon, but I couldn't eat; my stomach was in knots. Nobody explained what was happening to us, and every event seemed to become a long, drawn-out process.

Finally, the jail officer gave me a big, ugly green jacket, handcuffed me again and this time, as tears filled my eyes, I watched as they shackled me around my ankles. I felt as if the flames of hell were licking at my feet.

Still wearing the same clothes I'd worn the day before, I was loaded into a van with other inmates, both men and women. I had no idea where I was going as the big garage door heaved open, and I didn't dare ask anyone as we headed out through the streets of Madison.

As I watched through the window, I saw people going about their business, walking into stores, banks or office buildings. They had no idea how lucky they were to be free, to walk and drive wherever they wanted! How I longed to be a normal person again, just like them. I couldn't believe my own circumstances, shackled in a van hauling me off to prison like a criminal.

Soon we were in an area of Madison I didn't recognize, and then we hopped on the highway. It was a cold, winter day and the ride seemed endless. We finally pulled into a garage at what I soon learned was the Dodge Correctional Facility in Waupun, Wisconsin.

The guards herded us like cattle into an open area where we waited for hours to be booked as offenders. After filling out paperwork I was told I was an intake prisoner, a transition program between sentencing and hard core prison. A guard led me into a shower room and I was ordered to wash and Kuell. I learned Kuell was a toxic smelling shampoo that kills lice and germs.

I was so afraid, naked in the open shower. I pushed a button to turn on the water, but there was no temperature control and poor water pressure. I cleaned myself as quickly as possible in the cool stream and dried off with a small white towel that I hoped was bleached. I had no hair conditioner after the acrid shampoo and no facial or body lotion. It was my first realization that the little luxuries in life were over. The toiletries I took for granted at home were banished in an instant. I dressed in green elastic waist pants, a factory type shirt that buttoned down the front and white Keds. Men and women wore the same clothes.

After the shower they took my photo. I was taken down a long hallway to a small room with a wooden bunk bed, two chairs, a small wooden desk and that ubiquitous open toilet. Another lady was already in the room and immediately complained to the guard about her medical condition. I could tell she was chemically addicted. She was totally irrational spouting wild stories and excuses trying to get her way. This woman terrified me. I was so relieved when staff finally moved her to another room.

Now I was alone in the cell. I heard talking and keys clanging as a sergeant occasionally walked the hallway. Otherwise I was totally alone with nothing to do. I couldn't play with my kids, grab a magazine off my coffee table or munch a sweet apple from my kitchen. What in the hell was I doing in this place?

Soon, a flap on my door opened and a tray of food was shoved through. Prisoners on intake had to stay in the room for meals the first seventy-two hours of confinement. A lady came with a cart of books and I snatched a couple romance novels wanting to occupy my mind and escape into someone else's problems. Oh, how I wanted to call home and talk with our girls. They needed to hear Mommy's voice. All our lives were flipped upside down and we were spinning three hundred miles an hour.

That first day on intake, I filled out a form that was the only means of communicating with the staff. I asked the floor sergeant if they had any jobs because I was willing to work. I was so used to multi-tasking with many children in my care that the idle time freaked me out.

That night I donned the big sleep T-shirt they issued to me and was glad to sleep without the wacky woman in the bunk above me. The next day, the staff issued clean clothes, the exact same green ensemble as the day before. I tried to read the romance novel but was relieved when my door opened and a tall, solidly built sergeant entered.

"We have a swamper position if you want to work," he said.

I had no idea what a *swamper* was and it certainly didn't sound very glamorous. But it couldn't be worse than staring at four walls in a tiny cell for hours on end, so I took the job. After completing my intake hours that Sunday, I went to find out what a swamper does. Another inmate, named Nancy showed me the ropes. Nancy was about my age with long, dark hair and a medium build. She showed me an area where clean clothes and towels were stored for the other inmates.

"We receive the dirty clothes and clean some of them," she explained. "The rest goes to a large laundry area."

We scrubbed showers and mopped down the hallways. The job certainly lived up to its name but I was thankful it kept me out of that claustrophobic room from six in the morning until nine at night. Nancy was friendly and we delivered newspapers and books to the female inmates on our floor for them to read in their rooms. Swampers had the special luxury of going outside in a fenced-in area to shovel snow. We were the only inmates allowed outside. I never thought shoveling snow and cleaning bathrooms would be a privilege.

All inmates got one hour of gym time five out of seven nights a week. I was glad to run on the treadmill as I was used to jogging a few miles each day. I also lifted weights while many ladies played volleyball or walked around the gym. I needed the exercise to expel my overbearing tension.

We had a church with a prison minister on Mondays and a tiny library was open once or twice a week for fifty minutes. No rooms had TVs or radios. My family immediately sent me money for canteen hoping to make my incarceration as comfortable as possible. I was relieved to see toiletries on the canteen list.

My first order was for a comb, toothbrush, toothpaste, bar of soap, body lotion, deodorant, shampoo, hair conditioner and dental floss. I also purchased a pen, paper, envelopes and stamps. The sergeant commented that I didn't buy junk food like the other women. I wanted to take care of myself as best I could.

For meals, we walked through a cafeteria line and received plates and bowls of portioned food. You couldn't ask for seconds, and any leftovers were discarded. We ate in a small dining hall at round silver metal tables with four seats attached. We had fifteen minutes to eat.

The food was blah with lots of processed meat, carbohydrates like white bread, noodles and rice with very little seasoning. The cold breakfast cereal was my main nutrient and substance.

Some inmates were cordial while others stuffed food into their mouths. It was probably better food than they could scrounge up outside prison. I longed for a decent home-cooked meal. But I had so much on my mind, my appetite was nil.

I filled out visiting forms for Dave, our girls, my parents, siblings and their wives and other close friends. I sent these forms to them which included a questionnaire they had to answer. They sent the forms back to Dodge for processing.

During my three weeks at Dodge, I met with a social worker. She told me I was headed to Taycheedah Correctional Institute the women's maximum security prison in Fond du Lac. Indirectly, she told me I couldn't trust many people in the big house.

"They may try to get you to buy things for them with your money."

I was so naïve. After all, I was used to helping others. As I was about to face such a cruel world inside prison walls, I was frightened for my safety.

My third week at Dodge, I was finally allowed to make a fifteen minute telephone call. I scheduled the call for 11:45 in the morning on Thursday, knowing my girls would be eating lunch before Carrie left for Kindergarten.

The floor sergeant told me how to work the phone near his work area. The dialing instructions were lengthy because all prisoners had to call collect. I punched in the numbers and waited with my heart pounding in my chest. I heard two rings.

"Hello." I melted at the sound of Dad's wonderful voice.

"Hi, Daddy, it's me!" I heard him gulp, then we both had tears.

"It's so good to hear your voice, honey." We didn't speak long because Dad knew I needed time with each daughter.

"Hi, Mommy!" Carrie squeaked. "When are you coming home?"

It was a question that broke my heart. I told her I wanted to be with her so much and prayed I would have her in my arms soon. I talked to Allison for a few minutes and she told me about her toy dog and wondered why I was not with her. Jenny babbled into the phone and more tears streamed down my face. I spoke a few words to Mom and Dad and the fifteen minutes were quickly spent. I had to remind myself to be thankful for this connection, however brief.

That same week, I received notice that my appellate attorney, Dean Strang, was going to visit me that Saturday, March 8, 1997. Steve Hurley worked with Dean and considered him an excellent lawyer; he recommended I use him to file an appeal. I was eager to start the gears cranking to get me out of this horrible place. The sergeant commented that professional visits were usually Monday through Friday.

Saturday came and I was called to the visiting room. They had confiscated my contact lenses during my processing, as such luxuries were banned in prison. Unfortunately, my state-issued glasses had not arrived, so my vision was extremely blurry.

I entered a huge visiting room and two sergeants checked me in.

"I have not met my new attorney yet," I told them. "And I can't see well without my glasses. Can you direct me to him?"

They pointed to a table far across the room. As I neared the area my eyes began to focus and my heart leapt. There at the table was Dave! I was so surprised and happy to see him that I jumped into his arms and held on tight. His bear hug felt heavenly.

"I talked to Dean and he told me he had to reschedule your meeting for Monday," Dave told me. "So I took his place."

My dear husband had driven five hours to see me, knowing I would be in deep despair. The sergeant who checked me in now called me back to the desk.

"Who is that visiting you?" he asked. "I thought you were meeting your attorney."

I froze, hoping he wouldn't turn Dave away. I explained the situation and he chuckled and blessedly sent me back to visit with my husband. I still treasure those three hours of sanity, bonding, family updates and sheer joy with Dave.

I was thrilled on Monday when I finally met with Dean Strang. A guard led me to a small, private conference room where he was already waiting. He was about an inch taller than my five-nine and looked quite dapper and intelligent with his jet black hair, small round glasses, designer suit and tie.

I had huge hopes for an appeal, and was anxious for him to explain the process. As Dean laid out some folders on the table, he told me he was reading through the trial transcripts and other pertinent records and materials.

"I am noting all significant information to determine which appeal factors are strongest to address," he said. "Then I will meet with Steve Hurley and begin composing the issues."

That seemed like a long process, but I was relieved when Dean said he had already filed the necessary papers so the appeal would take place.

"We have ninety days to compose and file the brief."

My stomach turned. Ninety days? That meant at least three more months in prison. Dean could only tell me the details of this process and I trusted his knowledge and abilities. He departed after a couple hours and left me clinging to new threads of hope.

The day before the state of Wisconsin hauled me to Taycheedah, I received a soft case with my new glasses. Excitedly, I pulled them out and put them on. They were big, round, dark red frames that jutted beyond my face, making me look like a clown. But I was so happy to finally see with normal vision, I didn't even care how they made me look. I knew I needed to have a clear focus before I entered maximum security prison.

CHAPTER FOURTEEN

Just as I was getting used to the routine at Dodge, the three weeks were up. On Friday, March 14th, it was time to move to Taycheedah. The Dodge people would have to look for a new swamper. That day dawned cold and snowy which was typical for Wisconsin in mid-March.

The correctional system did virtually nothing to prepare me for this massive transition into hard core prison life. I had a million questions about the cell size, food, freedom to walk about and of course, how I would fare with the other inmates. I dressed in state underwear and the monotonous green outfit. Thankfully, the prison system allowed me to take my toiletries, along with my Bible and up to twenty-five letters from friends and family.

I rode in a van through more foreign territory. Billboards for familiar stores and restaurants were actually a comfort, allowing me a few moments of normalcy on this otherwise bizarre journey.

I drew in a long breath when we arrived at the gates of Taycheedah. Beyond the razor-topped fences loomed the forbidding prison, a dreary gray fortress that would be my residence for years to come! I was still in utter disbelief that my worst nightmare was here. And now, I had arrived in Hell.

The staff moved the line of new prisoners into the lower part of an old building, where they strip-searched us again. I cringed as they inspected my naked body. I learned that strip searches were routine any time we left the prison grounds, which included court appearances.

Following the humiliating exploration, the staff issued more green shirts, pants, underwear, socks, one pair of canvas Keds, a towel and bedding. I was with a group of five other women, and after we gathered our new belongings, they marched us outside on this cold winter day to a large building that I soon learned was the maximum security section. I said a few words to my fellow inmates, but mostly just listened to the other ladies chatter as I looked over my new surroundings. I was frightened as we entered this huge space, and my eyes gazed up in wonder at the two levels of cells. Unlike the men's facility that had rooms with wooden doors, the women's had rows of blue doors and a metal railing along the top tier. It looked more like a warehouse than a place of human habitation. My heart pounded in my chest as I watched the female prisoners moving about.

I stood there terrified, waiting for guidance on the next step of this process. I saw a large desk area, probably an intake center, with various staff members sitting around it. The staff took us into a room with big windows where a towering black sergeant told us he would come back and conduct an orientation.

We waited and waited. One hour went by, then two hours. The sergeant finally returned. "I'm too busy to do the orientation," he announced. "Gather your things and I'll assign each of you a room." He did give us all a handbook, which was the extent of my introduction to maximum security prison.

Time dragged as I waited for my turn to be assigned a space. At last they told me I was on the second level near the end of the north tier. A guard opened the automatic door and I walked into the tiniest closet of a room I'd ever seen, measuring eight-by-six feet. Straight in front of me and in full view of the small window on the door was the familiar metal toilet beside a miniature tin sink.

The only other furnishings were a bunk bed with metal drawers below the lower one, and a small metal cabinet with two shelves. My only outlet to the world was a teeny window with bars across it at the end of the bed.

My new roomie was sitting on the bottom bunk. "Hi, I'm Jen," she said in a friendly tone. She looked extremely young as she tossed her long, fine, light brown hair away from her face. "You can put your things on the top bunk."

Jen was watching her thirteen-inch television, the largest you could have in the rooms. Her belongings were on one of the shelves and she pointed to my drawer. My heart sank when I saw the sponge foam mattress with the heavy plastic covering. The pillow was also covered with thick plastic and crackled like a bag of potato chips in my arms. I resolutely set up my bed and packed my meager items away.

"I'm freezing in here," I said.

"You can wear one of my thermal shirts," Jen offered and pulled it out of her drawer. To my surprise, I noticed that Jen was wearing normal street clothes. She told me family and friends could have stores send me clothing as long as it met prison codes. They were not allowed to mail me a package from home because of the risk of smuggled contraband.

I couldn't wait to get out of my prison costume and wear something that actually fit me. I also wanted quality walking shoes so I could exercise. My legs and feet ached from the thin-soled Keds.

I stored my few possessions on my shelf and then hopped onto the top bunk and tried to get comfortable. It was the only place to sit in the cramped space. I felt suffocated, locked in a room smaller than the master bathroom of my home with a total stranger. Fortunately, I wasn't claustrophobic, but the prospect of living in these conditions for any length of time was unbearable.

I soon learned that Jen was twenty-six years old and serving two life sentences for a double murder. Of course, I didn't sound much better with my baby homicide charge. Jen had a bubbly personality and was extremely nice to me at a time when I truly needed kindness. She told me about mealtimes, how to sign up to shower, do laundry and use the telephone. At that time, she had a janitorial job in the building and I was eager to begin work myself. There was no way I could sit in our tiny closet of a room all day and just stare at the walls, deep in my personal misery.

That first night, I tossed and turned on the crunchy pillow, desperately missing my husband, babies, family and friends. I finally fell into a fitful sleep, only to be abruptly awakened at two-thirty in the morning when staff charged into the room and ordered Jen to "get up for a UA!"

I was utterly startled. What in the hell was going on? The guards ordered me to step outside the room. It was cold and dark with a few hall lights on. I heard commotion in my room but had no idea what was going on with Jen.

A few minutes later, a guard directed me back into the room. Jen was already in bed. I climbed onto the top bunk and lay there in a daze in this strange environment. Finally, I did manage to fall asleep.

The next day, I asked Jen about the early morning raid.

"You'll get used to that," Jen said matter-of-factly. "They were performing a urinalysis for drugs. It happens periodically, usually in the middle of the night."

Talk about more humiliation! Jen told me the guards watched as she sat on the tin toilet and produced a urine sample. In time, it would happen to me, too, several times a year.

Some inmates stole other inmates' prescriptions or visitors smuggled in drugs, so their urine did test positive. The prison rarely did anything about the positive results, such as actually treating the drug addictions. The prison could put inmates into segregation for a few days if they refused a urine analysis (UA) or had a dirty result. But such issues were generally ignored. With few repercussions for positive testing, I thought the random urine tests were pointless. I actually think those early morning raids felt more like punishment and degradation, with lots of alarm tossed in.

Jen told me if the prison doctor prescribed drugs for an illness, the inmate had to take the medicine in front of the staff. Although they had to stick out their tongues to show they actually swallowed the pill, some prisoners were adept at manipulation, hiding pills in their mouths. They collected drugs this way to sell to other women.

I was finding myself in a very bizarre world.

Jen and I shared stories about our charges. She was from a nice family in Milwaukee, but had gotten mixed up with gangs and made some poor decisions. I don't think she pulled the trigger, but she helped plan the killings, drove the getaway car and was put away for life.

I gave her a brief scenario of my case and she felt very sorry for me. "I remember that story on the news," Jen said. "It sounded like the baby was beaten up pretty bad."

I quivered, hearing her accusation. "That's not true," I insisted. Nobody seemed to get my story right, so I didn't share any more details. My case was so medically complicated, I kept it between my attorneys, family and close friends. I later learned this was smart because the prison was rife with snitches. In some cases, prisoners spewed lies about other inmates to district attorneys. Those lies were actually used in court so the snitch could get time reduced. I was glad I had a friendly roommate in Jen but wondered how I would manage in this rough environment.

The first couple of weeks at Taycheedah were awkward. Being confined to one small room and longing to be at home caring for my girls and Dave were devastating.

Neighbors from Waunakee got together and sent me a thirteen-inch color television. They also ordered jeans to be mailed to me, but they did not match the prison specified tint and had to be returned. Talk about insane! The prison gave us a denim swatch sample to view, but did not allow us to send it to our family to match.

Instead, my friends had stores quickly send me khaki shorts, some colored T-shirts, two sweatshirts, gym shorts and tennis shoes. It took almost four weeks for the prison property department to process the clothing, but I was so grateful for these few luxury items, and I cherished the supportive running shoes.

It was good to be out of the prison greens, and in the beginning I wore my own clothes all the time. This included going to meals, trips to other buildings and visits. Later the rules would change.

Friends from Waunakee also sent me newspaper articles about my case. One story in the *Capital Times* said my dear friends at Crossroads United Methodist Church still strongly supported me. They continued to pray for me and raised nearly five thousand dollars for a legal defense fund for my family. The church members said the verdict raised troubling questions about our justice system. The paper quoted one church member, Grace Fonstad, who said, "They focused on the wrong thing…not solving the death of a child, but laying blame."

"I was in court all week and I saw reasonable doubt throughout the trial," Barb Werner, the pastor's wife, told the paper. "People are very upset. They feel if they can do this to Audrey, they can do this to anyone."

The article also said some day care providers in Waunakee now refused to take children under the age of two. I felt blessed to have such strong support behind me. But nobody was able to produce a get-out-of-jail-free card for me.

I quickly settled into the monotonous routine of prison life. Breakfast was served shortly after six in the morning and dinner as early as four-twenty in the afternoon. Each section of the building rotated on a meal schedule. It was the same cafeteria food as that in Dodge, served on plastic trays with plastic silverware. There were no choices or extra portions.

Some meals were extremely meager and my stomach growled. I craved fresh vegetables, fruit and lean meats, but they were in short supply. Sometimes we got lucky when the kitchen served apples or oranges or a rare banana.

At first, friends and family sent me fruit from an outside vendor and I received a large variety. This was a delicious treat, but after a few years the staff didn't want to handle it anymore. That was the end of my private supply of fresh fruit.

I continued with my exercise for fifty minutes each day the gym was available, usually five days a week. But that was often cancelled. I was used to lots of vigorous exercise, so I craved it and I found it almost unbearable when the confined space I was in didn't allow me to get the exercise I needed. The prison also had a day space area where the inmates could share social time. I sat and talked briefly with my fellow inmates, but most of the time, I felt alone, as I could not relate to the struggles most of these women had faced throughout their lives. I felt sorry for them, but many did not see that their own choices and attitudes had caused most of their problems. I kept the conversations very general and purposely avoided forging close friendships. I was both wary of these women and out of my depth. Certainly, I felt unable to guide them.

We inmates could sign up for a shower every day. The shower time was not restricted, but often, guards watched closely to make sure nobody lingered too long. The shower stalls had blue doors that started about two feet off the floor and rose about five feet. Each door had paper-punch-sized holes, which did not provide full privacy, but it was still better than an open shower area. Because there was no temperature control, I often lathered and rinsed quickly under a stream of chilly water.

Doing our laundry was limited to twice a week.

But my favorite sign-up sheet was to use the phone to call Dave, our girls and my parents. The calls could last up to thirty minutes and became the highlight of my life inside prison. I just lived for this contact! The calls were expensive, however, and a three-dollar connection fee and fifty cents a minute often added up to a three-to-six-hundred dollar a month phone bill for Dave.

We felt it was worth it, however, as we all needed as much contact as possible. I was not going to lose my connection with my daughters for any amount of money!

After a few weeks, a sergeant assigned me to work on the yard crew. This meant I was out of bed by four-thirty in the morning on snow days to shovel snow. Fortunately, the prison provided boots. When it snowed a lot, I shoveled many long sidewalks, emergency exits and other areas, but I didn't really mind. I needed the fresh air. I was also assigned to indoor tasks. The physical labor kept my body busy and allowed me to fall into a deep sleep each night.

I knew I had to maintain mental focus and continued hoping I would get out soon on appeal. Without that faith, I knew I could crack inside these regimented confines.

Soon the prison approved my friends from Waunakee for my visiting list, and I looked forward to my time with them. The prison allowed four visits a week with only one on the weekend, and my friends coordinated and filled the slots. I treasured my time with each of them, especially hearing about life on the outside that I ached to stay connected with, even though I was no longer there.

Finally I learned that Dave, Mom and Dad were bringing the girls for their first visit on March 22nd. I had not seen them in a full month and was overwhelmed with anticipation. I also feared that baby Jenny wouldn't recognize me. *How would I cope with that?* I wondered, already feeling the pain of that possible scenario.

I could barely contain my excitement as I waited for twelve-thirty to arrive. I walked into the visiting room and Allie and Carrie ran over to me, squealing, "Mommy!" It was pure joy to hold them in my arms. I led them to a table with Mom, Dad, and Dave holding Jenny. I hugged them all so tight I thought I could feel their little hearts bursting with joy.

Carrie and Allison wanted my full attention and talked non-stop. Then, Jenny reached her arms out to me and seeing this, I felt tears running down my cheeks. Holding my girls and sharing this time with my family was as close to Paradise as I could come.

The visiting room had a small carpeted play area for children with toys, books and a little round table with chairs. It wasn't home, but the girls loved the playthings and their time with me. I read them a few books, built a tower with blocks, sang songs and tumbled on the ground with them. It felt so happy and normal. For those few precious hours, the prison seemed to melt into the background. Once again, I was with the people I loved most on earth, and it didn't matter where we were as long as we were together.

As I played, hugged, kissed and nestled with my babies, Mom, Dad and Dave worked in some conversation, but they knew the children mostly needed to connect with me, and vice-versa. The two-hour visiting limit ended far too quickly and I cried when it was time to say goodbye. Our two older girls clung to me and begged me to return home with them.

"Why can't you come with us?" Carrie asked, confusion all over her sweet face.

Dave had to pull the girls away and it wrenched my heart to see their tears. Was it too much for them to see me, and then be torn away after just two hours? I sobbed on the long walk back to the maximum security building, mulling over the situation.

I knew this was torture for all of us and thought of the long five- hour drive back home for my family. I knew it was a lot of responsibility for Dave and my parents in a van with three little girls who needed so much attention, especially after seeing me. And yet, I was desperate to wake up from this nightmare and be with them, whatever it took.

CHAPTER FIFTEEN

Summer arrived and I was outside in the sweltering heat working on the yard crew. No loose T-shirts or shorts were allowed; instead, we had to wear long, state-issued green pants and a short-sleeved polyester blend shirt.

I pushed a heavy lawn mower for up to six hours a day across acres of prison land. If we had abundant rain, the grass thrived and we were busy. Some of the women on yard crew were lazy and complained constantly, so I found myself taking on a heavy load. I didn't mind the exercise at all; it was good for me both physically and mentally. I was used to working out and being active.

I had learned to ignore the other prisoners. I did my work and stayed to myself most of the time. My whole focus was on maintaining my sanity until an appeal set me free. As to my compensation from the state for my blistering work keeping the grounds tidy, I was paid a whopping thirty-two cents an hour.

In late July, my attorney, Dean Strang, submitted my post-conviction motion in district court. This was the first step in trying to get me a new trial on the lesser charge of second degree reckless homicide, or acquitting me altogether. Unfortunately, his initial motion went before none other than Judge Moeser. It seemed highly biased to give it to the judge who had sentenced me, but the Wisconsin appeals process starts with the court and judge that tried you. This was very discouraging, but I was relieved to finally get the motion underway. Dean advised me that this period could take up to eighteen months. When he told me this, my heart sank.

Dean's sixteen-page motion emphasized that the prosecution had not offered sufficient evidence that I had "utter indifference for human life." He cited my hysteria on the 9-1-1 tape and my concern for Natalie after she fell ill. He pointed out that Judge Moeser had refused testimony about Natalie's father's indifferent behavior.

My new attorney also stressed that the state's nine medical witnesses were "cumulative," meaning they spouted the same testimony over and over. This was unfairly prejudicial to my case.

Then, too, the judge had improperly dismissed a juror, and allowed Joanna Evanoff to testify about the alleged library incident, even though she had not actually seen me strike a toddler. Joanna was not a credible witness, as her testimony was only speculative.

A compelling part of our motion concerned an orange-colored stain on the inside back of Natalie's jacket that the state had introduced at my trial. Gretchen Hayward had questioned Cindy Beard on the witness stand at length about this stain. Cindy testified she had brought a half jar of peaches for Natalie to eat that day. The prosecutor implied that I had fed these peaches to the fussy baby, which added to my frustration that morning and that she later vomited the peaches onto her jacket. Cindy testified she never would have let the child leave her house with such stains.

In my motion, my attorney wrote that the state was obviously implying that the stain occurred at my house the morning Natalie died. When I was on the stand Hayward brought it up again. "Did you put the peaches in the refrigerator?"

"No," I testified.

"Where were the peaches?"

"I didn't know there was any food in the bag."

Hayward had me describe how I had laid Natalie's jacket out on the floor before I put her into it. I explained how I had opened it up with the zipper spread flat.

"The jacket wasn't dirty like this, was it?" She asked, holding up the stained jacket for the jury.

"I did not observe the condition of the jacket that morning."

"Have you ever seen Natalie come to your place with a jacket that had this kind of mess on it?"

"I have never seen those stains on that jacket until today," I answered honestly.

Later in her cross-examination, she brought up the peaches again asking if I'd ever fed Natalie peaches before. "Do you recall Cindy telling you there was either cereal or peaches in the bag?"

"No."

To add insult to injury, Hayward suggested I had fed Natalie the peaches and grabbed her jacket to wipe off her mouth rather than using a burp rag or napkin.

This peach stain was an outright fabrication. I had never gone into Natalie's diaper bag that morning except to retrieve the jacket Cindy had placed in the bag for our stroll to preschool. The baby was not even taking her bottle, much less eating peaches! Investigators did not find a half jar of peaches in the bag nor in my house. The coroner did not find peaches in Natalie's stomach at the autopsy.

The peach-colored stains were also found on the back of Natalie's car seat. They ran under the cushion and were soaked in underneath. But Natalie never had her jacket on while in her car seat in my care that day. Natalie had spit up formula *after* I lifted her from the car seat. These off-white formula stains were also found on Natalie's shirt and sock and the front of the jacket.

The EMTs and emergency people noted that I had a similar formula stain on my white cotton sweater that morning. If I had fed Natalie peaches, it would show on my white sweater.

My attorney, Dean, noted that Cindy gave Natalie Amoxicillin, a pink liquid antibiotic, that morning at home and theorized that Natalie projectile vomited onto her jacket while in her car seat before arriving at my house. This could explain the orangey stain. I have no idea why the stain wasn't tested before the trail, possibly because we didn't anticipate that it would be used as a significant piece of evidence from the DA. But in this appeal, Dean Strang saw it as hugely important.

It was a significant sign that Natalie was ill *before* arriving at my house that morning.

In closing arguments, my attorney correctly guessed that Hayward planned a rebuttal fashioned around the stains that he would have no way to answer. The stains became an important point in the prosecution's final argument. They used other themes, too, but the stains became a key factual theory of the state's case, both in evidence and to support and advance their fabrications.

Dean suggested that Cindy was mistaken about bringing the peaches-- or she had lied on the stand. He said the only way to find out for sure was to test the stain to determine if it was peaches or Amoxicillin.

The state fervently refused and Judge Moeser did not rule to test the stains.

In my motion, Dean asked the court to cut to the chase. He said if the state was unwilling to test the stains, I would pay for the testing. The state had no good argument for forbidding me from sponsoring the tests. Yet the judge still refused. It seemed to me he was highly biased with the state.

To this day those stains have never been tested. The state responded that the peaches were not really a big deal in the trial. In other words, it was no big deal that they had invented it. The peaches were splashed all over the testimony, and painted an inaccurate and highly prejudicial picture of me and what had occurred that morning.

I still thought Natalie choked on her formula that morning. I saw the formula come out of her mouth and nose and onto her clothes and my sweater, and so I paid keen attention when Dean told me about a letter he received from Lorraine Endres, one of the volunteer EMTs who had responded to my house that morning.

In the letter, Lorraine said, "I hope I may be helpful in pointing out some areas that should be checked to help the jury and judge see how unfairly Audrey was treated."

Lorraine said she attended a continuing education class six weeks after Natalie died. One of the sessions was taught by none other than Dr. William Perloff, head of the University of Wisconsin-Madison Pediatric Intensive Care Unit. In fact, he was the expert on ""Shaken Baby Syndrome"" who had testified against me at my trial.

Lorraine wrote that during the training session, Dr. Perloff put a true-life case on the screen but said he didn't have the name. Immediately, Lorraine recognized the case as mine. Perloff told the students that the babysitter had claimed the baby choked on milk, but no milk was in the airway.

Lorraine was stunned and wrote in her letter to Dean that her EMT report and Police Chief Roberts had both specifically stated that a milky substance was found in the baby's nose and mouth. The Med Flight doctor had also said he saw milk in the airway.

"Why did Dr. Perloff lie about that?" Lorraine asked in her letter. "If he lied about the milk, what else did he lie about?"

Lorraine's letter was three pages long and asked why the parents were not put through the same scrutiny that I was. "Is it not unusual for parents, especially new parents, to be upset when a child cries so much day or night? But who takes in extra children if they have a problem with kids crying getting on their nerves?

These are some of my concerns along with others. If I can be of any help, let me know." The letter was signed "Hopefully, Lorraine Endres."

I was utterly touched that Lorraine had taken the time to write that letter and spell out what she knew was true and had been suppressed during my trial. Finally, somebody in authority was actually on my side!

Dean appreciated the letter too, but said it had no legal impact on the appeal process in my case. He used it as background knowledge.

It was a brutal summer as I awaited the state's response to our motions. During hot and dry spells the grass died out, so I only worked an hour or so a day and detested the time confined to my prison cell. In maximum security, guards locked us in the cells all the time except for meals, showers, work, and maybe a few hours of exercise, library or social time. Many days we returned from dinner just before five p.m. and were locked in until six thirty the next morning.

Of course, there was no air-conditioning and the brick walls sucked in the heat and pressure-cooked those of us inside. We could purchase a small plastic box fan and open our barred window, but that merely circulated the stifling air. Our toilet sweated, leaving water on the floor, so Jen and I plastered newspapers around it to absorb the moisture.

My salvation was talking to my girls on the phone. I signed up as often as I could because this time was crucial to us, and it also got me out of the stifling cell.

I cherished any visiting time I could get with friends, and my parents made the trip every other weekend. On the alternate weekends, Dave usually visited with the girls. Sometimes he would spend the night with friends in Waunakee and other times he made the rugged round trip in one day, which meant a thirteen-hour day alone with three little girls. I knew it was difficult for everyone but I refused to lose contact with my children. Dave was a saint as he handled everything necessary for us.

I was so lucky to have Jen for my roommate. She was surprisingly kind and respectful to me. Her parents visited her once a month and she worked as a janitor, cleaning bathrooms and hallways in the main areas of the prison. We never had an argument, even though it was difficult to share such cramped conditions with another person. Instead, locked in our cell for long hours, we read, wrote letters or watched television. We each had our own small TV set, but if we liked the same program we would watch it together. If not, we used headphones with our own televisions. Fortunately, our work schedules varied and we each had a couple of hours a day alone in the cell. Many times Jen mingled in the day space-- a little area with tables during social time-- to give me some privacy, and I did the same for her.

We were fortunate because many of the other inmates had roommate problems, ranging from sloppiness and snoring to stealing, rudeness, disrespect and sexual issues. I was fortunate that I never experienced any sexual threats. Because we controlled the lights in our cells, some inmates were up all night while their roommates tried to sleep under the harsh glare.

Hygiene was also an issue for many of the prisoners. We had to buy all our own toiletries from the canteen, which provided hygiene products, snacks, and extras like writing paper, greeting cards and stamps. We could order what we needed, but deliveries arrived only once in ten days, requiring us to plan and budget carefully. I was blessed that my family gave me money for items like soap and shampoo, but many women had no money at all for even the basics. Some inmates received state pay (five cents an hour) but that was only for women unassigned to jobs or medically unable to work. The sundries were priced as they were in regular stores, so basic products like toothpaste, deodorant and soap were too expensive for some inmates, and even those who worked couldn't afford many canteen items at their modest hourly wage. As much as I wanted to help others, we were not allowed to buy canteen goods for fellow inmates and would get a disciplinary ticket if we were caught doing this.

In August, I was assigned to help paint the gym ceiling. I spent hours and hours on high scaffolding, craning my neck as I rolled the paint onto the ceiling. I focused on a limited area so I wouldn't look down quickly and lose my balance. I've never been comfortable with heights, and the stifling, arduous task stretched on for five weeks. Because I was missing precious gym time during this project, I wanted it finished quickly. Thanks to the outdoor running track we could use at appointed times, I was able to walk or run during the paint job, which provided therapy for my body and probably saved my sanity.

Autumn was a welcome relief from the heat, and my mowing job turned into a raking assignment, and more indoor painting. However, the months dragged by as each evening I returned to the oppressive closet that contained my hard bed and meager belongings. I spent many nights crying softly into my crunchy pillow, wondering what my family was doing in our spacious, comfortable home.

The holiday season was especially depressing that year. On December 21st, Dean Strang called to say the state had finally responded to our motion. My heart thumped as he revealed that the state had systematically denied all the points in our motion, saying my hysteria and life-saving measures only indicated my thinking *after* committing the offense, and said little about my state of mind when I supposedly performed the lethal act.

"The jury could reasonably infer that the defendant called 9-1-1 because she realized her conduct was forceful enough to kill Natalie and feared being blamed for her death. She was remorseful at having violently assaulted a helpless infant or was frightened or repulsed by Natalie's apparent lifeless body. These are all consistent with guilt." I found these words bordering on extreme cruelty, and was devastated, but to my surprise, Dean took it in stride, saying he'd expected it. It was now up to Judge Moeser. Dean was doubtful of any possible new trial from this motion because judges rarely reverse a conviction handed down in their own courtroom. And all this just a few days before Christmas!

The prison showed no signs of the holiday except for a small artificial tree in the visiting room. I woke up in the same bleak cell on Christmas morning, knowing my girls were peeking into their stockings and opening gifts. I had suggested ideas for presents, but what the girls really needed was their mom beside them on Christmas day.

That afternoon, Dave and the girls made the long trip to visit. The girls lit up over the fake tree in the visiting area. Fortunately, they were still young enough to ignore the reality of their surroundings.

I had saved some treats for them that my mother had purchased, as well as some candy from the vending machine. We all made the best of it, but I could see the haunting pain in Dave's eyes. It had fallen on him to manage this holiday alone with our girls, and then drive all this way to brighten my Christmas. I knew I should focus on the true meaning of Christmas, but my absence in our home created an emptiness that permeated every moment we were together.

The long wait for Judge Moeser's ruling was excruciating. In the winter, my yard job switched to shoveling, but if it didn't snow I was confined to my room like a caged animal. I was sad, bored and always cold. Our bedding was limited but I had one warm blanket and another I folded over the mattress for a bit more softness. The state-issued green jacket was thin, but thankfully a friend sent me a Polartec fleece jacket and I wore that daily. I braced myself against Wisconsin's freezing weather when we had to walk outside to other buildings for meals, work, visits and other activities.

My maintenance job was not providing enough time out of my bare room, so when I heard about a job in the kitchen I transferred jobs, grateful to finally have regular work hours. At first, I worked in the "dish room." One can only imagine the stacks and stacks of dirty dishes in that massive institution! My new job started at five in the morning and stretched into the afternoon, but I actually welcomed an activity that kept me busy and took my mind off my depressing situation. I was soon promoted to pots and pans, which meant lots of heavy scrubbing.

A twinkle of hope arrived near the end of March when Dean turned my entire trial transcript and Natalie's medical documents over to several experts, asking them for a review of the information and an opinion. We were thrilled when Dr. John Plunkett, a coroner with the Minnesota Regional Coroner's Office, wrote that there was no scientific data to support the conclusions about "Shaken Baby Syndrome" that the doctors had presented at my trial.

Dr. Plunkett explained that retinal bleeding is not exclusive to "Shaken Baby Syndrome" and can be caused by infections or resuscitation efforts. He also verified that there was no data to conclude when a retinal hemorrhage occurs relative to a brain injury.

It can either appear at the time of the injury or develop later.

The prosecution had theorized that children with severe head injuries do not have a lucid interval, but Dr. Plunkett cited other cases where children appeared normal after brain injury, but later fell ill and died.

This physician was a distinguished coroner, with many published articles in medical journals. In his letter to Dean, he enclosed one of the articles he'd had published in the journal, *Child Abuse and Neglect,* the previous November. He said the same journal would publish another article in the Spring that he'd written about lucid intervals following brain injury.

Not surprisingly, my very favorite part of his packet was a short cover letter which read, "I'm very optimistic, but I tend to be an optimistic person. Perloff and those folks have it absolutely, flat out wrong, and they've had it wrong for twenty years. There's going to be hell to pay."

For his testimonial, I was grateful beyond words.

Dr. Janice Ophoven, a pediatric forensic pathologist in Woodbury, Minnesota, also reviewed my case for Dean. She believed that the timing of Natalie's injuries could not be established with certainty. "Onset of symptoms in cases like this can be widely variable." She said the infant was "clearly suffering a seizure when she was found in the bedroom and the lack of air before Med flight arrived could have caused the damage stated at the autopsy." She also clearly noted the pre-existing brain injury.

Her final statement was like a gentle lullaby to my ears. "It is my opinion based on the findings and history of this case, the injuries could have occurred prior to the transfer of the child to Ms. Edmund's care."

Dr. Plunkett and Dr. Ophoven were bright beams of hope for me. Finally, these experts had provided new information that could clobber the prosecution's false case against me.

Another four months dragged by before Judge Moeser's decision arrived in a letter from Dean Strang. It was written July 23, 1998. My fingers shook as I opened the envelope and I truly hoped the doctors' new input had swayed Moeser in my direction. That hope dissolved when I read in Dean's letter that Judge Moeser had denied all our claims.

He wrote in his decision, "The issue is not whether a trial is perfect but rather if it's fair."

Dean wrote that Moeser's decision was not well reasoned. "It will do little or nothing to hurt our chances on appeal, although obviously it will do little to help them."

One caveat: the judge did find that questioning the ousted juror when I wasn't in the room was an error. But he held that his error was "cured" the next day when he talked with me, so his decision was harmless.

My attorney ended his letter by saying he would file the notice of appeal immediately and we would get on with it. This meant we were moving to the State District Court of Appeals.

In utter despair, I dropped the letter onto my lap. I had already spent seventeen horrible months without my family in tight confines. Why couldn't we have sidestepped the local court, where we knew Judge Moeser would deny our pleas? The state was so quick to accuse and convict me, but reversing their mistakes and fabrications was taking an unconscionably long time.

How would I manage another eighteen months in these harsh conditions?

CHAPTER SIXTEEN

Immediately, Dean got busy with my appeal. He planned to restructure and strengthen the points made in the motions filed before Judge Moeser and was confident my case would progress once in the Wisconsin District Appeals Court. I trusted him, but cringed when he said this part of our journey could take another whole year!

Prison was not a humane environment, and although I survived within it, I never really adapted. My mind was always with my family, and the happy life I knew existed outside these bars and cement.

However, no matter what I was thinking, I always gave my best at my prison jobs, no matter how menial the task. At this point, I was still working in the prison kitchen and arrived there just before five in the morning. I didn't mind rising early because it helped keep my body and brain in motion.

After washing literally hundreds of dishes, I took a permanent position preparing food and stocking the serving line. It was a good thing I exercised regularly, because this job put lots of miles on my running shoes and kept my arms in shape hauling pans laden with food. I did such a good job, I actually worked my way up to forty-two cents an hour!

Fortunately, I felt safe working in the kitchen. Prison management pretty much watched over the food areas and I never saw violence there, but a few inmates had sharp tongues and lazy work habits. Some women were delusional and thrived on fantasies, or acted out scenarios they saw on television. One woman pretended she was a movie star. It was sad and bizarre, and I wondered why the prison never treated those with mental illnesses.

Inmates were not required to work, but for me, it was essential. Whenever I was locked in my small cell, I longed to be out and busy. I tolerated my cohorts and cherished the few women who were hard workers.

One of them was Gloria. In her late fifties, short and hefty, Gloria was the motherly type who pulled her short gray hair back into a stubby pony tail, which was required for kitchen work. Although I avoided prison friendships in general, I realized Gloria and I worked hard and well together in the kitchen. Soon, we began talking, sharing our feelings and information about our families, and encouraging one another to hang in.

Gloria was serving an eighteen-year-sentence for forgery and embezzlement. She told me she just wanted to provide well for her three children and found it easy to steal the money. She never expected the consequences to be so harsh. This was typical reasoning among inmates serving time for financial crimes. When their first thefts weren't immediately detected, stealing became a lifestyle.

Gloria had two daughters in their twenties with children of their own. Her son, Laramie, was eighteen when Gloria went to prison. Soon after, Laramie was diagnosed with cancer. As Gloria shared her heartache with me, I cried with her. She was unable to help her dying son, who was living with a relative while undergoing grueling cancer treatments. During this difficult time Gloria's roommate moved to the medium-security section. I wanted to support Gloria through her grief, so we both went to the prison staff and asked if we could share a room.

The prison staff rarely allowed room or roommate changes, but this time they made an exception and approved my transfer immediately. I packed up my scanty belongings and moved in with Gloria. Jen was wonderful and understanding, and was quickly issued a new roommate.

As I carried my box into Gloria's cell, she pushed up her big framed glasses and wiped tears from her eyes. Gloria would turn out to be an excellent roommate. Even though we worked the same job shift and were together just about twenty-four hours a day, she was respectful and tidy, both very important qualities for me.

I was glad I was there to lend a sympathetic ear when Gloria needed support as Laramie's health continued to spiral downward . She did the same for me when I longed to hold my husband and daughters in my arms.

Back at home, Dave was a warrior maintaining our household

and tackling the long trip with the girls for bi-weekly visits. I remember when Allie was newly potty trained. She ran to me in the visiting room and promptly pulled up her dress to show me her pretty panties with tiny flowers on them. Allie was always my girly-girl who loved to sit on my lap and play with my earlobes.

"Mommy, why don't you wear your pretty earrings anymore?" she asked in her sweet little girl voice. Allie always loved earrings. She also smoothed over my fingernails and asked why I no longer wore nail polish. She was so perceptive, she even noticed my eyes weren't adorned with makeup and my lightened blonde hair had grown out completely.

The prison did not allow hair dye on the premises, and we had to ask other inmates to cut our hair in a small room next to the guard's desk. The prison approved blow dryers, but not curling irons or electric rollers. A shiny square of metal hung in our cell as a mirror. The canteen sold one type of makeup foundation in two shades and some eye shadow, but no mascara. I didn't bother much with makeup behind bars.

The transformation in my looks really bothered Allie. Here I was, only thirty-seven years old, but my burdens and the resulting stress had sprinkled my naturally dark hair with streaks of gray. I must have looked like an old lady to Allie.

Each time they visited I was afraid that baby Jenny wouldn't recognize me, but she always curled up in my lap and clung to me. Carrie sang various songs she'd learned at school and was proud to perform in her school programs. I held back tears as I watched her dance about, knowing I would not be in the audience taking pictures or videos and clapping for her performance.

I hated when it was time to leave and the girls always burst into tears. "Why can't you come home with us?" Carrie pleaded. She was much too young to understand why her mother had to remain in this strange place. I don't know how Dave managed the long ride home trying to comfort three broken hearts. Each time they left, I dragged myself back to my room, where Gloria was always kind and understanding. She had her own pain as her son continued to decline and my whole world felt heavy and sad.

My parents kept their home in Hudson, Wisconsin, but were living at our house about an hour away in Minnesota, a godsend to our girls and Dave. They cooked and cleaned, loved the girls, helped Carrie with homework and even participated at her school. They wrote to me several times a week, sharing stories and sending lots of photos, and had the girls draw pictures or write little notes. My heart leaped when I received their thick envelopes. I could see my babies growing and learning in every way and cherished the contact we all shared, despite my inability to be there with them.

Dave worked long hours and often didn't return until after six in the evening. When he arrived, dinner was on the table, the house was in order and the girls were safe

But it was also difficult for him to sacrifice his privacy with my parents living with him. Like many men, he enjoyed a beer or cocktail in the evening after work, but my mother did not approve of drinking. I know the situation was tense at times, but Dave handled himself with great aplomb and never wavered in his support for me. I was very reassured that both Dave and my parents were providing love and strength in my home until I could return.

I called my family almost every evening and talked to each person; it was the highlight of my day. Yes, the calls were expensive, but I was blessed that Dave and my parents could afford them. The calls were priceless for our bonding. Carrie would get on and chatter about something that happened at school, making me simultaneously happy and sad as I listened to her stories.

Mail was a daily highlight for me and usually included up to six letters or cards from family and friends. This contact was a strong connection with normal life on the outside. My own routine was so mundane that I loved hearing what others were doing, from their job triumphs to their happy family events.

The prison staff opened all our mail except for legal correspondence, which we had to open ourselves in front of a guard. The staff also confiscated anything considered contraband. Once my friend, Jill, sent me some seasonal return address stickers she designed and printed on her computer to make it easier for me and fun for the girls to get letters from Mommy with address labels for every season. The guards would not let me have them, so I had them forwarded to my mother, who used them to send letters to me.

Issues like these were irritating. Some of the guards were coarse, but most of them were respectful. Many inmates tried to forge friendships with the guards to get special privileges, but the prison firmly forbade such contacts. I did my best to act cordial, but talked to the guards as little as possible, preferring to find sustenance from those friendships I'd made before my living nightmare began.

We had no access to computers or the Internet, and I had little understanding of this phenomenon. Friends and family sent me various articles from the amazing monster called the Internet, but we were limited in the types of articles we received, to prevent circulation of pornography or illicit information.

I wrote thousands of letters by hand, which helped pass the time and keep my mind occupied. If we were sending mail to another inmate, we had to leave it unsealed for the guards to read. Otherwise, we could seal our own letters. Friends sent me pre-stamped envelopes which helped save me money, given all my letter writing, but soon the prison outlawed those, too.

The many pesky rules and demands felt like constant punishment. But I was, after all, in prison. The guilty inmates deserved the crackdown, but it felt cruel and inhumane for me as a law-abiding citizen wrongly imprisoned.

Around this time, I was watching Oprah on my little television. Her guest that day talked about writing a "gratitude journal," showing appreciation and thanks for even the smallest blessings in our lives. I loved the idea and began writing every day on white, lined paper, about the many things I was thankful for. The smallest things pleased me, like nice weather, walking outside, the many people who supported me and my children. Yet, some days I had to reach deep inside myself to find even one thing to write about. Other days, my appreciation poured onto paper and I could fill a page.

My gratitude journal helped me shift my focus, if even for a moment, to the good in my life. It helped deflect my attention from my appalling circumstances, which continued to haunt me.

Fall came and went and I spent my second Halloween, Thanksgiving and Christmas in prison. The fall and winter were always an excruciating time of year for me. I longed to celebrate the holidays baking cookies with the girls, decorating the house, wrapping presents, visiting Santa, and creating the magical excitement that is Christmas. But that wasn't the biggest reason for my despair. My imprisonment, which kept me from raising my children, was devastating. When would someone believe the truth and get me out of this hell hole?

It absolutely crushed me that my young daughters' Christmas memories revolved around driving hours and hours to visit their mom in a sterile room with a little fake tree, then driving home without me. No amount of presents could assuage that pain. The season held little joy for Dave, too, who had to manage it all. Meanwhile, I clung to the true meaning of Christmas and prayed I would not spend another one like this one.

Meanwhile, Dean called or visited on occasion and I was always eager to hear of any progress on our appeal. He filed his arguments, which were very similar to the points he'd made to Judge Moeser. Dean explained that the appeals process would not involve a trial, but that the two sides would make their arguments in writing, as I'd just experienced at the circuit court level.

"When all the documents for the appeal have been filed," Dean said, "the case is submitted to the judges, who will decide the appeal." I learned that most cases were assigned to a panel of three judges. They would carefully review the circuit court records, including the transcript, and review the briefs filed by the parties. Applying the appropriate legal standards using previous cases and statutes as guides, the judges would then decide the case.

It sounded fair and impartial to me. At least I wasn't facing Judge Moeser again. I began to feel the renewed stirrings of hope. The arguments were filed in due order and it became another long waiting game. Dean said the appellate judges could grant extensions, which would drag the process out even longer. I knew that my freedom and sanity were riding on these three judges and their ability to recognize the truth, at last.

The ruling came down on June 24, 1999. I will never forget that day. My heart pounded as I opened the letter from Dean, only to find that the three judges had unanimously rejected all of our arguments. They decided the evidence in the original trial was sufficient to prove utter disregard for human life, and that there was no error in Judge Moeser's rulings, the juror removal or his instructions to the jury.

In other words, the appellate judges upheld the conviction

and I would remain in prison. Dean was devastated, and I collapsed--my mind, body and soul nearly comatose. I held the letter and stared straight ahead as I reflected on my twenty-eight months in prison. I had held on because I had hope. Now that hope was stomped. I wanted to scream out, but guards would come, deem me insane and lock me in solitary confinement. Yet, if I held this rage inside, it would consume me.

These dueling thoughts left me in severe confusion and pain. How on earth would I get out of this nightmare?

Dean was quick to tell me he would immediately take my case to the Wisconsin Supreme Court. Another sparkle of hope glimmered, and that was all I needed...hope.

Gloria and I continued to live and work together. While we tried to boost each other out of our depressed slumps, the reality was that Gloria's son was dying. It actually gave me perspective. Despite my travails, I did not have a terminal illness and one day I would get out of prison, while Gloria's harrowing situation was final.

Exactly two months after the District Appeals Court decision, the State Supreme Court declined to review my case. Because the appellate court gets to decide which cases they will hear, and had decided to pass on mine, the lower court's decision stood and I would remain in prison.

I was glad they had made that decision quickly; this cleared the way for Dean to take my case to the United States District Court in Milwaukee. Surely the federal court would uncover the ghastly lies that were keeping an innocent mother in prison and away from her three small children.

After two-and-a-half years in maximum security prison, I needed this hope—needed it desperately.

CHAPTER SEVENTEEN

As the months wore on, I found that prison life was wearing on me. The repressive environment bred frustration and irritation, and sometimes fights broke out among the inmates in the cafeteria, gym or outdoors. My heart would begin to pound at the sight and sound of violence so I quickly fled those frightening scenes. I avoided loud, obnoxious people at all costs, but thankfully I was never personally threatened.

Some nights, inmates yelled for the guards, their wails easily filtering through the walls, awakening many of us. Usually the prisoner claimed medical problems, but it was mostly a bid for attention. Many women suffered poor health because they had abused their bodies with drugs, cigarettes, junk food and a lack of exercise.

I'd already had two bad colds, and others suffered hacking coughs or flu. Some inmates became seriously ill with chronic conditions, including cancer. We had to fill out a form to receive medical or dental attention, but it could take weeks to see the prison doctor. In fact, it practically took a life or death situation for a doctor to see an inmate right away. Instead of treating people early on, the prison allowed conditions to fester until an ambulance had to haul the inmate to the hospital.

While I exercised and watched my diet to maintain my health, illness plagued me in other ways. When Gloria and I were still roommates in maximum security prison, her son Laramie finally passed away at the age of twenty. It was devastating for us both, each in our own way.

Soon after, my father was diagnosed with lung cancer, introducing a new source of constant worry and guilt. I knew that my conviction had ravaged Dad and no one had expected I'd still be in prison almost three years later, with no end in sight. Add to that taking care of three active little girls, and it was no wonder that Dad's health deteriorated.

Fortunately, his first lung surgery was successful and I was greatly relieved he didn't have to bear radiation or chemo. How I longed to be by his side to comfort both him and Mom during his health crisis. The best I could do was reach out to them in letters and phone calls. When Dad was in the hospital I was able to go to my social worker's office and use the phone to call him. The money for these calls came out of money I had saved from my prison job.

During his recovery, my parents moved back to Hudson and a neighbor cared for the girls while Dave was at work. I know it was difficult for all of them, but Dave never complained or commented about his lot; I think he was still numb and thought I would get out soon.

As the new millennium of 2000 dawned, I lay awake in my cell and envisioned the celebrations playing out across the world. I prayed this milestone year would bring a change of fortune for me. And it did, but in an unforeseen manner. That epic year began with a new roommate.

After three years in the cramped maximum security rooms, prisoners would appear before the Program Review Committee, which reviewed the inmate's records, job evaluations and behavior reports. Gloria was at the three-year mark and the committee recommended her for a medium security section, so she was moved to the dorm where she could enjoy a lot more freedom.

I was very happy for Gloria, who needed a boost after losing Laramie.

I braced myself for a new roommate, and a woman named Joyce arrived to join me. She'd been moved from another room and plopped her heavy body onto the lower bunk, her short, dark hair stabbing out from her head framing a pale face. Joyce was very simple and childlike and I soon realized she was mentally confused. She was serving forty years for child abuse and neglect. Her husband had been the actual perpetrator, but Joyce had done nothing to protect her children and was charged accordingly. Now, Joyce went to school at the prison.

Fortunately for both of us, we got along well, talking occasionally and watching TV together.

Around the same time, I got a new job at Badger State Industries (BSI). The Wisconsin Department of Corrections runs BSI as a vocational training and work skills development program. Out of six hundred inmates, I was one of about twelve chosen to work this supposedly prestigious position doing computerized engraving for signs, name plates, door plaques, and metal name badges, to name a few. Soon I learned how to silkscreen shirts and other cloth items and later tackled computerized embroidery. I was happy to have a job where I could do more mentally challenging work. My jobs were recorded in my file and I received excellent work reviews.

BSI taught manufacturing and production techniques at various facilities and the inmates made products for state, county, municipal and non-profit agencies. The prisoners mastered crafts such as furniture construction, textile products, and metal stamping like license plates.

BSI also ran two dairy farms, a state-of-the-art creamery that provided milk and ice cream for the prisons, a steer feedlot and a cash crop operation. Other prisoners worked a computerized recycling program.

BSI was located right on the prison grounds in a separate building. My shift began at eight in the morning and I worked until three-thirty, all for a pay boost to fifty-cents an hour. I eventually worked my way up to a dollar an hour, which was considered excellent pay in prison. I deposited my skimpy paychecks into a savings account and the prison kept the interest.

It was about this time that the prison cracked down on the dress code. Up until then we could wear our own solid-colored T-shirts, sweatshirts, our own colorful jackets and dress pants or blue jeans. This regular clothing confused the guards, who couldn't always differentiate prisoners from staff or visitors. Under the new rules, the inmates were limited to blue jeans, grey t-shirts, grey sweatshirts and two pairs of grey gym shorts.

Talk about morbid! Stripping all color from our clothing was another drain on our psyches.

Joyce was all right as a roommate, but I was thrilled when word came three months later that the Program Review Committee had recommended moving me to the medium security dorm. It happened quickly--I'd returned from work one day and a guard handed me a large cardboard box. I was so excited I didn't even feel nervous about this abrupt change.

The dorm had two different wings and each section housed two sets of about eighteen bunk beds bolted to the floor in the shape of a U. A partial wall separated the two U's. It was a wide-open space and the only privacy was in the restroom or shower. The guard assigned me to a top bunk because many inmates were physically unable to climb up to the higher bed. Each inmate had an open metal book case with shelves and one drawer under the bed with a lock. I put my nicer clothes and personal belongings in the locked drawer.

Even though the living quarters were institutional and drab, offering no real privacy, the dorm felt like freedom at last, and I was so grateful to be there. Now, for the first time in three years, I was not locked into a tiny room, I could shower when I wanted, use the phone, and go outside to a small fenced area with picnic tables.

Like maximum security, the dorm didn't supply the other necessary toiletries except for a free toothbrush with hard bristles. For our menstrual periods, the prison issued an allotted number of sanitary pads each month. If we needed or wanted more, we could buy them along with tampons from the canteen.

The dorm did require new survival skills, however. I didn't actually feel physically threatened, but soon after I arrived, I noticed things missing from my drawer. Stamps, instant coffee I made with hot tap water, and toiletries would disappear while I was in the shower or at work. Someone was breaking into my locked drawer!

After enduring this for awhile, I told the guard and she reluctantly moved me to another area of the dorm. These professional thieves could bust into a locked drawer in moments. The staff largely ignored the crooks and shuffled the victims around to solve the problem. I felt lucky to move to another bunk and was relieved to see that things did improve.

I spent a lot of time outdoors as I reveled in the fresh air and perception of freedom it brought me. I didn't know anybody, and Gloria had already moved out of the dorm and into a medium security room, which was considered a privilege.

Some women would sit at the picnic tables and provoke loud arguments. When that happened, I immediately left the area and sat on my bed with my headphones to listen to the radio or watch the small TV on my metal shelf at the end of my bunk. That was the only way the prison allowed us to listen to music or TV programs.

Only about half the women could afford the luxury of a television and the prison officials forbade us to share our radios or TVs with anyone else.

My interaction with the other women remained the same. I seldom shared my previous life with other inmates and tried to be patient with some of the obnoxious behaviors often displayed. I certainly got an education in alternative lifestyles! These insights made me very thankful for all the good people in my private life; they were a strong ray of light in my otherwise dark existence behind prison walls.

I lived in the dorm for three months while my appeal slowly moved through the United States District Court in Milwaukee. Dean recommended I hire appellate attorney William Theis in Winnetka, Illinois. He filed a petition with the federal court for habeas corpus relief, which simply asked the federal judges to investigate whether the trial court had violated my personal liberties. Again, I clung to the possibility that these judges would finally see through the lies and bias against me, and finally get me out of this crazy prison.

In the summer of 2000, I moved to a locked room in the medium security building. The space was definitely larger and nicer than the maximum security rat hole, but I hated the confinement. The room had the familiar toilet, but now a curtain surrounded it for privacy. I finally had a key for my room, but the doors were locked from the outside at nine p.m. and opened again at six a.m.

Another negative was that showers were scarce in this building with only three stalls on each hallway for dozens of women. When I returned from work or exercise, I had to rush to the shower before I was locked in the room for the night. I absolutely detested this aspect of my smothering detention.

My new roommate was a woman named Bonnie who was in prison on drug charges. She was upbeat and kind, which helped me survive my days and nights. The only positive aspect of my new medium security room was that I could lock the door and nobody could steal my things.

In July, Mom and Dad brought the girls for a visit. Although Dad's cancer was supposedly in remission, he looked unusually pale and exhausted. Soon thereafter, my parents moved back in with Dave and the children, and I knew it must be a strain on Dad's health. I cherished whatever time with him and wished I could lift his burdens.

That day, as I watched my precious family walk away from me, Dad suddenly collapsed. Although he was still inside the gate, I could not get to him. The look of terror in my mother's eyes shot fear into my heart, while Carrie looked frantic and Allie began to cry. The guards called an ambulance and I watched in despair as they scooped up Dad and carried him out of my sight.

When I could, I called Mom later and learned that she had followed the ambulance to the hospital with the children in the car. The doctors had determined that Dad was developing diabetes and that his blood sugar was so low he'd briefly passed out at the prison. My poor Mom had managed to locate a motel for the night while handling three frightened children, with no extra clothes or supplies.

Fortunately, Dad stabilized and Mom drove them home the next day. His doctor back in St. Paul ran some tests and found--to our deep sorrow--that the cancer was back. I was absolutely devastated by the setback and wanted desperately to help my family. Once again, the cruelty of my needless imprisonment almost crushed me during that time.

Then, in late August, a full agonizing year after the Wisconsin Supreme Court refused to hear my case, Bill Theis, as my new attorney, filed the preliminary memorandum supporting habeas corpus in Federal District Court in Milwaukee. The twenty-page brief declared my rights had indeed been quashed in Judge Moeser's courtroom.

In the memorandum, Bill said my case came down to one stark question: Who injured the baby? Nobody at my trial disputed that Natalie had died from traumatic injuries. Either I had administered them or her parents were the culprits. Medical experts testified the injuries could have been inflicted as early as one-forty in the afternoon the day before Natalie died. That meant that Natalie's parents could have been responsible.

Bill said the circuit court had allowed the state to present extensive evidence and testimony that Tom and Cindy Beard had been loving, demonstrative parents. If that was true, these testimonials would support the contention that they had not shaken, choked or battered Natalie. And if they didn't do it, I was the obvious suspect.

Now, facing those testimonials, I had powerful contradictory evidence and witnesses who could have affirmed that the parents, especially Tom Beard, did not act concerned or grieving when Natalie was dying. State witnesses said on the stand that Tom held and cuddled his baby often, yet I had several witnesses who would have testified that Tom would not touch baby Natalie in the hospital, stood at a removed distance from her, and abruptly left her hospital room. Neither parents showed grief or emotion, according to a statement from the hospital chaplain that is shown in court documents.

Judge Moeser had not allowed my witnesses to testify, saying people react differently to grief and it would confuse the jury. But my attorney declared that I must have the opportunity to present my contradictory evidence. He said the jury was given a one-sided presentation which left it with little choice but to convict me.

My attorney also cited other federal cases where the emotional reaction to the death of a loved-one was considered relevant and sometimes damning. In my case, the parents' reaction to Natalie's grave condition could have been evidence of guilty knowledge. Bill said the jury was unjustifiably limited to the picture of Tom as a loving father who enjoyed holding his child. The jury was not allowed to see the portrait of that same father who would not come close to her and showed no emotion as she lay on her death bed. I had also witnessed that he was uncomfortable around her.

Bill declared that this new evidence would not confuse the jury, but would instead allow the panel to consider my side of the story, which was where my rights had been violated. I had not been given the right to present a defense after the state had introduced evidence about the parents. The judge had also denied me due process when I was barred from rebutting the state's evidence.

I was impressed with Bill's brief: it appeared to be well thought out and skillfully written and it infused me with new hope.

My parents continued to live with Dave while Dad underwent radiation therapy, and several members of my church blessedly drove him to treatments while Mom handled the girls. My folks stayed with Dave until right before Thanksgiving, when Dave told me over the phone that Dad was extremely sick and he believed it was time for them to let go of their responsibilities to our family, return to their home in Hudson and focus on caring for themselves.

A neighbor ran a day care center in her home, so Dave placed the girls with her. Jenny was there all day and Allie and Carrie arrived after school. This arrangement was extremely stressful on Dave because he had to be home by five to pick up the girls and then handle every household task on his own. His newly added burden consumed me with sadness and guilt.

The radiation treatments continued to zap Dad's health and it became harder and harder for him to swallow. Soon, he lost weight and grew weaker and weaker. It was clear the end was near and Dad was placed on life support. However, after two weeks my mother and brothers discussed the situation with doctors and decided to halt life support but keep him in an unconscious state on morphine.

I hated that I was locked away from him. I couldn't imagine never seeing him again. The life support was removed on a Sunday and I called home every evening. The girls knew Grandpa was very sick and missed him. Dave was thoughtful and helpful as he visited the hospital every day. Mom was now sleeping at the hospital, staying by Dad's side until death parted them.

On December fourteenth, I called in the evening and talked with Carrie. She told me that their daddy had kept them home from school so they could visit Grandpa at the hospital. "Then we went to see Santa Claus," Carrie said. "And that's when Grandpa died."

Even though I knew the end was near, I gasped in shock. It was one of the darkest days of my life. I sat in my gray clothes in my gray room in my black mood and mourned his loss. I felt totally alone and isolated from the family I wanted to hug and comfort. Of course, I was not allowed to attend my own father's funeral, yet another abomination among many as I struggled to survive my unjust imprisonment.

My brother, Gary, had been stationed in Iraq with the Navy before the war began. Word of our father's illness went out to him, and the phenomenal Red Cross flew him home within twenty-four hours. He had five precious days with our father before Dad passed and then took a two week leave after Dad's funeral and drove to Minneapolis to spend time with Dave and the girls. He was a wonderful comfort to the entire family.

Back in my locked room, I actually felt Dad's presence. It was as if his spirit was now free and he could be with the daughter he loved so much. I leaned on his essence and desperately missed him.

Several years before, Dave had lost his own father suddenly and still carried profound feelings he rarely shared, but my mother's deep mourning and need to talk about Dad became a great strain on him.

Handling another close family death was almost too much for Dave on top of his weighty responsibilities. It was easier for him to push the feelings inside. I worried about him, but couldn't get him to open up.

Mom never returned to our home with Dave and the girls. With Dave's blessing, she needed to take care of herself. Now, even more than before, our world seemed dark, blurred and increasingly sad. I kept praying, *Please let the Federal District Court see the truth.*

The wait was excruciating and I was about to begin my fourth year in prison for a crime I did not commit.

CHAPTER EIGHTEEN

January, 2001 was a difficult time for me as I grieved for my father and worried about Mom, Dave and the girls. I knew Dave was overwhelmed with responsibility and I was relieved when he asked his widowed mother to come from Detroit and help with the girls for awhile.

Everyone calls my mother-in-law "Mike," her childhood nickname for Millicent, and she definitely lives up to her masculine nickname. Mike is a brawny woman with long, graying hair slicked back and braided down her back. Her boisterous personality resonates through her husky voice and hearty laugh.

When Dave took me to Detroit to meet his parents for the first time, I liked Mike immediately. I recognized his mischievous sense of humor in her, and like Dave, she was sharply intelligent.

I immediately recognized Mike Edmunds as one strong lady with a deep love and devotion to Dave and his sister Leslie. She fawned over Dave, and was his fierce protector and advocate. In her eyes, Dave could do no wrong. I knew Dave was very close with his mother and she would be a strong support for him.

That January, Mike packed up some of her belongings in Detroit and moved in with Dave and the girls for what was supposed to be a temporary situation. I knew it lifted a huge burden off of Dave's shoulders because now he had his mother to grocery shop, cook and drive the girls around.

At the same time, I got a new cellmate. Petite and soft-spoken, Mary was in her late forties and serving a life sentence for killing her newborn baby. The tiny girl was her fifth child and for whatever insane reason, Mary had put the child in a box and placed it in a dumpster, where the infant died. The story sickened me. While I, too, had been imprisoned for a baby's death, I was not responsible for it, which was how I differed from the other inmates. Most of them were guilty, and I could never relate to their crimes.

Mary was very secretive about the details of her baby's death and never divulged why she had done it. But as a prison roommate, she was perfect. Mary was quiet, respectful, and had a big heart. She would sit on the bed in her prison-issued glasses, her brown hair tumbling to her shoulders and spend hours drawing and sketching. We got along well and talked often. She was from the Superior North region of Michigan, so her family was six hours away. Although her father visited once a month, her children rarely came to see her.

While my everyday existence was numbingly boring, I was extremely stressed as my mind swirled with things that were out of my reach and control. The girls were still trying to adjust to having lost Grandpa, and now their Grandma Jean was no longer living with them.

In addition, Mike, a grandmother they barely knew, had come to live with them. However, I knew Dave was more comfortable with his own mother in the house, which was understandable, and as my legal delays continued, Dave tried to allay my fears.

"Don't worry, my mother is helping," he assured me, saying he would continue to bring the children for visits and that he'd be there to support me.

But this soon changed. Dave was gradually finding excuses for not visiting as often. "The girls are tired," he'd explain over the phone, or he'd be too exhausted or too busy. His visits decreased to once every three weeks and eventually down to once every month.

I sensed something was bothering him, yet he wouldn't share his thoughts or feelings. He never even asked to work out a new visiting schedule, but I could see that something was eating away at him.

I knew it was a long, arduous five-and-a-half hour drive each way for my family, but Carrie told me later that when she was younger, it wasn't so bad. One time, her sisters were fast asleep when they hit the halfway point on their trip home. Suddenly, Daddy pointed out a huge, gnarled tree. "That tree is yours, Carrie," he explained. "Whenever you see your special tree, you'll know we're halfway home."

During all those grueling drives, while her sisters slept, Carrie forced herself to stay awake to see her special tree. The girls also waved to a pink elephant on top of a landmark gas station along the way. I was touched that Dave tried to ease this travel burden for the girls and made some lasting memories out of a brutal situation.

But I could tell he was actually crumbling inside.

I decided to call on my cousins, Kristy, Linda and Susie, my brother Wayne, his wife, Mary and my friends, Connie and Barb to fill in for Dave. They were good enough to combine their schedules to bring my girls every other weekend. Sometimes the prison wouldn't approve the driver's visit in time, so they had to let the girls off with another adult on my visiting list, then drive around Fond du Lac for a few hours. They were always generous and gracious under these awkward circumstances, and I appreciated their efforts and support from the bottom of my heart.

I found, to my dismay, that I was having less and less physical contact with my mother. After Dad died, she drove down once or twice, but as much as she loved the girls, she couldn't handle long-distance driving on her own. Her visits dwindled to occasionally catching a ride with relatives.

Early that summer, the prison notified me that I was up for parole in August! I was four-and-a-half years into my prison term. With the federal district appeal staggering forward, Dave rested all hopes for my release on the parole hearing. He was confident that the panel would see my excellent work and good behavior in prison and let me out.

I talked to other inmates about parole, and was disturbed to learn that they felt the process was a sham. However, I dutifully filled out paperwork and listed my prison achievements, if you consider going to work every day on time and actually performing my job an achievement. I was an exemplary worker and I knew my behavior reports were excellent. I also had to prove support from the outside and show I had a place to live if I was released. My record seemed golden for parole.

Another unknown factor loomed over me. Inmates told me I would speak with one person, not a panel, and the parole officer would ask me to admit to the crime and show remorse. That was exactly what Judge Moeser had stipulated in my sentencing. Dave thought if I lied and said I shook Natalie, I would be released so I could return to raising our children. But as tempting as the reward might be, it was not an option for me. Many inmates confessed responsibility at their parole hearings in hopes of getting out, but it never worked. In my case, admitting guilt would be a lie, and worse, it would be on my record forever!

With all the propaganda against me, I just couldn't create another lie to get myself out of prison. I knew if I faked a guilty confession, it would affect the medical arguments for future "Shaken Baby" cases. What kind of example would that be for my daughters? Should one lie to get what one wanted?

I knew we were living through a painful situation, but I felt we could manage somehow. I was not dying from a terminal disease. I was alive and in the girls' lives. We could make the most of this situation through visits, and in the end, my daughters would learn that their mother had stood up for the truth.

On the other hand, Dave vehemently disagreed. First of all, he thought the parole system would see that I was a good person with family support and would let me go free. But he also believed it was more important to get myself out of prison to raise the girls than to stick to my (true) story that I was innocent.

I just knew that I couldn't live with that lie, and that it would haunt me for the rest of my life. And even if I did lie, just to be released, other inmates warned me that admitting guilt would not necessarily give me a free ticket out. I decided to stick to my decision and await the hearing.

In August, a guard led me to a small administration room for the parole hearing. Inside sat a portly woman with glasses and a constant grimace. She barely looked at me as she perused my paperwork. My good behavior, excellent job evaluations, and loyal family meant nothing to her; instead, she ignored all the positive information and referred only to the structure of my sentence. I was serving an eighteen-year sentence and she said that four years were not enough punishment for killing an infant. Parole denied!

The meeting was over in about three minutes. The parole denial crushed Dave, who now felt we had very different priorities. His was to get our family back together. Mine, he felt, was selfish. He did not agree that truth and integrity outweighed my ability to be free to raise our children.

Of course I understood his mindset--of course I wanted the same thing myself. It was definitely a lose/lose choice to have to make, but I never wavered from the truth and had to trust that our girls would grow stronger from this vital life lesson. One day, I told myself, I would get out of this awful place with my name and the truth intact, along with the respect of my daughters for refusing to tell lies to regain my freedom especially knowing that it wouldn't have gotten me out of prison anyway!

The Saturday after Labor Day, I called the girls. They told me that Daddy was on his way to see me, and Allie was upset because she'd wanted to come, but Daddy wouldn't let her. I immediately felt a sense of deep foreboding. Dave never came to visit alone. My heart pounded, and I was very apprehensive as I awaited his arrival later that morning.

When I walked into the visiting room, I saw Dave with a can of soda in his hand. He immediately grabbed my arm and said, "Let's go outside and talk." This was not the Dave I knew! I was shaken to the core as he pulled me outside, and then, before we could even sit down, he blurted out, "I can't do this anymore. I filed for divorce."

Everything blurred as my world crashed around me. Feeling wobbly, I sank down onto a bench. No wonder I'd felt him pulling away all summer --and now our marriage was collapsing!

"I know you've been through so much," I began, trying to find a way to bring him back. "Let's get a counselor to help us make it easier for you."

However, Dave shook his head at the mention of counseling. "I've done enough. You need to get an attorney." Dave's mind was made up, and he actually moved away from me. "We need to get the girls down here and explain the situation to them."

I burst into tears, but he refused to discuss it further and left abruptly. A kind staff member helped drag me, sobbing, back to the cell, where Mary was sitting on her bed. Although she listened sympathetically, there wasn't much she could do to help.

As I began to recover from the shock, I first felt deeply wounded and then angry towards Dave for giving up on both me and our girls. He swore there was no other woman--so why would he break up our family? What had happened to our marriage vows and his promise to be there with me, for better or worse? Once again, I was being punished for something that was completely out of my control.

CHAPTER NINETEEN

The next several weeks were a mad scramble as I tried to find a divorce attorney. The thought of even more legal bills frightened me, but I had friends contact lawyers in Minnesota to explain my circumstances. My biggest fear, of course, was losing contact with my children.

Finally, the day arrived when Dave brought our young daughters along with him for the dreaded visit. We sat at a picnic table outdoors, with me and the girls on one side facing Dave alone on the other.

When they heard his devastating news, they all cried and clung to me. Carrie was approaching the pivotal age of eleven and was now in the fifth grade. Allie was in second grade, and sweet little Jenny was in kindergarten. They had already suffered through so much that now the divorce announcement was another resounding blow.

I assured them that I would always be their mother and would never give up on them, knowing that they dreamed about my returning home so we could be a family again.

Carrie, Allie and Jenny knew from the beginning that I was in prison because a baby died in my care, and that it was from injuries I had not inflicted. Often, Carrie told me she knew I hadn't hurt the baby. She had been there that day and told me she saw me helping the baby. She had always held the belief that one day I would get out of prison and that our life would return to normal. Now, her parents were divorcing and her dream would never come true.

Over the next few months, I stumbled through my mundane existence by day, and cried into my pillow for hours at night.

Finally, my friends found me a divorce attorney named David Warg. We first met over the phone and eventually he visited me in prison. My biggest concern with the divorce was maintaining my contact with our children. I also wanted to make sure Dave and I would share custody when I was released from prison.

The Dakota County divorce court in Minnesota appointed an attorney for our girls, a "Guardian Ad Litem." His name was David Jahene. Once again, I was surrounded by Davids--my husband, my divorce attorney, this Guardian Ad Litem, and even my work supervisor were all named David.

The Guardian Ad Litem interviewed my husband, his mother, Carrie, Allie and Jenny in our home. He also met with me in prison. Although I was always a bit wary to meet with court-appointed people, I liked this David immediately.

"Audrey, you are Carrie, Allison and Jenny's mother and I can see you have maintained a steady and loving bond with them," he began. I was immediately relieved to hear that. He said that the girls needed continued and frequent contact with me and recommended visits at least once a month, more during time off from school, and at least four phone calls a week. He also said that Grandma Mike was not a substitute for their real mother.

Over the next few months, Dave urged me to finish the divorce quickly. "Let's just get it over with," he said. However, I held my ground and told him my needs were just as important as his.

His attorney tried to convince the court that I could spend eighteen years behind bars and continually referred to me as a "felon," acting from the guttural level of the prosecution that Dave had once so detested. The entire divorce process was ugly and painful.

Throughout the next few months, Dave and I talked sporadically on the phone. Christmas was awful that year. The kids visited, but I did not see Dave again until the following May, 2002. He was staying with Shelley's family in Waunakee and was scheduled to play golf with her husband while Shelley brought the girls to visit me. It rained, so Dave decided to bring the kids himself.

Jenny was in a cast after breaking her leg on a trampoline but the visit went smoothly and I was relieved; I wanted the girls to see unity and harmony between their parents. I asked Dave a few times what he and his mother were telling the girls about me or the divorce and he said they told the kids nothing.

That summer, I received the devastating news that the United States District Court had ruled against me and that I would remain in prison. My attorney, Bill, was outraged. He had hoped that the corrupt politics behind my earlier appeals would end at the federal level, but the justice system was obviously still broken. My personal liberties had clearly been violated in the trial and Bill could not believe that the federal district appellate judges wouldn't follow the law and release me.

2002 truly would be a dreadful year for me. First, I lost my husband; then, I lost the federal district appeal, and slowly my friends began to pull back as well. It wasn't an intentional rejection; they remained staunch supporters, but they had their own busy lives to focus on, with growing, thriving children to care for.

I was grateful that my friends continued to write, and several continued to send me clothing when I needed it. A few even sent me magazine subscriptions, which I loved.

Shelley remained my devoted friend and met Dave and other relatives in Black River Falls to pick up the girls. The Perkins Restaurant was right off I-94 and the girls loved the big moose out front. It was the halfway point between Dave and Waunakee. Shelley was wonderful, making the two-hour trip there and back to see me, bringing the girls with her. She took turns with her daughter, Michelle and my friend Barb Rowe, dividing the responsibilities between them.

During visits to Waunakee, Shelley did fun things with the girls. She took them to swim at her country club, allowed them to have friends overnight at her house and on the Fourth of July took them to see the fireworks in Madison. Shelley also shopped with them and even took Carrie to get her first bra. To make it a special occasion, they went to Victoria's Secret, where Shelley bought her *three* expensive bras! Carrie loved them and felt feminine and special. I was so grateful that Carrie had Shelley to help her through that feminine milestone, and longed for the day I could commemorate similar occasions with my younger ones.

But as my prison sentence dragged on, while she remained supportive, even Shelley's visits fell off. Now, she was going through her own divorce and I understood that my situation was more than she could emotionally handle at that time. The same thing happened with my other friends. It was sad for me because I yearned for outside contact, yet I totally understood that my continuing incarceration was wearing everyone down. I began to realize that I had to be strong on my own.

I was determined to hold onto what I had. Several inmates had commented on my close relationship with my daughters, which was rare in prison. Many of the women had no outside support, as I did, because their families and friends were angry about their crimes and wouldn't cooperate with child visitation. The negative family situations among the other inmates actually made me realize that I had to forgive and move on. If I were to teach by example, I would have to let go of hatred.

In September, our divorce was finalized. The judge granted Dave physical custody of our daughters, but that was only because I was in prison. I was greatly comforted that I never lost legal custody.

Dave said I could take any items I wanted from the house, so I sent my cousin with a truck to gather and store my belongings. Dave and his mother picked out things I owned before we married.

"Why is Daddy packing your stuff away?" Carrie asked me over the phone. "Where will it go?"

I tried to explain that I would need some things to set up a home when I was released from prison, but the idea seemed to confuse the children, so I dropped it.

Dave kept all the furniture and possessions we had bought during our marriage, but I was so distraught over the divorce, I ignored the paltry payout. For me, contact with the girls was more important than fighting over possessions.

I ended up with a small financial settlement that Dave was supposed to pay over four years. Dave was angry about the large phone bill, so the court ordered me to send him twenty-five dollars a month out of my tiny prison paycheck for the phone calls. He argued that I should pay the entire bill, but the judge ruled that Dave earned a substantial income and *our* children needed the phone contact with me.

I paid those twenty-five dollars every month until I was released from prison. The judge also allowed me to send up to one hundred dollars to each child and whoever the caregiver was every December. Therefore, I sent four hundred dollars to Dave each Christmas, scraped together from my dollar-an-hour wage. I was trying to keep peace and maintain communication. After working all those years in prison and saving every dime, I was still virtually destitute.

Attorney Bill Theis got busy preparing the papers for the United States Seventh Circuit Court of Appeals in Chicago. This was to be our last stop on the appeals treadmill. Bill filed the brief at the end of July and of course the state delayed until September to file its brief.

When school began again for the girls, I contacted their teachers. I wanted to be sure my daughters had strong connections with them. The teachers and the girls' classmates knew I was in prison. Fortunately, nobody teased or ridiculed them about this unsavory situation. I was proud that my girls never seemed ashamed or embarrassed when friends came to the house and learned that their mother was in prison. The girls always strongly affirmed that I was innocent.

The teachers sent copies of my daughters' report cards and class assignments, and were just wonderful with the girls.

After the initial turmoil, the girls never brought up the divorce. They were too young to really understand what was going on. Their lives hadn't really changed because I was living away from home, and during most of their visits, the girls talked about their adventures with friends, their team sports, birthday parties and fun in Waunakee. I realized this was their everyday reality and was grateful that they weren't dwelling on the negative, but Dave interpreted this as meaning they were doing fine without me and didn't need the constant contact.

In November, 2002, the judges in the federal Circuit Court of Appeals granted us oral arguments for our habeas corpus suit. Bill Theis was ecstatic, saying this was a rare and hopeful sign. I did not attend the hearing on November 13 in Chicago but Bill told me the judges seemed open with their questions. He felt confident we finally had a chance to state our case.

You can only imagine our utter desolation when that mighty court sent down its judgment right before Christmas. They concluded that the exclusion of evidence concerning Tom and Cindy Beard's demeanor did not violate my constitutional rights.

I thought Bill Theis would have a coronary, he was so livid! He just could not figure out why the federal judges didn't see that the laws had been ignored in my original trial.

I had to reach deep within my soul to keep from sinking into a deep depression, and throughout my entire incarceration, I maintained a close relationship with God. I am a devout Methodist and I attended Bible study sessions two nights a week in prison. There, we talked about not letting our past problems impede our future progress. My faith was the wall upon which I leaned during those crushing blows. But after that final setback, I began to wonder if God was listening.

Yet as the horrible year of 2002 ended, an amazing coincidence arrived. I knew in my heart only God could have arranged this chance meeting and little did I know it was about to transform the rest of my life.

CHAPTER TWENTY

The chance meeting actually occurred when my habeas corpus suit was in federal court. I was told that Keith Findley, a clinical law professor at the University of Wisconsin Law School, was attending a public meeting at the University of Wisconsin Hospital in Madison. Keith just happened to be the co-director of the Wisconsin Innocence Project, an amazing program where law students help prisoners prove their innocence.

After this meeting, Dr. Manucher Javid, a staff neurosurgeon, approached Keith and told him about a case that had bothered him for years. Dr. Javid had nothing to do with Natalie Beard's medical treatment or my trial, but he had heard about it at the hospital and during the media blitz of my trial. He told Keith Findley that my case was riddled with inaccuracies and he was baffled by the guilty verdict. He felt I was innocent and suggested Keith's group of law students look into my case.

Today, after working on numerous cases, Keith does not remember that random meeting with Dr. Javid at the hospital, but I will never forget him telling me about their encounter. Once again, I felt a powerful surge of hope when Keith contacted me to introduce himself. I had seen victorious news stories on television about successes from the Innocence Project.

Keith told me the group receives an average five requests a week for representation, and out of the roughly five thousand requests they've had in the ten years since the program started, the Innocence Project takes on only a dozen or so new cases each year.

"We're usually working on thirty-five or forty cases at a time," Keith explained. "We're very choosy, and the case must have substantial new evidence for us to take it on."

At the time Keith contacted me, I already had a lawyer working on the federal appeal. Keith told me the Innocence Project couldn't step in until all my appeals had been exhausted. That requirement was finally met in June, 2003. Keith called me soon afterward, and I was grateful beyond words that I had what seemed to be a promising new chance for freedom.

Keith contacted Dean Strang, who confirmed his belief in my innocence and suggested that Keith's students re-interview the witnesses.

Several students joined my case and talked with Dr. Javid, who told them that Forensic Pathologist Dr. Robert Huntington, who had performed Natalie's autopsy and testified against me at my trial, had changed his mind. Dr. Huntington had even written an article stating that symptoms can be delayed after a brain injury!

This new information was stunning and the students immediately interviewed Dr. Huntington. He proceeded to admit that he was uncomfortable with his testimony at my trial and was prepared to testify on my behalf. This was huge! Dr. Huntington had been the primary pathologist on my case, and he was risking his reputation to admit that he'd been wrong! I finally felt the wheels of justice beginning to grind in my direction.

Fortunately, my daughters were having a ball that winter. Carrie was eleven and mastering skiing at Buck Hill. Allison was in the Girl Scouts and Jenny had enrolled in swimming lessons. Grandma Mike was still living with them, but eventually she bought a townhouse to live near Dave and the girls.

Our visits and many phone conversations were filled with the girls chattering about friends, shopping and sleepovers. Jenny loved to have me talk to her pets, and had her Siamese cat, Sake, meow over the phone.

"How do you get Sake to talk to me?" I asked.

"I give her a little pinch," Jenny laughed. "Vista, the yellow lab, knows what you look like because I showed her your picture."

How I ached to be home and sharing daily life with my girls!

Late in June, the girls visited me for almost eight wonderful hours. They still have vivid memories of going through security at the prison's front gatehouse and the staff scanning a metal detector wand over their bodies. Allie would cringe when the metal clips on her bib overalls set off the alarm, so the guards helpfully suggested they not wear them. Unfortunately, overalls were in style at the time and Allie wanted to show me some of her adorable pairs.

On that visit, we set sadness aside and played outdoors on the swings, ran in and out of the playhouse on the grounds and played games. It was a slice of heaven for me. As I lay on the carpet in the playhouse next to Carrie, she pointed to her feet. "Mom, I'm wearing a size eight shoe now," she beamed. "I have big feet like you."

Carrie had just completed elementary school. I couldn't believe it--my little girl was growing up fast, and I'd had to watch her do so from afar. My heart twisted at the thought of losing any more precious time with my daughters. We all cried when it was time for them to return to Shelley's in Waunakee.

In July, all three girls headed to church camp in northern Minnesota five hours away. I called that morning and Jenny cried on the phone because it was her first time at camp and she was afraid to go. I longed to cradle her in my arms and kiss away her fears, but all I could do was remind her she would be in the same cabin with Allie. It was a long six days for me without phone calls, but I wrote letters and was happy when the girls returned with glowing stories about swimming, horseback riding, crafts and new friends.

School began after Labor Day and Carrie now had to leave the house before seven in the morning to attend middle school. This was the first year the girls would be in different schools.

In October, Jim Rhinerson, a student with the Innocence Project, came to the prison to meet me. It was great to see the eagerness in his young eyes as he told me he had lots of studying ahead. My attorneys handed over eight boxes of trial and medical materials for his fellow students to read, and Jim told me they would search for new medical evidence that would favor my claim of innocence.

While the team plunged into research and my girls adapted to a new school year, I was dealing with some new upheaval in prison. I had lived in the larger room with Mary for almost two years, but I still hated the tight confinement. Nobody had access to our room except staff, so at least my possessions were safe and I had more privacy than while in the dorm.

But that summer, the prison moved many of the medium security prisoners, including Mary and me, to a new building that was actually built to house maximum security inmates. It was pristine but oppressively small, at least three feet less in depth than my old cell.

I was back to living in a shoebox with no open windows and a tin toilet. I found that this punishing change really affected my morale, and after a few months of this fresh torment I asked for a transfer back to the dorm. I detested being locked in this cramped space and I especially needed access to the phone.

Mary and I talked it over, and even though she hated the confines, she didn't like the lack of privacy in the dorm. A few months after my request, Mary stayed behind while I moved back to the chaotic, yet more open environment. Although Mary had a life sentence for killing her baby daughter, I heard later that her attorneys got her out after serving sixteen years. I was happy for her knowing she was, deep down, a gentle woman and deserved a second chance at life.

The year 2004 began with me still living in the prison dorm. Then, in late January, my friend, Connie, drove Carrie and Jenny through a massive snowstorm for a visit. Allie was at a winter camp for Girl Scouts and Connie dropped the two girls off at eight in the morning. We all ran to the playhouse, our refuge from the reality of prison, where we painted wooden ornaments, watched videos, played games and ate snacks. Although three other inmates were using the playhouse at the same time with their children, it felt just like the girls and I were home on a winter Saturday.

Eventually, we ventured outside and were delighted to find plastic sleds. The prison grounds actually had a hill, so we slid down together. However, I didn't own any boots and my tennis shoes and state-issued clothing were soon cold and sodden from the snow. I barely noticed though, as I was thrilled to be sledding again after so many years. I pulled Jenny on the sled back up the hill and slid down many times with my daughters in my arms.

Then, we played on the swings, jumping off in mid-air into the snow. I had tissues with me to wipe runny noses and hugs to warm the girls. After more than an hour of snow fun, we went inside for lunch. When we were finished, we spent the rest of our visit being artists with paper and bright paints.

At three-thirty, Connie returned and was waiting for the girls in the visiting room. They ran to her and chattered on and on about the fun we had, but I could see sadness in Connie's eyes. That was when she told me her dad's lung cancer had returned. My heart sank.

This dear friend, who was already suffering so much personal stress, had taken the time to bring my girls to me. Now she faced a five-hour drive home. I hugged her close, yet it wasn't enough. How I wanted to comfort Connie properly, but there just wasn't the time.

I left a mourning Connie and my two crying children, returned to the concrete jungle and looked around, thinking; *This is not my home. How I hate being here, away from my daughters and friends who need me.* I sank onto my flat mattress and wondered how my eyes could produce any more tears. I was suddenly exhausted from seven years of crying, disappointments, anger and frustration.

Now, all I could hope was that the Innocence Project would finally end my nightmare.

The first wave of law students was indeed busy researching my case. They read through tons of medical research literature about child abuse and "Shaken Baby Syndrome." They compiled this information, which was invaluable, and passed it over to the next group of students.

Unfortunately, law students could only serve one year with the Innocence Project, so that May, a new group of students signed on to my case and had to read through all the trial transcripts, police reports, medical documents and the new research the first students amassed.

Shelley Fite was one of the new students. She told me the idea of freeing an innocent person deeply inspired her and felt honored when she was accepted as a member of the team.

During the first week of orientation, the new students gathered around a table. Here Keith Findley presented the various cases the Innocence Project was working on.

"Some were new and others needed additional work," Shelley said. "We could request which case we wanted, but each student worked on about ten cases over the course of the year."

Shelley said she was interested in my case because it was unique and scientific, thus an opportunity to learn something new. Also, she said many of the students were drawn to my case out of sympathy for my family situation.

It took the students all summer to read through the mountain of material. "It wasn't very sexy," Shelley said. "It just meant reading tons of files. We were trained to figure out exactly what happened in the case. One of the Innocence Project's strengths is that the students are passionate. But an entirely new group had to relearn everything each year."

Ryan Worrell was another second wave law student on my case. "Keith told us Audrey's case would take diligence and persistence, and I signed on immediately," Ryan said. He and Shelley took the new research to the next level.

"We started looking at foreign jurisdictions like Japan, Korea, Great Britain, Canada and Australia," Shelley shared. "We realized courts all over the world were starting to question 'Shaken Baby Syndrome,' so we looked into the legal aspects."

The students learned that the United Kingdom had ordered a massive review of all cases where parents were imprisoned for allegedly shaking their babies to death and had already overturned several convictions.

Shelley and Ryan pored through databases at the University of Wisconsin Medical School searching for literature. "Many of the legal articles were old, and we were looking for updated information," Shelley said. "Ryan and I compiled a folder with tons of medical articles plus we met with Dr. Javid and Dr. Huntington."

Keith later told me that Shelley and Ryan were the two students who really shaped the case. He said the students were excited to learn about new medical and legal aspects while working to set me free.

After her year was up, Shelley left the project, but my case inspired her to take a job as an appellate attorney with the state's public defender's office after she graduated from law school. Ryan remained loyal to my case and continued to check in and help even after he graduated. The ardor from these brilliant students touched and impressed me and I will forever be grateful for their tireless work on my behalf.

That year, Dave met a woman who worked at a restaurant. The girls told me he often left them alone while he was with his new girlfriend. Allie and Jenny watched television or played games together during those evenings. Sometimes Dave took the girls to eat at the restaurant, but for the most part, his relationship with the girlfriend was separate from the girls. They took it in stride, but I was concerned when Dave proposed, concerned about how it would all work out for our daughters and this woman.

Meanwhile, my daughters continued to make the long trek to visit me. During the summer, the visitor's shorts had to be the length of their longest finger when their arms hung down at their sides. The style for shorts that year was ultra skimpy and the girls had to tug their shorts as low on their hips as possible to meet this requirement.

Whenever we sat outside at the picnic tables, the guards watched us carefully on surveillance cameras because some visitors smuggled in unapproved items and passed them while outdoors. We were told to keep our hands in sight at all times to prevent passing contraband and to avoid inappropriate touching. The prying, suspicious eyes irritated me. The girls were alert and often told me to get my hands on the table.

That summer, Allie desperately wanted pierced ears. She spent a week in Waunakee, attached some magnetic earrings to her ear lobes, and kept them on for days. When she arrived at the prison, she was excited to show me, but I noticed the earrings were stuck to her ear lobes. I tried to gently remove them but they were wedged tight. Allie burst into tears.

I led Allie into the visiting room and a volunteer I knew from Bible study saw Allie's great distress. I was frustrated because the prison forbade me from entering the ladies' restroom with my own daughters. The volunteer and my friend, Shelley, took Allie and after a major painful effort, finally pried off the earrings.

Tears streaked Allie's face as she returned to me with red, puffy ear lobes. I held her and told her to use hydrogen peroxide for a few days to prevent infection. I didn't even have hydrogen peroxide to help her.

Shelley told me it was always difficult on the drive home after their visits. The girls cried and spat anger, so Shelley would bribe them out of their tears with dinner at a fast-food restaurant. She also bought Allie her first bra and taught the girls how to shave their legs.

I was aware that my daughters would miss me more and more as they entered their confusing teen years. How obliged I felt towards Shelley for her enduring support!

In the winter, my friend Barb Zanter drove the girls down for a visit one frigid Saturday. The prison had no sheltered area for visitors to wait, so Barb opened her long down jacket, drew Jenny close to her body and zipped it up. Carrie and Allie jumped up and down to circulate their blood and warm themselves. No matter how harsh the conditions, we were all determined to be together and maintain our strong relationship.

That December, 2004, I finally got a transfer out of the Taycheedah hell hole and into the John C. Burke Correctional Center, a minimum security facility in Waupun. I requested the move in early fall and it happened abruptly on one of my Fridays off work. I was on the phone with friends when a guard called me to the officer's desk that morning.

"We're packing you up and you are going to minimum today," they told me.

I was ecstatic! I watched as the staff inventoried all my belongings and packed everything from my TV, radio and clothes to food, legal papers and photo albums into seven boxes. Two hours later, I was out of the gate and on my way to my new quarters.

The drive to Waupun took about a half hour. I stared in awe out the window, studying normal people entering restaurants or filling their tanks at gas stations. It was close to Christmas, so I enjoyed various holiday decorations along the route. The move didn't frighten me because after eight tortuous years at Taycheedah, I was aching for more freedom.

The sergeant who drove me and several other women gave us a general rundown on the building set-up. "There are head count times when you must return to your rooms. If you have any questions, feel free to ask a staff person."

That was my only orientation and I could already tell I was entering a more relaxed environment. The van chugged onto the grounds surrounded by the familiar prison fence, but I was amazed to see a red brick building with a blue roof. It was much smaller than the morbid Taycheedah and looked more like a large restaurant or nursing home. The sergeant led us inside and my heart glowed at its openness. She then led us through the cafeteria, which she explained was also used for visiting. Room wings branched into separate divisions with both an upstairs and downstairs.

I was relieved that they didn't require a strip search or sanitizing shower. Instead, they simply handed us our boxes and gave us a key to our rooms. Oddly, they took away the hot pot that Taycheedah had allowed for heating water. They also confiscated the eye shadow I purchased through canteen at Taycheedah. This lower security facility banned them. Strange, but I was glad to give up these small items to live with more freedom, which included more gym time and an outdoor sitting area with a large field with a walking/running trail.

When I got to my room, other inmates told me my roommate, Wendy, was away at court for a few days. It was wonderful to have the room to myself for that short time while I became adjusted to my new residence. The room was almost like the medium security rooms at Taycheedah with the metal beds and tin shelves. The window opened, but still had bars. I loved that I could shower at any time before ten at night in the communal bathrooms down the hall.

I settled onto my skimpy mattress that first night in minimum and prayed I would not spend much time here. Surely, the Innocence Project would spring me from prison.

As I closed my eyes in exhaustion, I had no idea that this nightmare would loiter for several more years.

CHAPTER TWENTY-ONE

When my roommate, Wendy, arrived back from court, I was relieved to see that she was friendly, clean and respectful. She was serving time for drunk driving. We shared a room for several months until she was released. The roommate turnover was faster at Burke, but many inmates stayed for years serving out their sentences for a variety of crimes, including drunk driving, embezzlement, molestation, and vehicular homicide.

Many of the women were kind, but others were obviously content and loved to bask in the free room and board. For them, prison felt safer than the life they'd lived outside of prison. I continued to keep my distance and even though the prison staff was much nicer and even called me by my first name, I didn't forge close bonds. Any dispute with other inmates or unusual links with staff could be used against me at parole time.

I was highly relieved to wear my own clothing during visits. The girls first came to see me at Burke soon after my arrival, close to Christmas. They were so excited to see me out of the drab clothing and wearing a colorful sweatshirt and jeans, and our visit was much less structured. I could actually handle money for the first time in years! I don't know who was more excited about that, the girls or me. At Taycheedah the girls, Dave or my parents had to put coins into the vending machines for various treats because the prison had banned inmates from touching money.

Burke decorated a bit for Christmas with a tree and some garlands, bows and lights at the end of the hallways. This visit felt happy and festive, and later I actually got to decorate Christmas cookies to serve to the inmates at meals, which felt cheerful and even, in a way, normal.

Christmas Eve fell on Sunday that year and for the first time, the prison held a church service, which I cherished. But on Christmas morning, I still awoke in my sterile room without my family. I choked down the cinnamon rolls that were a special treat for breakfast and appreciated the turkey lunch, but there were no

Christmas programs, music or festivities. The highlight of my day was talking to the girls on the phone and imagining myself sharing in the magic of the holidays.

Soon it was back to my humdrum life. For the first thirty days at Burke, I was required to work on the grounds, so I was back to shoveling snow. After that, I returned to Badger Industries, this time an off-campus job from seven to three o'clock, five days a week. My days off were Saturday and Sunday. I now sorted computer parts and performed a load of clerical work processing orders, all for the astronomical pay of one dollar an hour, tops.

I wore jeans and a solid colored shirt to work and back at Burke, but about a year later they cracked the whip and mandated the drab grays and greens we'd worn at Taycheedah. I could still wear the colored shirts to work, but had to change out of them when I was back at Burke.

The prison packed a tasteless bag lunch for workers, so I supplemented my meager meal with food I bought from the canteen when I was at Taycheedah. For some reason, Burke's canteen offered a skimpy food choice and I was always hungry for something tasty and fulfilling, especially seasonal fruits and vegetables.

Despite my new independence, my life soon settled into pretty much the same stale existence. We still had designated times for meals, and the food was better and more plentiful, but that eventually changed to the same dreary slop they served at Taycheedah.

I did enjoy the freedom to go outside when I wanted to walk or exercise, but the visitation hours were limited to only two evenings a week and weekends. At least the girls could visit me both Saturday and Sunday, whereas Taycheedah had limited us to one visit on the weekend.

On February 21, 2005, I met with Sharon Williams of the Wisconsin Parole Commission. I had never trusted the parole system and was angry but not surprised when this rigid woman slapped me with an eighteen-month parole deferment. Williams said I needed an extra year-and-a-half of punishment because my offense had involved a loss of life. She insisted my claim of innocence was "apparently evidence I was not sufficiently rehabilitated."

Meanwhile, Keith Findley was wonderful and instructed Shelley Fite and Ryan Worrell to quickly write up a memorandum requesting a shorter deferment, which they sent to the Parole Commission Chair Lenard Wells.

The Innocence Project included letters and e-mails from my family and friends. I cried when I read the letters from my daughters.

Carrie wrote, "I wish my mom was home because I need a mom. Dad isn't enough!"

Allie said, "I need her home because she's my mom and I need her with me. I don't even remember her being home. I was only three. It's been more than seven years. I think she's had enough years of punishment."

Keith talked with Lenard Wells about the request and Wells said my crime was serious and involved a baby's death. He wanted me to show remorse.

"But Audrey maintains she's innocent," Keith insisted.

Yet Wells said it was not up to him to decide if I was innocent, so I remained in prison.

By that spring, I noticed a change in the girls. They were getting into activities with friends and at school, which is normal and expected at their ages. I continued to write and call several times a week, but scheduling visits became a challenge as the girls got older. They wanted to see me but dreaded the long drives and time away from their active lives and friends. The court ordered regular visits, but Dave did not insist that the girls visit. He was still distracted by his young girlfriend. It was a confusing and painful time for all of us.

Carrie turned fourteen that summer and I felt her pulling away. She was now a teenager and resented forced visits that interrupted her life. I continued pushing for the regular visits. Phone calls and letters were just not enough. I felt we needed the physical contact but the visits dwindled down to once a month, and often the younger girls came without Carrie.

My mother still grieved for my dad and could not drive the kids herself, but she rode with other people and was on my visitors list, so she brought the girls whenever she came. Dave never visited me and no longer even followed my legal case. It was as if we'd never been married or had a loving life together. It hurt deep down, although I tried not to think too much about "what might have been" and "if only."

At that point in my incarceration, I felt isolated, deathly bored and totally baffled by the relentless injustice of my situation. I can barely remember the details of those trying years from 2005 to 2007 because it was a long, numbing, dreary period of incessant waiting.

In early 2006, I met with Paul Maske, who was in charge of the Community Custody Program at Burke. He wanted me to join the program, which meant I could work at businesses that contracted with Burke and earn a worthwhile wage. The program was considered an honor reserved for hard-working prisoners. My social worker supported this move, but only if my parole deferment was shortened. I was thrilled at the idea and grateful when Keith had his students pounce on that and quickly write up a new memorandum to the parole commission chair, once again asking for a shorter deferment.

"If Ms. Edmunds is actually innocent, demanding that she admit guilt and take responsibility for the crime is to require that she lie in order to achieve a better recommendation for deferment," the memorandum stated.

We were only asking to shorten the deferment by three darn months, but the parole commission did not budge. I wanted to scream with outrage and so did Keith and the students.

In May, a new round of students joined my case, including Steve Grunder and Nicole Moody. A few weeks later, on June 2nd, while they were still reading through my mounting case material, Keith filed my post-conviction motion in Dane County Circuit Court. Unfortunately, it was once again going before Judge Daniel Moeser. Keith motioned for a new trial based on newly discovered medical evidence.

Judge Moeser agreed to schedule a hearing for late July, but my nemesis, the prosecution's Gretchen Hayward, told the court she needed six months to file her written response to our motion. She argued that our proposal had no basis and that Judge Moeser should deny the hearing.

Keith was flabbergasted. Six months to answer a brief? This was preposterous! It was typical to get about forty days to respond, and most post conviction motions are usually resolved within a few months.

AUDREY EDMUNDS

"It's absolutely absurd to think this hearing should be denied when we have listed a mountain of new medical information," Keith told me. He was prepared to go to the hearing that moment and told Judge Moeser, "We have an innocent woman in prison, and she should not have to wait six more months."

The judge granted the state a few months to respond and they finally filed their brief in November. Keith promptly filed his own response, calling the state's information "wrong." Judge Moeser decided to hold a hearing on the new medical information but ended up scheduling it for January and February of 2007, right in line with the state's six-month request.

Keith and the students were certainly getting an eye-popping glimpse of my life over the past ten years. Keith knew that my case was complex but he also recognized that the state wanted to drag it out to make me suffer even longer. The students had not seen Gretchen Hayward at my trial, and were stunned when they witnessed her acid tone, steely looks and uncompromising attitude in court. They felt a sense of profound disgust emanating from her, and were shocked that she showed no signs of backing down, despite the massive new medical evidence.

Keith's hearing to present the new medical material was scheduled for January 25 and 26 in 2007. The day before the hearing, I dressed in Burke's prison greens to go off-grounds, and a Dane County deputy transported me to the county jail in Madison. The familiar booking process took hours of waiting in a filthy holding cell with other women, and involved fingerprinting, the mug shot, a strip search and a visit with the nurse. When that series of indignities was over, they issued me their prison blues and locked me into another cell.

I slept deeply that night out of sheer exhaustion and awoke in the grimy cell with no toiletries to prepare for my day in court. The jail did issue a small toiletry kit after twenty-four hours, which included a tiny plastic comb, a bar of soap, a toothbrush and toothpaste. I had not been jailed for twenty-four hours yet, so I hopped in the shower and was relieved to find a dispenser of liquid soap to wash myself. One of the other inmates gave me a dab of her toothpaste, which I rubbed across my teeth with my finger.

169

When the guard came to get me for my court appearance, I was wearing the same crumpled clothes I'd slept in. Clean clothes were issued only twice a week in Dane County Jail. I was mortified when the guard clanked a set of handcuffs around my wrists in front, then led me through the maze of hallways to the courtroom.

It was here, in my rumpled condition, that I finally met Keith Findley in person. A slender man, he stood about six feet tall and looked to be about fifty years old with dark, curly hair. He exuded warmth and kindness and I was very grateful to have him by my side.

I reached out my hands, expecting the guard to remove the handcuffs, but he shook his head. I had to wear them through the entire day of testimony, struggling to write notes to Keith with my hands bound together. It was the ultimate degradation.

I looked around the courtroom and was thrilled to see my mother, aunts and uncles, cousins and friends from both Waunakee and the Twin Cities area. I also noticed a slew of reporters, but I didn't see anyone on behalf of the Beards.

Despite my humiliating appearance with the wrinkled blues and state-issued granny glasses, I was excited to get away from the tedium of work and prison and finally hear the evidence the Innocence Project had compiled to defend me. I had gotten farther than ever this time, and felt I might finally win my freedom.

I said a short prayer to God, and the proceeding began.

CHAPTER TWENTY-TWO

Keith was the main litigator, but his students, Steve Grunder, Molly Gena and Nicole Moody were by his side for this hearing. What a great chance for them to see their hard work in action in the courtroom.

To my great relief, Gretchen Hayward had finally retired! Now, Assistant District Attorneys Mary Ellen Karst and Shelly Rusch represented the state. Again, hope surged that this time I would prevail.

Keith called Dr. Patrick Barnes to the stand first. Barnes was an eminent pediatric neuro-radiologist at the Packard Children's Hospital at Stanford University in California. He specialized in the imaging technologies like CT and magnetic resonance imaging (MRI) scans for diagnosing conditions of the brain and spinal cord in children.

He had worked with these radiology images for thirty years, lectured, wrote numerous medical journal articles and consulted on many court cases. He had even testified for the prosecution in the highly publicized "Nanny" case in Boston back in 1998, when 19-year-old British au pair Louise Woodward was convicted of involuntary manslaughter for the shaking death of eight-month-old Matthew Eappen. The story was all over the news in America and England, and I'd followed it with interest on my tiny television from my prison cell.

Barnes looked over my court case and admitted that back in 1996, when my case was tried, he would have testified just as the prosecution doctors did against me.

"The only difference in the 'Nanny' case is there was a huge skull fracture and the pattern of the injury was different," Barnes testified. "But I would have looked at the imaging in Audrey's case and said this is child abuse."

The doctor had based his decision on the infamous triad of brain bleeding, brain swelling and eye hemorrhages that was considered specific for child abuse and "Shaken Baby Syndrome", and prior to 1998 had been universally accepted in the medical community. Dr. Barnes admitted he had used the triad in his practice and to testify for the prosecution in numerous court cases. Now, he said, he regretted it!

"Since that time, evidence-based medicine standards have been applied to the old literature prior to 1998," Barnes testified. "I was a contributor to that old literature."

In other words, Barnes realized that instead of automatically labeling a child showing the triad of symptoms as a "shaken baby," now the medical community had to look at *all* the details of the case.

"Did the baby have a preceding infection? Did it have any bleeding or clotting problems? Were there any problems, particularly with infants under six months old, at the time of birth?" Dr. Barnes said.

When doctors looked back at some of those cases, they found that many so-called "child abuse victims" had had significant medical problems before they showed the triad of symptoms, including Natalie Beard!

Keith asked Dr. Barnes about Natalie's ear infection, for which she had been on antibiotics the day she fell ill at my house.

"Is that significant in this case?" Keith asked.

"It certainly could be, because ear infections, even if treated with antibiotics, can spread to the brain. That is a source we have known about for centuries."

"So a simple ear infection a week before could be a cause of what happened here?"

"That's right," Dr. Barnes testified. "When you look at this CT scan, you can see there is fluid or thickening in the ear. So that's one of the things I would report to the doctor to consider as a potential source of the problem."

Keith brought up Natalie's birth records that showed she had a bruise on the back of her head, which likely happened during the birth process.

"Trauma at birth can set up a subdural hemorrhage that becomes chronic, forms a membrane, and then re-bleeds later," the doctor reported.

Dr. Barnes said a re-bleed could occur from normal activity, a slight bump or even be triggered by infection.

This testimony rang true to me. It could explain why Natalie was often fussy and didn't reach developmental milestones on time, like rolling over and sitting on her own. But this had never been considered or researched in Natalie's case.

I was riveted when Keith asked Dr. Barnes if choking on formula could cause injuries like Natalie's.

"If that caused the airway obstruction, the lack of oxygen to the brain . . . yes."

I was relieved that some of the other circumstances the prosecution ignored in my original trial were now, finally, being presented. This powerful testimony finally felt correct. I could never figure out why Natalie's case was not thoroughly investigated from every angle. The police, medical and prosecution teams completely ignored obvious evidence, like the propped bottle and the fact that the rescue workers and I all reported seeing formula trickling out of Natalie's nose and mouth that day.

Keith told Dr. Barnes that Dr. Turski, the neuro-radiologist at my original trial, had testified that subdural hematomas are almost always traumatic, resulting from some type of blow to the head or shaking.

"I know Dr. Turski very well. He's a very good neuro-radiologist, and that's what we all would have said at the time."

"For years," continued Dr. Barnes, "the medical community had stuck to the same old theory about the force involved in ""Shaken Baby Syndrome"," describing it like "a high speed car crash" or "falling from a two-story building."

"That story has no scientific basis," Dr. Barnes said. "I'm embarrassed that I testified to that in the past."

Dr. Barnes input was remarkable because he was explaining how the medical landscape had changed dramatically since my case went to trial. After years of testifying for the prosecution, this educated and ethical doctor was actually admitting that he'd been mistaken! He felt so strongly about righting his wrongs that he'd taken time out of his busy schedule to fly to Madison and state under oath, without payment, on my behalf. His powerful testimony moved me deeply, and gave me renewed optimism that the wrongs done to me might finally be righted.

Next on the stand was Dr. George Nichols, a forensic pathologist in Kentucky who had performed at least ten-thousand postmortem examinations and supervised thirty-thousand autopsies during his lengthy career. He had thoroughly reviewed all aspects of Natalie's case.

"Based on the knowledge that was available to you in 1996, how would you have diagnosed this case?" Keith asked.

"It would have been hypoxic ischemic brain injury due to a choking event, due to asphyxia (suffocation) from formula," Dr. Nichols testified. "I came to that conclusion because the attendant (Audrey) noticed some type of abnormal breathing."

Nichols noted that the police officer first on the scene had also noticed a large quantity of formula in the nose and mouth of the infant. But later, when Natalie stopped breathing, rescuers intubated her and reported they didn't see formula in Natalie's airway.

"Before the intubation, a mask was used to do CPR," Nichols stated firmly. "This will remove any formula present and push it down into the lungs. If you look at the medical records in the hospital, the child developed blood-tinged froth hours after the admission and had an abnormal chest x-ray. I believe that represents an aspiration pneumonitis."

Nichols testified that without the history I'd provided and the similar report from the police officer of a choking event, he would have irrefutably concluded "Shaken Baby Syndrome". But he was looking beyond the triad of "shaken baby" symptoms and considered the entire scenario of events I'd experienced that day.

Dr. Nichols also reported that new research done by computers in 2006 show choking events can produce internal pressure that can rupture capillaries and cause bleeding in the brain and eyes.

I agreed heartily with this explanation, since I'd always believed Natalie choked that morning on formula. But why did a seven month old baby choke while feeding? My ears perked up at Dr. Nichol's continuing testimony.

"There's a subdural hematoma present, which may well produce minor degrees of brain swelling resulting in the child's inability to feed safely," Nichols said. "It could be a pre-existing brain injury, which interfered with the child's ability to breathe and that caused the choking, which entered into a sort of spiral."

Dr. Nichols also agreed that the medical community now largely debunks "Shaken Baby Syndrome" and that doctors instead consider all the factors surrounding each individual case. I could not fathom why that hadn't been the obvious protocol ten years before.

Dr. Horace Gardner, an ophthalmologist, took the stand next. He shared that *any* kind of pressure in the brain is transferred to the eye, which can cause bleeding!

"In the 1950s, researchers injected salt water into the brains of monkeys. Increased pressure in the head caused the two things seen in this child: hemorrhage in and around the optic nerve and bleeding in the retina."

Keith asked Dr. Gardner if he could conclude when the trauma occurred simply by looking at Natalie's eyes.

"Absolutely not."

Dr. Gardener had also changed his thinking about "Shaken Baby Syndrome" and testified extensively how science had changed.

The testimony ran until five o'clock and I left court that day feeling renewed. Back in jail, I was relieved to escape the horrible handcuffs. The guard gave me a toiletry kit and placed me in a large female confinement area, called a "pod." It was much cleaner than the cell with more freedom. At least seven other women were sharing the pod, which had the omnipresent metal beds and a sitting area with a large television. Some ladies played cards at a table, while one walked swiftly around the area for exercise. Fortunately, everyone was very nice.

That night I was so emotionally drained, I fell into a deep sleep. We were awakened at five-thirty the next morning and served breakfast at the kitchenette just after six. Many of the prisoners went back to sleep, but I jumped in the shower and eagerly awaiting my next trip to court. The staff was extremely nice to me and most of them knew about my case from the heavy media coverage. Yet, they still had to lock me back in the handcuffs.

It was hard to believe ten years had passed since my trial. I was now almost forty-six years old, my blonde hair long-ago grown out and replaced by gray streaks. Another prisoner trimmed it to right below my shoulders with straight bangs. I longed to pretty myself up and wear beautiful clothes again, but nothing could nullify my buoyant attitude that day. I was finally hearing the truth being spoken in this court of law.

The mad scientist from the *Back to the Future* movies was first on the stand that day, only now Dr. Robert Huntington looked more like a jolly Santa Claus with his fluffy white hair and full beard. Dr. Huntington was the forensic pathologist who'd conducted Natalie's autopsy.

Dr. Huntington had testified against me at my trial, declaring Natalie had died from "Shaken Baby Syndrome". Now he told the court he had based his testimony on the common medical thinking of the time.

"What caused you to change your opinion?" Keith asked.

"A study done by Dr. Mary Gilliland concluded that there could be, and in roughly a quarter of cases was a 'lucid interval.' That is an interval between injury and the effects of that injury appearing."

Huntington remembered this study when, in 1999, he performed an autopsy on a young child named Maria Hernandez. Maria was brought to University Hospital in Madison about nine o'clock in the morning with bruises on her face, head and body, which Huntington surmised were obvious signs of a beating.

The house staff looked after her and the young pediatric resident doctor on the case described Maria as clingy and irritable but perfectly alert.

"She wanted to be held, but she was responsive," Huntington said. Even a CT scan in the afternoon failed to reveal any brain injuries or abnormalities.

The medical staff continued to monitor Maria throughout the day, writing on her chart at one thirty-two in the afternoon that she was "agitated." Less than a half hour later, the entry was that she was "drowsy." At two o'clock, a nurse wrote "awakens, agitated, clinging to mother." At about seven in the evening, a doctor wrote in Maria's report that her "eyes were not tracking."

"The child was displaying many of the same symptoms that Natalie Beard experienced when she was dropped off at Ms. Edmunds' house, namely irritability and vomiting," Keith stated. "Do you agree with that?"

"That does appear to be the case."

Getting back to the case of little Maria, Dr. Huntington continued that around two o'clock the next morning, a nurse entered Maria's room and noticed she was struggling to breathe. Maria's eyes were not responding to light correctly and from that point on, the little girl declined rapidly and died from what Huntington found during the autopsy: "Hemorrhages on the optic nerve, subdural hemorrhages and a really badly swollen brain."

Maria had displayed the classic triad of "Shaken Baby Syndrome," but Huntington was stunned that, despite severe injuries to this child and sixteen hours of observation in the hospital, trained personnel had not detected signs of serious brain injury.

"What lesson did you draw from the Hernandez case?"

"That lucid interval is a distinct, discomfiting, but real possibility."

This powerful testimony made me want to yell with relief. If these doctors and nurses had not recognized signs of a serious head injury, how could they expect that I would know Natalie was in serious trouble that morning when Cindy brought her to my house? In 2002, several years after Dr. Huntington was exposed to Maria's case, he wrote a short letter to the Editor of the *American Journal of Forensic Medicine and Pathology,* stressing the possibility of lucid intervals after serious brain injury.

"So based on all that, do you believe there could have been a lucid interval in the Natalie Beard case?"

"Yes."

"Are you now comfortable with the testimony you offered on this matter at Audrey Edmund's trial in 1996?"

"No, sir, I am not. I hedged a bit, but I wish I had hedged more."

Here was the actual doctor who had performed Natalie's autopsy boldly refuting his previous testimony before the original judge, Daniel Moeser. I thought it took amazing courage and decency to admit that he was wrong. I sat in that courtroom as one after another of our medical experts, considered tops in their field, humbly confessed to making this same mistake.

Dr. Peter Stephens was a forensic pathologist who flew in from Cedar Rapids, Iowa to testify at my hearing.

"Most of us in 1995 would have testified along essentially

similar lines. We would have all agreed on shaking and would have agreed on a 'no lucid interval'."

Now Dr. Stephens supported a different diagnosis. "If you're going to assign a cause, especially one which carries significant consequences to somebody, you ought to exclude other possibilities."

I was the one who had been living those significant consequences and I was grateful to these ethical doctors, who were now trying to undo the damage they'd caused so others would not have to face false accusations as I had.

Dr. John Galaznik, a pediatrician at the University of Alabama, was last on the stand for us. He described the original study on "Shaken Baby Syndrome" dating back to 1972.

"By today's standards, it is appalling," Galaznik testified.

He explained how Natalie's body shut down and testified that everyone, including me, the rescue workers and medical personnel who treated Natalie when she was first brought to the hospital, described her choking.

"At 8:44, Chief Roberts arrived and observed gasping breathing. At 8:47, EMS arrived and said breathing ceased as they walked through the door. At 8:53, no heart rate is found and they start CPR. There is a loss of respiratory function which ends in cardiopulmonary arrest at 8:47, typical of a choking event," Glaznik testified.

He said if the baby was severely shaken, the child might not be lucid but the breathing would continue, much like a boxer knocked out in the ring. The referee stands over the unconscious fighter counting him down, but he's still breathing on his own.

"Given Chief Roberts' testimony and the CT scan, the trauma scenario does not work for me." Galaznik said. "Everything I see is consistent with the choking and not so consistent with the trauma explanation in this case."

Also, Dr Galaznik said new medical articles state the lack of oxygen in a choking incident leads to brain and retinal hemorrhages, which doctors in my original trial said could only be caused by trauma.

The state took their swipes during an aggressive cross-examination. They tried to discredit our witnesses and make them appear not to be qualified. But I left court that Friday feeling jubilation I had not felt during this entire nightmare. I had just listened to the doctors describe what I knew all along. The truth!

The guard brought me back to the jail pod where they locked me up for another two days. Several friends, including Shelley, Tina Hinz and Pam Annen visited me over the weekend for about a half hour. I was always grateful for my friends, but our conversation now took place through a tiny hole in the glass shield between us.

On Monday, Dane County finally transported me back to Burke. I was relieved not to have to undergo another strip search at the prison. I returned to my prison job sustained by the powerful testimony from seven compassionate doctors. All of them had taken off work, left their families and commitments, and come to testify on my behalf.

The Innocence Project does not charge inmates for its services, but relies on donations to pay for expert witnesses. Many wonderful friends donated money for my defense. My mother gathered three-thousand dollars from family and friends, and an amazing woman named Carolene Hoffman donated another thousand. One precious friend from church named Grace Fonstad provided two hundred dollars. I appreciated every penny, including twenty-five dollar donations from various friends and church members.

It all added up to eighty four hundred dollars, which covered airfare and expenses for the wonderful doctors who testified. All waived their usual fees except for Dr. Galaznik, who agreed to a reduced rate of one thousand dollars for the time he'd spent researching the case.

These doctors had given hours of their precious time sifting through all the documents, examining slides, scans and tissue samples. And in the end, they did what they knew was right. They spoke the truth.

While the hearing buoyed me to a new level of strength, I knew I faced the state's follow-up a month later. Would they slam shut the door to my freedom again? I couldn't bear thinking of another disappointment. But this time, I had a feeling things might turn out very differently.

CHAPTER TWENTY-THREE

The hearing arrived on February 22, and this time the Dane County van battled a typical Wisconsin blizzard to get me to Madison. I stared out the window at the frozen landscape. Few people were out in the storm, and I was disappointed—how I hungered to see people living normal lives!

I muddled through the same degrading booking process but was blessedly placed in the large pod, rather than in the dingy cell. Before the hearing, handcuffs bound my hands again, and a taser was attached to my leg. The taser was a new precaution because another inmate had gotten unruly during a court appearance. So now, seventeen-hundred bolts of electricity could jolt through my body if I got out of hand!

Keith read me some of the state's responses to our brilliant new medical evidence and I dreaded hearing the prosecutors repeat their falsehoods once more.

The courtroom was much emptier than in January and I saw only a few friends were scattered in the sparse audience. I figured the fierce snowstorm was keeping everyone away. With the steel handcuffs digging into my wrists, I forced my attention to the state's first witness, a pediatrician from Kentucky named Dr. Betty Spivack.

Spivack rambled on endlessly, confusing me. Even the prosecutor had trouble keeping her on point.

Keith leaned over and asked if I understood what she was saying, and we both shared a quick laugh. Even the judge grew impatient and tried to focus Spivack.

During her hour-and-a-half testimony, I managed to pick up that this witness did not believe that Natalie had choked. But most of her answers sailed beyond my levels of interest or comprehension. I was relieved when she was finally dismissed just after three in the afternoon.

Milwaukee County Medical Examiner Dr. Jeffrey Jentzen took the stand next. He had testified against me at my original trial and said he had re-reviewed the medical charts, autopsy report and other data surrounding Natalie's death. He had also assessed the Maria Hernandez case that Dr. Huntington had shown to demonstrate lucid intervals after brain injury.

This witness testified that he would not change his testimony if I was retried today, and that he did not accept the re-bleed theory, saying the old subdural bleeding appeared localized, according to Huntington. He denied that pneumonia was caused by formula, saying it was consistent with a child who underwent resuscitation efforts and was placed on mechanical support.

"I believe the child sustained a traumatic head injury, developed acute onset of neurological symptoms, became unresponsive, and dipped into a coma based on the brain swelling which led to brain damage."

Dr. William Perloff took the stand on Day Two. He was the medical director of the pediatric intensive care unit at UW Children's hospital, the self-proclaimed "Shaken Baby" guru who had testified at my first trial. He also refused to budge from his original testimony.

"Having re-reviewed Natalie Beard's medical records, autopsy and all other reports, can you describe what caused her to die?" the prosecutor asked.

"She died from inflicted trauma brain injury. That is, she was shaken. In her case, there was clear evidence of impact." Dr. Perloff went on to describe ten elements that led him to his conclusion.

I was relieved when the state testimony ended just after one o'clock on the second day. Keith told me the state had offered a tough-fought hearing. He thought they had made the points they needed to make and acknowledged that some of the new developments had given us an inch, but he admitted it is always hard to listen to the opposing side's evidence.

Keith told me Dr. Perloff seemed like a pleasant man who spoke with confidence about his firm belief in ""Shaken Baby Syndrome"." But I felt this: Dr. Perloff was remaining ignorant about all the facts in my case.

Honestly, the state's testimonies meant absolutely nothing to me. They could have paraded a million esteemed doctors to the stand to present their acclaimed beliefs, but *belief* will never outweigh what I truly experienced that day. It enraged me that I had to continue hearing all this meaningless medical rubbish when I had flat-out told them the truth! No matter what their research, theories, formulas or experience said about Natalie Beard, there was only one truth: I did not shake or inflict a traumatic brain injury on that child. The state's presentation was pure conjecture. I was always thoroughly beaten by the ongoing lies.

Judge Moeser scheduled oral arguments for March 8, 2007. It was a chance for both sides to summarize their arguments. Keith asked me if I wanted to attend in person, but I declined because it was so difficult to go through the process of transporting me back and forth from and back to jail. Instead, I sat at a phone in the guard office at the prison and listened to hours of final arguments. At one point, the staff and other inmates needed to use the phone, so I had to hang up. The main gist was this statement made by Keith:

"It's simply no longer true that all doctors agree with the shaking hypothesis or even that traumatic or intentional injury had to cause all of Natalie's problems. A big divide has developed and it has all become very controversial."

He firmly stated enough new information had been presented for a jury to weigh reasonable doubt.

The state argued that our evidence was not convincing. "What's been presented here…aspiration, choking, resuscitation… is not new. It probably and reasonably will not change the verdict in this case."

I was relieved when it was all over, even though it meant more waiting. Work occupied my body, but my mind enjoyed toying with the idea of freedom in time to share the summer at home with my daughters. I truly felt I had a strong chance to prevail this time.

Twenty days after the final arguments, a guard called me to the phone. My heart lurched when I heard it was Keith Findlay. I wanted so much to hear good news, but I felt paralyzed with fear. These phone calls had let me down way too many times to trust the judicial system any more.

"Audrey, I'm so sorry," Keith began.

Tears stung my eyes. I knew what was coming.

"Judge Moeser has denied our motion."

I felt as if somebody had pulled the plug and drained out my energy. This cannot be happening again, I told myself, even as my heart broke into a thousand pieces. Keith was on speaker-phone with several of the law students. "Moeser said the prosecution's evidence far outweighed our new medical findings." Keith read more from Moeser's eleven-page decision.

"The defense failed to show a reasonable probability that a new trial would produce a different outcome."

I was speechless, my mind reeling from the injustice. It wasn't up to Judge Moeser to decide which testimony was stronger…that was the jury's job.

Keith and the students were just as appalled, especially after working on the case for four long years. "This isn't the end of the road, Audrey," Keith said. "I didn't really trust Judge Moeser to look beyond the original absurdity. We have a better chance with the state appellate judges. We are not defeated!"

The students were kind and said they still believed in my innocence. I asked Keith why he believed I hadn't hurt Natalie Beard.

"It doesn't fit your personality, Audrey. It makes no sense. You were a trained, experienced child care provider who handled this difficult child with nothing but patience and your soothing, calm nature," Keith said firmly. "Put that with the prior brain injury prone to re-bleed and I feel it was pure bad luck that Natalie was in your care the moment she crashed."

I needed to hear him recite those facts again, even though they were already engraved in my soul. It was yet another of many depressing days. I cried for awhile, but then had to rise above it, as I'd done so many times before. Hope has always motivated and sustained me—even if the odds seemed insurmountable.

No matter what happened with the appeal, I had a mandatory release date of February, 2009. The state of Wisconsin requires inmates to serve three-fourths of their term unless they are released on appeal. I hated to serve out my time without clearing my name, but at least I would finally be free to raise my daughters, now ages sixteen, thirteen and eleven. I could not give up when I was so close to the finish line.

Keith and his students immediately filed for an appeal in the Fourth District Wisconsin Court of Appeals. It was a simple, one-page document to start the process. They ordered transcripts of the hearing and sent them to the court of appeals in mid-May. They now had forty days to file a brief.

During that time, I received a letter from my journalist friend, Jill Wellington. She was dumbfounded at my latest setback and could not understand why this travesty continued to plague my life. Jill constantly searched the Internet for information and updates about my case and felt my side of the story had never really been told. It seemed to Jill that every article talked about my heinous crime, but nobody presented my side of the story.

"I think it's time we start writing a book and give you a voice," Jill wrote. She had been one of my faithful pen pals over the ghastly years in prison, sending long letters and pictures that lifted my spirits. She told me in her letter that she anguished all those years, wanting to help me through her writing. But she lived in Michigan and the thought of gathering all the materials and interviews seemed overwhelming from so far away.

"Now I know the gist of the book," Jill said in her letter. "We will tell this story from your perspective. This is your story alone."

The idea thrilled me. That May. I sat on my steel bed and hand wrote pages and pages of information for Jill. She wrote back and focused me by asking specific questions to keep the information chronological.

Jill felt she needed to read the entire trial transcript and I remembered that my friend, Barb Zanter in Minnesota, had compiled all the testimony plus medical records through the years. I called Barb and coincidently, Jill's husband, Mark, was visiting Dave that same weekend. Barb drove the heavy box filled with thousands of text pages to Dave's house so Mark could bring them home to Jill.

The box was too bulky for Mark's plane ride, so he left them behind for Dave to ship to Michigan. Dave decided he should not have to pay for this, since he was no longer involved in my case, and saw no reason for me writing a book. Stoically, Barb picked up the documents from Dave and shipped them at her own cost.

Jill was floored when they arrived and declared the box a virtual gold mine of information. Barb meticulously organized the trial transcript into indexed binders. Everything was in that box, including Natalie's autopsy reports, medical data, plus transcripts of all my appeals.

Barb told Jill she'd felt compelled to gather and organize the materials and had wondered if they would someday be used in a book about my case. It really felt like divine guidance, because Barb's contribution was invaluable and saved Jill a ton of time and effort. Jill now set to work reading the mass of documents.

Without a computer or typewriter, I wore out my hand writing my side of the story in long-hand and it took awhile because I had to fit in the writing around my work hours.

It was a slow and tedious process. It took about two weeks for her questions to arrive at the prison and me to answer them and send them back. Sometimes I didn't answer the questions fully enough and Jill had more questions. She worked to pull out my feelings and emotions, but it was painful to dig that deeply, and I often dissolved into tears. Jill hated that I didn't have access to e-mail for quick clarification.

The whole process of writing was both frustrating and fulfilling, especially when Jill began to send the written chapters. At last, the truth would be told!

In May, I was finally granted community custody, which meant a better job at Findlay Industries in Beaver Dam. This was a huge honor and meant that I worked a regular job, with non-prisoners, for a stunning nine dollars an hour. I could actually sock away some real savings for my future.

The majority of community custody inmates worked at the Beaver Dam warehouse. However, I spent most of my time with another woman at their facility in Columbus, which meant an extra half hour commute on the bus. My unglamorous job was called a "purger." That meant I spent the day rummaging through all kinds of truck and tractor parts and moving heavy metal. Some parts could weigh as much as fifty pounds and I definitely developed some new muscles.

It was a grueling, dirty job, and we sorted through grubby parts and sometimes tossed brand new truck and car mats out because the company no longer needed the stock. I managed because I knew I wouldn't have this job forever.

For me, I was happy just to be off prison property and conversing with normal people. The manual labor also allowed me to fall into a deep sleep every night.

Everyone was nice to me, even though they knew I was residing in the state prison, but prisoners were not allowed to forge close friendships or ask co-workers for favors. The prison was adamant that we wear blue jeans and colored shirts, and I was always careful to follow the rules because prison sergeants would pop in for random checks and report prisoners who weren't properly attired.

Soon after I got the new job, I was granted my own room, a privilege reserved for inmates on community custody. I loved finally having my own space and the relative peace I needed to work on the book. The rooms were the same, but the singles were in a quieter hall with fewer women.

Of course, the prison tainted my happiness by charging me twenty-two dollars rent for every day I worked. So much for padding my bank account! All that heavy labor was being exerted for virtually no pay.

That July, I was thrilled on Carrie's fifteenth birthday when Keith and the students sent another memorandum trying once again to get me out on parole. I don't know why I got excited and set myself up for another emotional plunge--because the parole commission turned me down once again.

Fortunately, the book gave me new focus and was a source of excitement and energy. I could clear my name through the book because I refused to live the rest of my life with a tarnished reputation based on a wrongful conviction. I felt the burning need to share the truth and help others who, like me, had been falsely accused of the lie called "Shaken Baby Syndrome".

The girls continued to visit when they could, but Carrie took a job that summer at the country club near Dave's house. At the age of sixteen, she was preoccupied with work, friends, exercising and enjoying the freedom of driving her own vehicle. I rarely saw her, but talked to her on the phone when I could. At times she would chat at length, but other times it was hard to catch her at home.

I was proud of her for working hard and earning her own money. But I felt the distance with Carrie and hoped she had enough guidance to make good decisions as a teenager. Allie and Jenny attended summer camp again and loved it. My girls thrived on their busy lives, but I knew that my continued imprisonment was affecting us all.

At the end of July, the Innocence Project filed a motion asking if they could go over the page limit on their brief. My case was complicated and they needed more than the allotted fifty pages. The court allowed the increase, and the students filed the brief on July 27, 2007.

The state had thirty days to respond, but as usual, dragged it out and got a month's extension. At the end of August, they asked to prolong the deadline to mid-October. They also wanted to increase the page number. The waiting was torturous, but I continued filling my time and mind with my work and my book.

It took two more months to pull everything together. Finally, my case was turned over to the Court of Appeals on December 7, 2007--eight long months after Judge Moeser had turned me down. I actually allowed myself to dream of sharing Christmas at home with my girls.

As winter moved in, I wore gloves, a fleece jacket, and a thermal shirt under my clothes at work. Many times, the garage doors were opened for forklifts to move in and out, bringing in the bitter cold. The rules forbade the other staff from sharing their coats with inmates, but several generously left jackets around that I gratefully wore.

One day a vendor brought ice cream, strawberries and some toppings as a treat. I hadn't eaten good ice cream in almost eleven years and I lingered over every bite! It felt so rich and special. Another time, a co-worker gave me some of her Cheez-Its. I ate each cracker slowly, allowing one after another to slowly melt in my mouth.

Sometimes our work unit held potluck lunches. What a treat they were! It was wonderful to taste good quality barbecue beef and delicious desserts. In prison, I'd learned to relish simple pleasures and tried to squeeze out every bit of enjoyment.

Christmas came and went—and there was still no news of

my release date. Jill and I continued to send our manila packets back and forth by snail mail in two week intervals. I was finding that writing about my ordeal was both agonizing and cathartic. It was actually excruciating to relive that horrible morning when Natalie fell ill, as were my long years in a maximum security prison. Jill said she cried while she wrote each chapter, but I wanted to stop weeping and start living again.

As I watched the ball drop in Times Square on my thirteen-inch television that New Year's Eve, I prayed that 2008 would finally be my magic year.

CHAPTER TWENTY-FOUR

January, 2008 crept along, as did my same mundane schedule. Keith told me the appellate judges would likely take three to four months to pore over my case and come to a decision. I expected to get word around my birthday at the end of April but the waiting was interminable. My hopes, as usual, were tinged with fear that this latest appeal would fail like the rest of them. Perhaps I'd have to wait another year for my mandatory release date. Another year of incarceration for a crime I hadn't committed.....

Meanwhile, I bundled up for work as best I could against what was shaping up to be a harsh winter, even by Wisconsin standards. By late January, we were already nearing the snowfall record for the entire winter season.

When I talked to the girls on the phone, they were excited about a ski trip to Colorado with Dave that was planned for February 7. They'd been planning the trip for months and were flying into Vail. I was happy that Dave was taking this trip alone with our daughters. Dave now had a new girlfriend and the girls needed and deserved his full attention.

January 31 was no different from any other numbing day in prison. I went to work and performed my lackluster job, then arrived back at Burke at four o'clock that afternoon, where I stood at the guard station waiting for a sergeant to check me in. A woman who worked in the hair-care room came out and pulled me aside.

"Audrey, I saw on the noon news that you were granted a new trial!"

I was so shocked, I grabbed onto the counter. "What?" I gasped. For a moment I was unable to comprehend what she was saying.

"It was the top story on the news!" she said, her face filled with delight for me.

My heart started to pound in my chest and ears. *No way!* I screamed to myself. I had expected to wait for months. My miracle had finally arrived!

The sergeant approached and I struggled to contain myself. She was an older lady and crabby as usual, so I hurried through check-in. The moment I was back in my room, another sergeant poked her head in and told me my attorney would be calling me in twenty minutes.

I fell upon my bed in utter shock. The news must be true if Keith was phoning. Sure enough, the call arrived at four-twenty that afternoon. I sat at the guard desk as Keith asked me, "Did you hear the good news?" He was on speakerphone with his students, Laura Bayerd, Anwar Ragep and other excited staff at the Innocence Project.

"Tell me what's going on," I begged, my voice quaking with emotion.

Keith told me that many of his students trolled the appellate court website daily looking for a decision. Keith had logged on to his e-mail that morning at work and read a message from a former student saying there had been an awesome decision in my case. Keith quickly clicked on to the appellate website and his heart surged as he read the entire brief. He ran out of his office shouting the astounding news to everyone in his path. This was a victory of incredible proportions for the Wisconsin Innocence Project! In ten years of existence, I was only the tenth innocent person they had gotten released from prison! Now, these dedicated lawyers were as excited as I was!

"We received word today that your verdict has been vacated and that you have been granted a new trial."

The information was overwhelming. "What? Vacated? What does this mean?" I had no idea what this new announcement meant.

"The appellate judges reversed the conviction! It no longer stands. It's as if you were never convicted of this crime!" Keith explained. "The state now has the choice to retry you or drop the case."

Words can never describe how I felt when I heard those words. I had waited eleven long, frightening, frustrating, desperate, lonely years to hear them and I couldn't believe, after all the setbacks, that my prayers were finally coming true.

"This happened amazingly fast," Keith said. "The appellate

judges said Moeser used the wrong standard in deciding if you deserved a new trial."

Was I hearing correctly? Had someone actually recognized the travesty of justice I'd been living with for the past eleven years?

Apparently, Judge Moeser had weighed the evidence and concluded the state's proof was stronger, but the three appellate judges unanimously agreed that he should have listened to both the new and old evidence and decide if a jury could find reasonable doubt. The decision was written by Judge Charles Dykman, the same appellate judge who had turned me down for appeal earlier.

"What we do now is file immediately for a hearing with Judge Moeser to get you out of prison," Keith continued, unable to hide his excitement. "You don't have a conviction or a sentence now, and it is correct and ethical to set you free."

Freedom? It was finally going to happen? With my name cleared? For a moment, my joy dissolved as I anticipated facing another lengthy trial. I shared my concern with Keith.

"The chances of you ever going back to prison are slim."

"Please, Keith," I pleaded. "The only way I can walk out these doors is knowing I will never have to come back. I could not face another round of prison later. I would rather serve out my term now."

"None of the exonerees who came this far in the court system had to return to prison," Keith assured me gently. Later, he told me it was one of those days that sends a chill down your spine. The Innocence Project worked on my case for five taxing years. Amazingly, that same week, their eleventh client was freed from prison after DNA evidence proved he had not raped a woman years before. It was a joyous week for the wonderful Innocence Project!

I immediately called my daughters but they had already heard the great news. They squealed with excitement, eager to know when I would be free. I told them it could be days or maybe a week, but it would be very soon!

I phoned my mother, and friends in Waunakee but everyone had seen it on the news and the news was crackling along the gossip circuit. I told Shelley to contact Jill in Michigan, but Patti Larson had already e-mailed her. It seemed I was the last to find out about my impending freedom.

On my way back to my room, still in shock, I shared my news with a few inmates, who were very happy for me. Then, I sank onto my bed and cried, my heart still pounding loudly. I paused a moment to thank God and to plead, "I'll follow your lead, but please, please don't let me out of here unless it's forever."

That evening, Shelley made the hour-long drive to celebrate with me. We hopped and danced in each other's arms, we were so excited. She spent two hours with me, gushing about all we would do once I was free.

Keith told me it shouldn't take longer than two weeks to get a hearing and Shelley said I could spend a few days in Waunakee with her but I wanted to check the kids' school schedules first. Our visit was giddy and surreal, and I was so grateful she was there to share it with me.

I barely slept that night, and on Friday, when I went to work, the celebrating continued as several workers had seen my story on the news and stopped to congratulate me. Most didn't know my circumstances and told me how sorry they were that I'd suffered so needlessly.

Over the weekend, my friends Don, Lois and Patti visited me. I made tons of calls to friends and relatives, and we were all staggered that the conviction had been tossed out and that I would soon leave this repressive place.

On Monday, I was working as usual when the supervisor approached and said I had a call in her office. That was odd, since I'd never gotten a call at work before. What was going on? I was very apprehensive to get a phone call at work as the prison had a strong rule stating that inmates cannot use the telephone off grounds of the prison facility.

The supervisor assured me that the center had approved this call. I was dumbfounded and had no idea what this call was about.

"She said her name is Laura," the supervisor said, handing me the phone. She left to give me privacy.

It was Laura Bayerd, the student from the Innocence Project, who told me they had filed on Friday for my release, and Judge Moeser had been kind enough to call them himself that afternoon.

"He says he is beginning a large trial this week and wants to squeeze in your hearing on Wednesday."

I whooped with joy! I could be free in just a few days!

After work I talked with Keith who asked me if I wanted to attend the hearing in person. I pictured myself at the hearing, and then proudly walking out of that courthouse with my family and friends. But Keith said the rules stipulated I had to be released from a state facility. That meant going through the awful transport process to Dane County and having to drive all the way back to the prison after the hearing. I didn't want to spend another second in prison, so I opted to attend the hearing by phone. I wanted to walk out of that prison that day of the hearing.

I called the girls, knowing they were leaving that Thursday on their ski trip and wouldn't be home until the following Monday. Jenny answered the phone.

"Sorry I couldn't come to the phone the other day," she apologized. "I was playing with a friend."

"Honey, guess what! I'll be able to meet your friend in just a couple of days because I'll be home!"

Jenny's shocked silence spoke volumes. Then, she almost broke my heart when she sobbed, "Mommy, I can't believe it! I have waited for you since I was a baby." She finally handed the phone over to Allie, who was clamoring to talk to me, too.

"Are you sure this is going to happen this time?" Poor Allie had been let down way too many times over the years and was afraid to believe that her mom's freedom was only a few days away. Then, she, too, burst into tears.

Finally, Carrie got on the phone. "Hey, Mom, you're finally getting out." Carrie was absolutely delighted and in awe about my coming home to meet her boyfriend, and see her off to the prom.

The girls were disappointed when I told them not to drive down for my release, as the weather forecasters had predicted a huge snowstorm moving in on Wednesday. It didn't make sense for them to drive all that way and back home, and then have to get up early the next morning for their ski trip. I knew that the girls had always pictured watching me walk out of that prison and into their arms, but circumstances were such that they'd have to forgo seeing that part of their dream come true.

"We will have a great time buying me some new clothes and make-up," I cheered. "We have a lifetime together ahead of us."

I talked briefly with Dave, who was cordial but reserved.

He told me I could meet the girls for dinner on Monday after they returned from their trip.

At four-thirty, my social worker, Jenny Feurstenberg, called me to her office. She told me the Dane County clerk of courts had notified her about the hearing and urged the prison to complete the paperwork for my immediate release on Wednesday. Jenny was very caring, and wanted to verify I had a ride home. My heart was racing because now I knew it was truly happening: I *was* being released in less than two days!

I returned to my room and started organizing my possessions. I purged unneeded paperwork and old magazines and piled up clothes for the prison to distribute to the other women. We were not allowed to donate clothing ourselves. I didn't want to bring those drab gray shirts with me. I hung onto a few pairs of jeans and one shirt to wear as I walked out.

I had to pause at times to shake my head in amazement. I was actually packing to go home to my precious girls. On Tuesday I went to work, knowing it was my last day. Everyone was happy for me, and I floated on a cloud of joy, stunned by how fast things were happening. Shelley said she would come to the prison to pick me up. My mother and brother planned to drive down from Hudson for the hearing, and Shelley suggested they stay for a few days and then I could drive back to Mom's house with them.

I contacted my friend Barb Zanter in Minnesota. She lived in Apple Valley, about a twenty-minute drive from Dave's house. She is a teacher, and with her daughter grown and married, she lived alone in a three-bedroom rambler house. She had told me often that I was welcome to live with her when I was released, and she was now very excited that it was finally happening. This would be perfect, as I needed to be near my daughters and they knew and liked Barb, who had often driven them to visit me.

The guards finally gave me boxes on Tuesday and I packed all my legal paperwork, journals and lots of letters I'd saved over the years. I was excited to think this would be my last night of eating tasteless food and sleeping on the stiff mattress.

I switched on the six o'clock news and learned to my dismay that a massive snowstorm was expected to begin on Wednesday morning, with more than a foot of snow by evening. Now, I worried about my mom and brother traveling through the storm on Wednesday.

I knew Jill was driving eight hours from Michigan on Tuesday and was relieved that she was probably in Waunakee already. No way could she miss my release. She also planned to attend the hearing in Dane County so she could snap pictures for the book. Then, she would join Shelley and Patti to drive to the prison to pick me up. Everyone had that dream in their mind of seeing me walk out those steely doors, and Jill wanted to capture it all in pictures.

I can't even remember my last dinner in prison except that it included some kind of canned fruit. I vowed to never eat it again. Amazingly, I slept well that night until about 5:30 a.m. By 6:30 I was in the gym exercising, and then did my laundry so the clothes I donated were clean.

After breakfast, I made my way around Burke, thanking people who had been kind to me over the three years at that facility. There were lots of well wishes, and I wanted to hug several of the ladies, but hugging wasn't allowed. Even some of the staff congratulated me. I gave away my laundry detergent, shampoo, conditioner, lotion and other toiletries to various inmates—now I could buy what I really wanted on the outside!

I still had difficulty fathoming that *today* was the day I would leave behind eleven years of hell.

With everything packed and ready to go, I sat around and waited for the noon court hearing. By then, the snow was falling heavily and I watched the progression of the storm on television. Blizzard warnings had already closed schools, libraries and the metro transit system.

Shelley decided to forgo the hearing and head straight to the prison with her sister-in-law, Shelly Borchardt, and her friend, Robin Ryan. She did not want me to have to wait any longer. Poor Jill had to make a decision…attend the hearing or go to Burke with Shelley. In the end, they decided to cover both places. Jill would attend the hearing to gather information for the book and take pictures and Shelley would photograph me walking out of the prison. It was a devastating compromise for Jill, who had re-lived my nightmare with me as we wrote the book, and had now driven so far to witness my freedom.

It turned out that getting to the hearing was a nightmare in itself. Snow had buried Jill's van in the motel parking lot, so my friend Patti picked her up. Jill was aghast at the weather conditions as Patti drove her around Waunakee to photograph my old house on Dorn Drive and the Beard's house in the same neighborhood. Jill lived in Michigan and understood hearty winters, but this was the worst snowstorm she'd ever encountered.

The weather deteriorated further—now, it was one massive whiteout. Jill said the wind blustered sideways and plastered the windshield with snow and ice and Patti had to stop often to flick the wipers back into action.

"I don't even see a road," Jill exclaimed, trying to peer out the windshield. "How can you see where you're going?"

Both women could only see out of their side windows, and they watched, terrified, as they encountered the disabled cars and jack-knifed trucks wedged in ditches.

"Fortunately, I know the route to the Dane County Courthouse very well," Patti told Jill reassuringly as she slid through a red light under a new assault of snow pouring down from the skies. There were at least five inches of fresh snow on the streets, too, and the car's progress was now reduced to a crawl.

"I don't think we're going to make it in time," Jill lamented.

"Hold on," Patti said. "I'll get us there." Much to Jill's horror, Patti went through every single red light for the rest of the trip.

Meanwhile, Shelley and the prison pick-up crew inched in their own misery towards Waupun. A trip that normally took an hour now stretched to two hours. Cars and trucks lined the ditches, but the crew bravely forged onward.

I stared out the window at the raging storm. My one thought was, *Even if I have to sleep in a snow bank tonight, I'm walking out of this prison!*

CHAPTER TWENTY-FIVE

Right at noon, I settled down at a desk in the guard station to listen to my hearing over the telephone. Keith told me he would try to get me out on a signature bond, but my mother was prepared to pay a five-thousand-dollar bond if necessary. Keith assured me it wouldn't be more than that since my original bond had been five thousand dollars.

Thankfully, Mom and my brother, Wayne, had left Hudson early that morning because of the storm, and had driven through heavy snowfall and whiteout conditions close to Madison. But they were now in place in the courtroom.

Meanwhile, Jill and Patti were finally pulling into the courthouse parking garage at noon. Jill told me they leapt out of the car and clambered through eight inches of snow that quickly filled their shoes. There was no need to look both ways before clomping across the street--the city of Madison was at a standstill! Even the university had closed down, which was rare.

By 12:10 p.m., a panting Jill and Patti had arrived on the tenth floor. Jill scooted into the media room next door to photograph the key players, and was relieved to see Judge Moeser enter the courtroom in his flowing black robe. The timing couldn't have been more perfect!

Jill snapped pictures but the glass had been tinted to block flashes from bothering court proceedings, so later we found that her courtroom pictures were blurred. She caught her breath when Judge Moeser put me on speakerphone. Jill had not heard my voice in eleven long years!

The hearing was short and to the point. Judge Moeser acknowledged the appellate court decision and read the statute that would release me. Even though this man had put me through so much misery over the years, I was grateful to him that day for expediting my hearing. I was cordial and thanked him for releasing me on the signature bond.

Very few outsiders attended the hearing. A few reporters braved the weather, and a local television station interviewed Wayne and my mother. Patti talked with several newspaper reporters. Jill whisked into the courtroom and captured a memorable moment on camera: a picture of Keith Findley signing the documents that would set me free.

Jill joined the others in the corridor when suddenly she looked down the hall and saw a perfect photo walking towards her. It was Keith Findley and students Laura Bayerd, Anwar Ragep and Steve Grunder, all wearing huge smiles on their faces. They simply glowed after the hearing! Jill lifted her camera and with tears in her eyes captured a truly inspiring picture of those precious people who had given so much of their blood, sweat and tears to free an innocent woman.

Mom and Wayne decided to head back to Hudson, but ended up battling the furious storm. Jill talked to the reporters and everyone realized driving to the prison to get pictures of my release was virtually impossible with the raging weather. The Wisconsin State Journal reporter, Dee Hall, said she would try to find a stringer near Waupun to take some pictures. Patti battled the elements back to Waunakee and dropped Jill back at the only motel in town. Apparently, nature had conspired to delay, once again, my return to Waunakee.

At twelve-thirty a sergeant told me my friends had arrived, but the paperwork was not yet ready. Taycheedah had yet to fax its portion of the release forms and Dane County was hustling to finish its part. At one o'clock the courthouse in Madison shut down because of the weather, and I was extremely thankful that the clerk of courts stayed on to process my release.

The Burke staff was very kind and told Shelley and the gals to grab a cup of coffee at a nearby restaurant. They would be contacted when the paperwork was ready. The wait was grueling as Shelley longed to see me out of prison, and we were all aware of the deteriorating road conditions.

Finally, just after three, I heard my name called over the Burke loud speaker with orders to bring my things to the property area. Several inmates helped me carry my boxes and I gladly turned in my state items. It took mere minutes for my release.

Joyously, I walked into the prison entryway and saw Shelley, Robyn and Shelly standing there waiting for me. We hugged with glee, but they all wanted to get me back to Shelley's home and handed me a hat, scarf and a beautiful pair of boots.

"These are yours," Shelley said. "You will definitely need them." Realizing I didn't have a heavy coat, Shelley let me wear one of hers, a lovely black quilted jacket. I pulled on the boots while my friends ran some of my boxes out to the car.

With snow gusting sideways, I picked up the final box and headed out the door of that infernal prison. I was over the moon with excitement, drinking in the freedom of actually walking to a car that would take me off the property.

The Wisconsin State Journal hired freelance photographer Hank Snyder from Beaver Dam to take pictures that the Associated Press would later send around the world. Hank was wonderful, and even helped us haul the boxes through the wild snow. He took a picture of the four of us huddled together in happiness, which appeared in many newspapers.

Exuberantly, I threw my arms into the air, wanting to hug it all in. Shelley did a great job capturing the moment, knowing Jill would kill her if she didn't get good pictures. As joyous as the moment was, we were all freezing and after bidding Hank goodbye we hopped into the car and for the first time in more than a decade, I rode past the barbed wire fences to freedom.

Shelley instantly gave me her cell phone and I stared at it in awe. I'd never used a cell phone before. I quickly called Carrie, who was in the middle of getting her hair highlighted, and announced, "I'm free, honey!"

Carrie squealed with delight. "This is so cool we can talk by cell phone now," she gushed like a typical teenager. "What are you doing?"

"I'm driving home in a heavy blizzard," I reported, "But I'm finally out of that awful prison. See you soon!"

Then, I called the younger girls who screamed with happiness when they heard my voice. "We didn't have to press any buttons to accept your call," Jenny marveled.

My two requests for Shelley when she picked me up were flavored seltzer water and almonds. Now, she pulled them out of a bag for me and I opened the nuts, savoring their wondrous flavor.

"I also bought you this," Shelley said holding up an adorable white T-shirt splashed with red hearts. I peeled off my drab gray shirt right in the car and put on the heart-adorned top. It was the perfect shirt for a released prisoner who was finally riding in a car with friends, and could now go anywhere her heart desired.

Shelley also gave me a gorgeous new purse that she'd filled with Chapstick, bobby pins, a makeup bag and other exciting things I hadn't used or owned for years.

The phone rang and it was Ryan Foley, a reporter with the Associated Press. Jill had met him at the hearing and given him Shelley's cell phone number because Jill had always wanted my side of the story told.

Dee Hall with the Wisconsin State Journal had also called but said the paper would likely shorten her story because of all the weather news that day. I was glad to finally talk to the media and share my happiness.

We crept along for two hours, but I didn't have a care in the world. In DeForest, we pulled up to a house that Shelley announced belonged to her sister, Linda. "She's a hairdresser and she is going to cut and color your hair!" We all laughed because everyone was tired of the gray and wanted me back to my original blonde. I was thrilled, and grateful to Shelley for this fun surprise.

As we walked in the door, I just had to scoop up Linda's eleven-month-old granddaughter. I hadn't held a baby since my own children were small. I cuddled her close to me as tears filled my eyes. Linda set out crackers and cheese which I gobbled down and then trimmed my hair. We all decided the weather was so nasty that we needed to forgo the hair color and get back to Waunakee.

Now it was dark, and the country roads were horrendous, but as we closed in on Shelley's neighborhood, the phone rang. It was Patti and Jill. "We've been driving around and around your neighborhood and we can't find your street," Patti said. It turned out that Shelley's street was buried in almost fourteen inches of snow!

We pulled up next to Patti's vehicle as Shelly gunned the motor and plowed through the piled snow with her four-wheel drive vehicle. Patti followed her tracks and we all parked in front of Shelley's gorgeous condo.

I burst out of the car, eager to see and hug Jill. Even though we had corresponded regularly by mail, eleven years had passed since we'd last seen each other. She stepped out of Patti's car and started to cry. "Don't try to get through this snow," she called to me. "We'll hug inside."

But I couldn't wait. I ran towards her, my boots sinking into the knee-deep snow. We fell into each other's arms in sheer exhilaration, tears streaking down both our faces. After all the months of writing together, we could hardly believe my tragic story would finally have a happy ending.

I will never forget stepping inside Shelley's warm, wonderful home. My talented friend had created a comfy, inviting atmosphere with her expert decorating sense. I marveled at her modern granite kitchen and hardwood floors and again, could hardly believe I was actually out of the gray walls of the prison and inside Shelley's beautiful living room. My gaze darted around the room as I absorbed the kaleidoscope of family pictures, heirlooms, flowers and other tasteful accessories.

Finally, I sank onto a fluffy couch and cuddled under a soft blanket, awed by my sudden good fortune.

"I'm ordering pizza," Shelley announced. "I hope they will deliver on a night like this."

A few vendors had brought pizza to my last prison job, but other than that, the only pizza I had eaten in the past decade was some sauce slathered on a slice of French bread with a bit of cheese.

Then, Jill carried in two large presents wrapped in Christmas paper. "These are for all the Christmases you missed."

She had bought me a pretty, pink nightgown and fluffy bathrobe, which seemed so sumptuous compared to the T-shirts I'd slept in at the prison every night for the past eleven years. Next, Jill rolled in a large suitcase. "My mother insisted I spend five hundred dollars of her money on you. This luggage is yours, too."

Deeply moved, I unzipped the suitcase and found it overflowing with clothes, towels, and other things I'd immediately need. Jill also handed me a beautiful black jacket that fit me perfectly.

It felt as if God was erasing the gray in my life and infusing it with beauty and color once again.

I ate two bites of pizza before the doorbell started ringing. I couldn't believe the number of friends who braved the storm and were now pouring into Shelley's lovely condo. Friends, folks from church and former neighbors hugged, laughed and chatted until late into the night. Many brought gifts I would need, including pillows and linens for the times when my daughters visited me in my new home.

About 10:45 p.m. Shelley's phone rang. It was my eldest daughter Carrie. She was excited to be going to Colorado at four the next morning, but she wanted to hear my voice and longed to be with me. We chatted for a short while and she told me she would call the next day when they were in Colorado.

This was truly one of the most incredible nights of my life.

After the party wound down, Shelley showed me to an elegant room on the lower level. The queen-sized bed was beautiful and featured the thickest mattress I'd ever seen. I lingered in the bathroom, marveling at the beautiful granite sink, the lavish toiletries and especially my newfound privacy.

I washed my face and used some of Shelley's scented lotion. Finally, I slipped the pink nightgown over my head and felt—for the first time in years—pretty!

The ecstasy of sinking onto that bed was beyond what I had dreamed of all those years. There was no crunchy plastic cover or aching hips against cruel steel. But the best part was the thick down pillow. I hugged it close to me and cried.

I am free, I told myself again and again. Finally, I fell into a deep sleep, eager to see what the next day would bring.

To our delight, crews had begun to clear the roads, so Shelley treated Jill and me to lunch at her country club. We met with a few friends, including some who didn't know me but had heard my story and wanted to meet me. The service at the club was impeccable and I was stunned when someone set down a gorgeous salad in front of me.

I had craved fresh vegetables all those years; now, I savored every bite and drank in the ambiance of friendship, beauty and delicious food.

Back at Shelley's, the doorbell rang and I fell into the arms of

Pastor Dave Werner and his wife, Barb, who had been my constant support since Natalie fell ill. They brought along dear Grace Fonstad, another church member who had defended me from the beginning. We spent a lovely afternoon, which included a reporter stopping by to write a feature story about my newfound freedom for the Sunday paper.

That evening, Shelley's brother and sister-in-law invited us over for dinner. They now lived in Shelley's old house on Dorn Drive. When they asked what I'd like for my meal, I told Shelley I craved steak and they were happy to oblige me!

Many of Shelley's window treatments and touches were still in the house that I'd visited many times in the past, so it was nostalgic for me to see it again. The dinner was delectable and Jill took pictures of me eating my steak and my first Freedom Cake. She wanted to capture all my firsts.

After supper, the door bell started ringing and former friends and neighbors welcomed me home in another unforgettable evening of pure joy.

Shelley invited Jill to stay at the condo, so that night she crawled into bed with me, then lay awake trying to stifle tears as she listened to my soft breathing. All those years she had worried about me in prison. She couldn't believe she was actually lying beside me, and that I was peacefully asleep and safe at last.

The next day, we had three important missions. The first was to color my hair blonde. Robyn came over and helped Shelley with the hair dye, and we were all stunned to see the transformation. I knew my girls would be thrilled to see me blonde and youthful once again.

After my hair was styled, I pulled a bright pink sweater out of my new suitcase and was delighted to find that it fit perfectly. My friends and I then made our way to downtown Madison on our second important mission of the day--meeting with the folks at The Innocence Project.

I truly felt like Rip Van Winkle, finally emerging from a long hibernation. Shelley punched in the address on what she called "a GPS system" built into her dashboard. I was amazed to hear a woman's voice guide us to our destination. Technology had zoomed while I was languishing in prison. I knew I had a lot of catching up to do.

We finally found a parking garage and sloshed through the wet sidewalks to the Innocence Project building. As we neared, two students burst from the side door and ran toward us. They were Laura and Anwar, who had waited way too long for this moment. They hugged me warmly and led us inside.

The fourth floor was abuzz with my impending arrival and staff stepped out of their offices to greet me and offer their congratulations. I felt like a celebrity as I made my way to a tiny corner office. Students who had worked on my case over the years jammed inside to finally see the woman they had worked so hard to set free.

"So this is the office where it all came together?" I laughed, delighted to be among such loyal supporters.

Excited chatter and overall bliss prevailed as everyone talked about what they had done to free me. I was proud and grateful to these young people who had worked so passionately on my behalf. Of course, the room lit up with constant flashes from Jill's camera, delightedly gathering more material for the book.

The only person missing that day was our mighty leader, Keith Findley. He was out of town getting the man falsely accused of rape out of prison. He did join us on the speakerphone, but I longed to hug him and thank him in person. It truly was a momentous day.

Shelley steered us around Madison and we called Patti Larson and Shelly to meet us at the mall for our final important mission…shopping! I had written to Jill many times over the years that I missed TJ-Maxx, a fabulous discount store that sells clothes and household goods. That was our first stop and again, Jill took lots of pictures. Shelley generously opened her pocketbook and allowed me to buy whatever I wanted, but I stuck with essentials like cotton tops, some pants, underwear and socks. Jill was busily texting pictures to my daughters on the ski slopes in Vail.

We stopped by a vision center because I really wanted to ditch the prison glasses and buy some contacts. Unfortunately, they couldn't fit me in that day, so we grabbed some pizza at the food court and shopped the rest of the afternoon. I picked up jeans, new running shoes and some small gifts for the girls. Then, thoroughly sated from our shopping extravaganza, we hauled the bags over to Patti's van.

"Audrey, it's time," Patti said, handing over her keys. "You haven't driven in eleven years."

Fortunately, at the John Burke Center, I was taken to a state license facility to renew my driver's license before I was released, so I settled in behind the wheel and blissfully drove to Shelley's house. This act alone truly made me feel as if I were back in the saddle again!

That evening, more friends gathered and brought in Chinese food, another spectacular taste sensation for me. Everyone kept asking me if I felt strange being out of prison, and some were concerned about how well I would adjust to regular life again.

I reassured them that I'd never actually adjusted to prison life, so I was now once more living my *normal* life again. It felt natural and I fell into step immediately. Although I'd have to update myself on advances, such as cell phones and computers, I knew what was most important: how to live an honest, happy, normal life.

The party wound down and Jill and I tried to sleep, but couldn't stop discussing the past three days, agreeing that we could catch up on sleep later.

My dear friend Barb Rowe offered me her daughter's car to use for the next few months—a wonderful gift as I prepared to leave Shelley's charming condo. The roads were now cleared after one of the area's worst snowstorms in history.

The next morning, Jill and I packed up to leave Shelley's charming condo. Shelley loaded Jill down with pictures and newspaper articles about my release amid the record-breaking snowstorm. Finally, Jill headed back to Michigan, a stressful eight hour drive which included navigating the entire chaotic length of Chicago.

I packed up my borrowed car and aimed north. Tears fell as I drank in the exquisite frozen landscape of Wisconsin. I could not believe I was free and driving with no restrictions. I planned to spend the rest of the weekend with my mother and other relatives in Hudson.

And next Monday, I would finally hold my dear daughters in my arms once again.

CHAPTER TWENTY-SIX

Driving west on I-94 towards my mother's home was heavenly, especially passing Knapp Hill, a dazzling valley area with stately old trees. For years I had dreamed of driving through this majestic countryside in northern Wisconsin, and now I was awed by its winter splendor.

Memories flooded back as I pulled into the driveway of my childhood home. I half expected to see my Dad hurrying through the dining room to greet me. I picked up an old picture of him that always sat on the mantel and stared into his loving green eyes. It ached to have him gone and I missed him terribly, but his presence permeated the house with familiar mementos and pictures scattered about.

Finally, I could be with my dear mother outside those stifling prison walls. All these years, she had made the difficult trek to see me in my dismal conditions. Now we were on our own cozy turf, sharing our bond as mother and daughter in the home I'd always loved.

Mom made coffee in the kitchen. It hadn't changed much since I last saw it eleven years ago. I plopped my suitcase on the bed in my old room. Now Mom had it set up for sewing, but my heart swelled with memories. The nostalgia was bittersweet knowing I had been locked away from this house and my parents for so long.

That evening, my girlhood friend Nadine visited. I met Nadine way back in junior high. We ran to the grocery store which seemed like a wonderland to me, selling any food my stomach desired. We picked up snacks and called five other junior high friends over for an old-fashioned gab fest. We ended up with eight giggling women in Mom's living room, rehashing old stories. Amidst the laughter, the phone buzzed several times. The girls called to find out how I was doing and couldn't wait to see me. It all seemed so normal, as if the past thirteen years had never happened. It was still hard for me to grasp that I'd actually been freed from that horrid nightmare!

Sunday dawned sunny and bitterly cold. Mom and I attended church at United Methodist in River Falls where she and Dad married almost fifty years before. The kindly minister knew my story through my parents and greeted me warmly. I was thrilled to finally hug Myrtle, my grandmother's neighbor, who'd known me since I was a small child. She had written to me all those years in prison, and even though she was now ninety, she had faithfully followed my story through my relatives in the area. Dear people like Myrtle touched me deeply.

After church, we visited my brother, Fred, and his wife, Sue. They called my nephew, Tommy, home and I couldn't believe my eyes when the little Tommy I remembered hulked in at full manly height with his buddies. I was definitely feeling the time warp.

We then stopped by my cousin, Al's, beautiful farm in the country. His wife Christy had stored my clothes for the past six years and I needed to go through them. They provided a storage unit at their farm packed with furniture, dishes, holiday decorations and clothes, my married possessions Dave had returned. Boxes and items were piled into the back of the unit and as much as I longed to dig through it all, it was freezing cold. I located the clothes hanging in a standing box with a metal rod and I hauled it back to Mom's.

I couldn't afford to splurge on new clothes, so I hoped to find a few items that I could use, but as I flipped through the items, I realized that these clothes were truly outdated. I ended up tossing most of them, which was cathartic, yet sad. The clothing represented my life long ago and had hung unused for years at Dave's house, much like my dangling fate. In prison, I'd often day-dreamed of various outfits I would happily wear again. Now I packed that part of my life into garbage bags and donated them to a local second-hand store.

Mom loved having me back home and pampered me with homemade cookies and her memorable coffee. She'd waited so long for her only daughter's homecoming--I knew she cherished my company, especially since her home, which had once rumbled with four children, was now quiet without Dad. However, she realized I couldn't stay, as I needed to live near my children. I did visit with Mom until late Monday afternoon and then prepared to go meet my girls.

Allie called me as the plane was touching down in Minnesota after their ski trip.

"Are you supposed to use your phone during landing?" I asked her.

"I had to," Allie giggled. She was so excited.

I talked to Dave and he told me to meet the girls at the Applebee's Restaurant in Lakeville at six-thirty. I was ecstatic and packed my car with as much stuff as I could, hugged Mom goodbye and headed to Minnesota. It was wonderful to cross the St. Croix River into St. Paul. Amazingly, I remembered my way around and every familiar sight enhanced my joy just being there.

I was shaking when I arrived at Applebee's, wondering which car in the parking lot belonged to the girls, but once inside I learned they had not arrived yet so I took a seat and waited.

Finally, the door opened and my three bouncing girls burst in. Tears flowed as they ran into my outstretched arms. We hugged and squealed, making a scene, and several of Carrie's friends dining at the restaurant came over to our table.

"Is this the mother you're always talking about?" they asked.

"Yep, this is my mom," Carrie said proudly. She had spread the word among her friends that her mother had finally been released from prison.

I was always thankful that my daughters were brave enough to tell people about my situation. They had been my strongest allies through it all. No matter what Dave and I tangled through, my girls never wavered in their support.

Dinner was divine. The girls wore Vail sweatshirts and showed me pictures on their digital cameras. Of course, the technology was remarkable to me. I shared pictures Shelley had printed of my release.

Jenny was thrilled that I would be home to celebrate her twelfth birthday in a few weeks. The last time I'd shared cake and ice cream with her was when she'd turned one.

After dinner, the girls wanted to go to Target across the street to develop their pictures. I was stunned when Carrie, the little girl I left behind in kindergarten, hopped into a massive Suburban and expertly drove out of the parking lot. Carrie's boyfriend met us at Target.

The quick development process amazed me, and while we waited for the pictures I couldn't help but lament that my little girls were practically grown. I stared at them, recognizing their faces and bodies, but knowing I'd missed so much.

As sadness overtook me, I forced myself to shift my perspective. Carrie was only a junior in high school and I still had her for another year of prom, football games, the homecoming dance, Christmas, her track meets and all the other excitement of high school.

It was so hard to kiss my children goodbye and not bring them home with me. *They are my children,* I told myself, *and it's normal to want to live with them.* I had to constantly flick off my sad thoughts and smile at these three amazing girls.

Over the next few weeks I learned that the state would definitely ask the Wisconsin Supreme Court to reinstate my first-degree reckless homicide conviction. I prayed the state would drop everything, since I only had a year left to serve in prison, but they roared ahead. I reminded God of our pact and prayed that I would triumph.

Keith was disappointed and told the newspaper it was time for me to get on with my life. He told me we would likely have to wait until early fall for a decision.

My shoulders slumped. Another six months of waiting? When would the nightmare really end? The dragged out legal battle continued to nag at me as Jenny's birthday arrived on February 18. Dave let her have a sleepover on Saturday night and Jenny invited me over on Sunday morning to meet her friends.

I was nervous as I rang the doorbell. I hadn't seen Dave in five years. I was clueless what to expect from him. The door opened and there he stood looking pretty much the same. He was congenial as he invited me inside, but I stood at the entryway of this strange house for a moment, the place where our daughters now lived. Three years earlier, Dave had moved out of the house we shared.

Suddenly, I heard Jenny and her friends bounding up from the basement, whooping with delight.

Dave showed me into the kitchen where Allie sat eating breakfast at the island. She jumped up and hugged me.

"Do you want some coffee?" he asked. We talked for a good

twenty minutes. The visit was a bit awkward and I'm sure Dave was nervous too. I will always care about him, but my feelings for him had changed. He was no longer my husband and the relationship we had once cherished was gone. This home was his, not ours.

That afternoon, I took Jenny and Allie to Hudson to see my mother. My brother Wayne stopped by and we laughed and played like old times. This happy life was so familiar and normal, it was almost as if the hell years had never happened.

I decided not to work right away so I could spend time with the girls. I had walked out of prison with eight thousand dollars, earnings from eleven years of hard labor. I also had a small nest egg in the bank from my trifling divorce settlement, and I had real job prospects. The insurance company where I'd worked before I married Dave offered me a job, plus I knew Don and Lavonne Zietlow, who own three-hundred-and-sixty Kwik Trip convenience stores in Minnesota, Wisconsin and Iowa.

Lavonne was part of a church group that had prayed for me in prison. She was very kind and wrote to me in prison even though she'd never met me. She and Don told the parole commission that they would hire me if I was released, and even when parole was denied, and assured me I would have a job with them when I was out of prison.

I held off calling them while I took the girls to Waunakee for spring break; both Shelley and I had planned a trip to the Wisconsin Dells, where we rented a condo for a few days. We played at the nearby water park and when we tired, we returned to the condo for pizza and movies.

On Friday and Saturday, we went to a restaurant in Waunakee called Brian's Diner. Many friends joined us for more celebration and emotional reunions. Then, Allie and I drove to the West Towne Mall in Madison and shopped together like a real mother and daughter. Every new sensation tickled my awakening senses.

That Sunday, I returned to Crossroads Methodist Church, the congregation that had opened its heart and arms to me. It was a joyous, tearful reunion at their new facility. Pastor Dave had retired, but the new minister cried and spoke of my ordeal during the service. The members of this church will remain emblazed in my heart for their endless love, prayers and support all those years.

Many people who didn't even know me wrote to me in prison and donated money for my defense. It was a special day of fellowship with these extraordinary folks.

Track season started in April for all my girls and I was busy with track meets. There was lots of excitement because Carrie was in the state finals, where she took third in hurdles. I loved experiencing this with her and not having to settle for listening to the aftermath over a prison telephone.

While sharing life with my daughters was wonderful, my nerves were frayed over the pending legal issue. I couldn't begin a new job with so much uncertainty about my future. But as I began to feel the financial pinch, I took work at the Lakeview Kwik Trip store for $9.35 an hour. It wasn't enough to make a living, but it was a start. I mostly needed benefits because I had chipped an upper right tooth in prison and despite my frequent pleas to see a dentist, it never happened. My teeth now needed expert attention.

I settled in as a cashier and was surprised at how much I needed to learn. I had to familiarize myself with all the products, the register, and handling money. My heart never engaged at this new job because I longed to spend more time with my daughters.

Jill was thrilled to have me out of prison to work on the book and my girls helped me set up an e-mail account, but the computer confused me. Like me, Barb was a throwback, too, still using the old dial-up phone modem and sans a printer. Jill, frustrated, was still trying to help me release my deeply held feelings and had hoped for a faster pace for our work together. I was forced to write by hand new information and send it to her via snail mail.

Fortunately, I got a cell phone and I was able to answer her questions a bit faster. On Jill's birthday on April 14, the Wisconsin Supreme Court decided not to review the lower court's decision to overturn my conviction. I was thrilled! Another hurdle overturned! I was so grateful that the judges had recognized the truth and had acted quickly.

Keith Findley was overjoyed as well, and proclaimed that at last his work was done. The only lingering question was whether or not the state would act on its option to re-try me.

I thought, *God, when will this ever end?*

Keith suggested I re-hire Steve Hurley and Dean Strang to represent me, so I drove to Madison to meet with them on April 19. They immediately asked for a new judge on the case. I could not bear to go before Judge Moeser yet another time, and I was delighted when the court assigned a new judge whom I'd heard was highly ethical. A hearing was set for May 28, and I was hopeful the state would drop my case that very day.

I constantly swept away thoughts about the looming court date as I celebrated my 47th birthday (and Allie's) with her on April 27. She spent the night with me at Barb's house and I was thrilled to awaken with her on our shared birthday. Barb's house was a twenty-minute drive from Dave's house, and with school and numerous sports and activities, it was hard for the girls to visit often. My new job also limited our time together. The challenge to spend time with my daughters seemed never-ending, and I longed to buy a home where my girls would have their own rooms and we could live like a family again.

I was livid when I learned the state had postponed the hearing twice, It was now scheduled for July 11, Carrie's seventeenth birthday. As I took time to cherish what freedom I still had, I basked in the summer sun warming my face as I walked to the car. I lingered in the grocery store studying the myriad of fresh foods that had been denied me for so many years. Even the rain didn't faze me; I was actually thrilled to feel it on my skin.

That was one important lesson I learned from my ordeal... the simple things in life are the most precious. I'd never stopped to notice dew on a flower before I was in prison. Now, just about everything in life intrigued and excited me.

Everything, that is, but the hovering court hearing which finally arrived. Steve and Dean asked if I wanted to attend, but Carrie had a soccer game that day. I decided I'd spent enough time in courtrooms and preferred to be outdoors in the fresh air with my daughters.

Carrie's birthday turned out to herald double joy: it was a celebration of her birth and the day I was reborn! I had not told my daughters about the hearing because even though they knew what was pending with my case, I didn't want to trigger any more fear in them.

I was at my mother's house that morning with Jenny, my niece, Sarah, and my nephew, Shane, who were visiting from down south. The kids were playing in the park across the street as I sat on my bed with my mother's cordless phone pressed to my ear. My heart pounded as I listened to the court hearing. The state announced that Cindy and Tom Beard did not want to face the ordeal of a new trial, so my case was dismissed.

What?! I couldn't believe my ears!

When the court adjourned, I thanked my attorneys and then ran into the kitchen and hugged my mother. For several minutes, we just wept together with happiness and relief.

Then, I raced across the street and gathered Jenny, Sarah and Shane in my arms. They looked confused until I shared the news and the all of us shouted with laughter.

"Mom, you should run a big circle of freedom right here in the park," Jenny said.

And I did! It was my own personal victory lap, fueled by immense joy and relief.

Allie was on the soccer field with her dad, so I called her with the news and she was overjoyed.

Then, I called Carrie at her soccer practice and left a message that I needed to talk to her right away. Two minutes later, my phone rang and I excitedly shared my news.

"Hallelujah!!" she whooped into the phone.

On that day, my nightmare finally ended. I no longer had a storm cloud hovering over me or vindictive, angry people controlling my life.

That August, I strolled along the shore at Lake Marion, the warm sand sifting through my bare feet. In prison, I had dreamed about walking this stretch with my children. Now, as we walked, I came upon a broken plastic shovel in the sand and stopped to stare at it.

"What's wrong, Mom?" Jenny asked, concerned.

"Nothing, honey. Everything is actually just right," I said and burst into tears. I wished I had a camera to take a picture of that shovel just so I could remember how lucky I was to be on that beach to see it.

Today, the simplest things remind me just how happy and blessed I am to be free-- to be a nurturer, a leader, a friend, and best of all . . . a Mom.

EPILOGUE

After all these years of study and conjecture in this case, we still don't know exactly how baby Natalie died that day. Doctors have stated the old brain injury could have occurred during the birth process stalling her maturation process and causing headaches that made her overly fussy.

Doctors have also testified in my case that a slight bump to the head or even an infection could cause the old injury to rebleed leading to the convulsion which caused her to choke on formula.

The prosecutors in my case have not backed down on their accusations. In a recent ABA Journal law article, Assistant Dane County District Attorney Shelly Rusch said that all the medical evidence points to either a violent shaking or some other "high-energy traumatic event" like a car crash, which didn't happen.

Yet, Dr. John Plunkett who studied "Shaken Baby Syndrome" cases for years and counseled my attorneys during my appeals process says it is impossible for a human to shake a baby with the force of a car crash. Plunkett says anyone making these insane claims needs to quantify the force needed to shake a baby that hard...especially without causing a broken neck or a single bruise or mark on the baby's body in the process. I do not believe anybody shook Natalie.

The most stunning and vibrant news since my release comes from Dr. Norman Guthkelch, the doctor who originally coined the phrase "Shaken Baby Syndrome" back in the 1970s. Jill contacted him after I saw him interviewed on a PBS special hosted by investigative reporter Joe Shapiro.

"I am 96 years old and arthritic," Dr. Guthkelch wrote in an email to Jill, yet he is collaborating with a distinguished lawyer in an effort to "restore some balance" to the "Shaken Baby" mania.

Dr. Guthkelch wrote: "If you read my original paper, you will see that I avoid criminalization of SBS, and indeed never use that phrase. In my time and country (England in the mid-1900s) shaking was an acceptable form of correction. I am not exaggerating when I say I am aghast--lose sleep--at the thought that what I intended as a suggestion to avoid physical correction of a naughty child has become a blunderbuss weapon to incriminate possibly innocent caregivers!

It is completely contrary to ethical or scientific medicine to assert that a given clinical picture, particularly one discredited by recent evidence, is in itself proof of criminal intent, especially in the absence of witnesses. I am aghast that any colleagues should declare under oath that, as a rule, one can deduce the intention of trauma from the damage actually inflicted. The name SBS was bestowed at a time when there was not a vestige of proof that only shaking could cause it."

Dr Guthkelch wrote, "Look in the medical dictionary! How many syndromes will you find that define an etiology? Very few. Usually it's the presenting feature or the discoverer that's mentioned.

Traumatology is NOT an exact science. Anyone familiar with the use of firearms will tell you that even a rifle held in a vice and fired ten times will cause ten different holes in the target. It's quite clear that ten different episodes of shaking will cause ten different patterns of injury. To attempt, after the fact, to associate the differences with the state of mind of the supposed perpetrator is pseudo-science.

I'm not saying you can't ever deduce intention from results," Dr. Guthkelch continued. "But if a doctor testifies that the injury is necessarily consistent with murderous *intent,* I want to ask him at how many murders has he been present?

This is no laughing matter, but I can't resist suggesting that you/we adopt the motto "SBS" or ALL-BS!"

This letter from the man who actually named the supposed syndrome that sent me to hell is my final vindication.

I am grateful beyond words that this kind man, in the last years of his life, is fighting to change what has put hundreds of innocent people in prison all over the world. I hope the prosecutors in my case will see that they were wrong to have created a false case against me. Dr. Guthkelch's statements should warn other prosecutors to look at all aspects of what appears to be a "Shaken Baby" case.

Today, I hope to use my nightmare to help others who are wrongly convicted. I want to alert people who serve on a jury that what they hear from the attorneys standing before them is not necessarily factual. Juries should listen to every angle of the story.

In my case, if the jury members had listened, they would have looked beyond the parents' pain and the agony of a dead infant and heard that Natalie had no external injuries, with conflicting medical facts tossed in. My case screamed for a verdict of "reasonable doubt."

I have released my bitterness because if I dwelled on the injustices I suffered, those feelings would block me from truly pursuing my new path. In March, 2009, I attended the Innocence Network Conference in Texas and met with one hundred other people who had been exonerated because of Innocence Project intervention. It was heart-wrenching indeed to learn about the many situations involved, and all had been falsely convicted and had served more than fifteen years in prison! Most were released because of new DNA technology.

I sat in on a session about "Shaken Baby Syndrome" and Dr. Patrick Barnes, who testified at my appeals hearing, spoke about my case. He explained that when a baby lacks oxygen for more than four minutes, the body starts to shut down. When rescue workers revive an infant by administering oxygen and other resuscitation efforts, the heart rate picks up to normal and then signs of "abuse" occur.

Behind me, I heard a voice whisper, "So when there's no neck injury, the baby cannot have been shaken!" The voice belonged to Barry Scheck, the attorney who helped start the Innocence Project and who defended Nanny Louise

Woodward in the Boston "Shaken Baby" case. I had breakfast with him the next morning and he knew all about my case and sadly shook his head at the suffering I'd undergone.

The conference was held shortly after actress Natasha Richardson died from the same type of injury that killed Natalie. It was a very similar scenario; Natasha suffered a seemingly small bump on the head when she fell during a ski lesson. The ski patrol officers said the actress was lucid for several hours, walking, talking and even making jokes. She returned to her hotel room and later suffered headaches and deteriorated quickly. Doctors at the conference talked about Natasha's tragic case, and I understood it all too well.

Keith Findlay, my Innocence Project attorney, told me my case is precedent-setting. It will help many others incarcerated for "Shaken Baby Syndrome" who are innocent. I know this is already true because I received an e-mail from Kathy Hyatt of Columbia, Missouri. In 2004, Kathy was a nanny for three children, including an eleven-month-old girl.

"I was feeding her on my couch, turned my back for a split second and heard a thud," Kathy wrote. "She fell off the couch. Her eyes were rolled back in her head and she was having trouble breathing."

Kathy called her husband, who hurried over to help her. The baby was rushed to the hospital and, thank God, survived. Kathy was charged with Class-B felony child abuse for what was considered "Shaken Baby Syndrome." My case was presented in court and it took Kathy's jury five minutes to agree on a "not guilty" verdict."

"You are my hero!" Kathy wrote.

That one letter warmed my heart and reminded me there are many other parents and caregivers still in prison falsely accused of abusing a child. It is my mission to educate the masses and stop this injustice from happening to anyone else. I remain active with the Innocence Project and continue to consult others who are still in prison wrongfully convicted.

As of this writing, I have been free for almost five years. Life is good and there are times I actually forget I was locked away for eleven long years. I was able to easily and quickly settle back into the routine of normal living.

My daughters are the joy of my life. Carrie and Allison are both in college. Jenny, the daughter I left behind as a one-year-old, is now a high school student. I get together with the girls often and attend all their school and sporting events. None of us dwells on the past and what cannot be changed.

I now live with a friend who is just a couple of minutes drive away from where my daughters live with their dad. Money is still tight as my job doesn't pay much more than minimum wage, and many people ask me if I will sue the state for the travesty of my interminable confinement. Unfortunately, Wisconsin limits compensation for wrongful imprisonment to five thousand dollars per year in prison with a cap of twenty-five thousand dollars, plus attorney costs. This does not include an adjustment for inflation.

This paltry payout has been on the books since 1980 and is sinfully small for someone who was ripped from her normal life and falsely imprisoned. Currently, of all the states with compensation laws, Wisconsin has the lowest compensation rates. Twenty-five thousand dollars for eleven years of my life would not even get me on my feet again financially.

In January of 2012, Assembly Bill 452 was introduced to Wisconsin State lawmakers which would increase that to fifty-thousand a year with no cap, with cost-of-living adjustments. The bill would also provide up to ten years of health coverage under the state employee health plans, temporary housing, education, job assistance and counseling.

The bill applies to anyone released from prison since January 1, 2006, which includes me. The Wisconsin Innocence Project worked with legislators to craft this proposal. I truly hope this becomes law!

I have talked with my lawyers, and Steve Hurley told me I am eligible for reimbursement, but under the current compensation law that would be very difficult to achieve. He told me I must show innocence, not the lack of guilt, in order to qualify. My case doesn't have clear-cut proof like DNA, and Steve said the district attorney's unchanged false position against me probably means that the compensation board would not view me as officially innocent.

Keith Findlay with the Innocence Project worked on the new bill with legislators. The new proposal would lower my burden of proof from that needed in a criminal trial to be more in line with proof needed in a civil case.

Steve tells me my case has haunted him every day and every night since the jury read my guilty verdict in court. He still stings from my conviction and feels he should have prepared me better for my cross-examination. At this point, I consider it water under the bridge and am grateful for what he has done for me.

Throughout all the heartache, I hope I taught my daughters to never give up when fighting for the truth. I chose to take the hard road, but we all made it through and my name has finally been cleared. And the greatest gift of my freedom is knowing that my loved ones and I can finally enjoy the glorious years ahead together…a family once again.

Isaiah 54:17
"No weapon formed against me will prevail."

THE INNOCENCE PROJECT

The Innocence Project is a non-profit legal center dedicated to vindicating wrongfully convicted people and reforming the criminal justice system to avoid future injustice. Created by Barry C. Scheck and Peter J. Neufeld in 1992, the project is affiliated with the Benjamin N. Cardoza School of Law at Yeshiva University in New York City and has burgeoned to include sixty-six projects in forty-four states. Canada, The United Kingdom, Australia, and New Zealand have also added Innocence Projects.

As of this writing, Innocence Projects have successfully freed more than 300 people in the United States, mostly using DNA testing, including seventeen who actually served time on Death Row. These people spent an average of twelve years behind bars before their exoneration and release.

DNA testing has changed the criminal justice system remarkably and is the springboard for most Innocence Project reversals. DNA is scientific proof that our legal justice system does convict and imprison innocent people. Thousands of inmates, mostly the poor and forgotten who have exhausted all legal avenues for exoneration, are currently hoping the Innocence Project will take on their cases.

Teams of attorneys supervise law students who handle the case work. Clients undergo extensive screening to determine if DNA testing can prove their innocence claims. My Innocence Project attorney, Keith Findley, and his colleague, John Pray, observed the growing use of DNA in court back in 1998 and started up the fourth Innocence Project in the country at the University of Wisconsin Law School's Remington Center.

The Project also works on policy reform, trying to minimize the risk of false convictions. Staffers work with legislators and attorney generals, and contribute to major reform. One important area is eyewitness identification. Surprisingly, eyewitnesses are remarkably unreliable. People are not good at remembering and identifying a stranger's face, and often forget details of an incident.

While they have no intention of lying, they often make mistaken identifications.

"Looking over DNA cases, eighty percent were placed behind bars because of an eyewitness identification," Keith says. "New procedures are now used in collecting eye-witness accounts, and the standards have changed with admissibility in court."

False confessions are also an important cause of wrongful convictions. Most people cannot imagine someone falsely admitting to a crime, but the Innocence Project finds fifteen to twenty-five percent of its clients falsely confessed because of extreme police tactics. We know this is true because DNA evidence has proven their innocence. Keith says laws have passed requiring police to electronically record interrogations to deter them from coercive practices. This requirement protects both the accused and the police.

Another leading cause of false conviction is mistaken or fraudulent forensic science, which was involved in my own case. DNA proved this in more than half of the two hundred cases exonerated with the help of the Innocence Project. Unfortunately, my case did not have DNA to help free me, but it was definitely a case of bad science that was used to convict me.

"It's very discouraging and disheartening that some attorneys can't accept that they have an innocent person," Keith says. "You would think the criminal justice system would have more humility. Some can't accept that they might be wrong."

Indeed, in my case, the prosecution has never backed down on their false claims. I feel they do it to save face, but they would gain much more respect if they would man up to the truth and admit they were wrong. I feel it is cowardly to refuse to admit they were wrong.

I thank the Innocence Project from the depth of my soul for setting me free. I pray that, with their continued compassion and diligence, Innocence Projects around the world will unshackle thousands more innocent people who currently suffer in prison and will bring significant reform to the system that unjustly put them there.

For more information about the Innocence Project visit the website: **www.innocenceproject.org**

AUDREY EDMUNDS

Audrey is the proud mother of three daughters: Carrie, Allison and Jennifer. She works tirelessly to consult and assist others who are wrongfully accused of Shaken Baby Syndrome and other convictions. She speaks publicly on radio and television and remains active with the Innocence Project. She resides in Minnesota where she is finally reunited with her children.

JILL WELLINGTON

Jill Wellington has been a journalist for thirty-three years including fourteen as an award-winning television news reporter in Michigan. She also reported for radio, wrote a weekly humor column for her local newspaper and has written three books. Jill resides in Michigan where she enjoys a second career as a portrait photographer.

ACKNOWLEDGMENTS

I have many people to thank for their dedication, support and love during my harrowing ordeal. Thanks to my daughters Carrie, Allison and Jennifer Edmunds for boldly standing behind me through the worst of times. To David Edmunds who carried a heavy burden all those years...I thank you.

I am deeply grateful to all the attorneys who worked tirelessly on my case including Steve Hurley, Dale Peterson, Dean Strang, William Theis, and Michael Bowen. And, of course, Keith Findley with the Wisconsin Innocence Project who headed the five year effort to clear my name and set me free and all the students who worked on my case. Your work is so important and appreciated.

My heartfelt thanks to all the doctors who took the time to research and testify on my behalf and to help change the medical community's thinking about Shaken Baby Syndrome. I will forever be grateful to Dr. John Plunkett, Dr. Robert Huntington, Dr. Mary Dominski, Dr. Patrick Barnes, Dr. George Nichols, Dr. Horace Gardner, Dr. Peter Stephens, Dr. John Galaznik, Dr. Manucher Javid, Dr. Norman Guthkelch, and all the other doctors who are working to clarify wrongful Shaken Baby cases. Lorraine Endres, I deeply appreciate all you did for me.

My family and friends were my source of strength and comfort. Thank you to my parents Jean and the late John Glasbrenner, my brothers Fred, Wayne and Gary Glasbrenner and their families, Uncle John and Aunt Alice Hanson and their family, Uncle Ed and the late Aunt Betty Hanson and their family, dear Aunt Kristi who is now in heaven, and Scott Tiegen, Shelley Murphy, Patti Larson, Tina Hinz, Barb Zanter, Connie Peterson, John and Barb Rowe and their families, Don and Lois Ehley, Grace United Methodist Church, Crossroads United Methodist Church, Grace Fonstad, Nancy Bergstrom, Kim Rixen, Debbie Theisen, my friends since junior high Kim, Jodi, Nadine, Nancy and Maureen.

I will never forget the kindness of everyone who prayed for me, sent letters or money and those I have met since my release who are caring and supportive.

And, to my dear friend Jill Wellington, who used her journalism skills to pull this all together so the truth could finally be told.

AUDREY EDMUNDS

My heartfelt thanks to my family who supported me throughout the five long years it took to write this book, and to my mother Edna Mae Holm who is also an author and read and provided input as I wrote. To my precious cousin Kathy Gangwisch who also read and edited as I wrote. Also, deep gratitude to Barb Zanter who gathered all the trial transcripts, appeals transcripts and medical documents and organized them brilliantly.

Thanks to our editor Claire Gerus. I enjoyed working with you! Thank you to TitleTown manuscript previewer, Nicole Whitaker.

Also thank you to my dear friends who urged me forward and provided input including Debbie Moore, Barb Handley-Miller, Jacky Newcomb and Lari Becker.

Audrey's and my warmest thanks and appreciation to Tracy Ertl, the owner of Titletown Publishing. She put her heart and soul behind Audrey's story so it can be told and save others from the faulty science of Shaken Baby Syndrome. You do important work, Tracy! Also much gratitude to Erika Block for the wonderful design of the book.

Most of all...thanks to my dear friend Audrey, who taught me to embrace and appreciate the everyday joys in life. She is the strongest woman I know!

JILL WELLINGTON

Me at 4 years old growing up in a loving home with my three brothers.
(Courtesy Audrey Edmunds)

Our house on Dorn Drive in Waunakee, Wisconsin where the baby fell ill.
(Courtesy Jill Wellington)

Me holding baby Carrie while visiting Jill Wellington in Michigan during the summer of 1992. We were surrounded by babies and toddlers. I was used to caring for children and loved it. (Courtesy Jill Wellington)

Celebrating Carrie's birthday July 11, 1996, just four months before the trial. My girls were only one, three and five when I was taken from them.

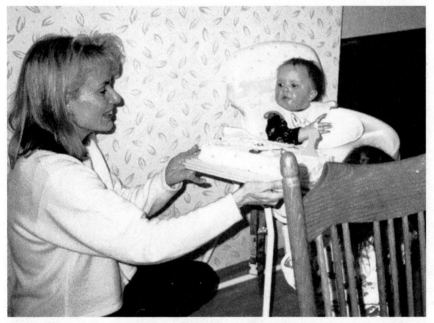

Wearing my happy face for Jenny's first birthday in February of 1997. Inside, I was frightened out of my mind because two days later I was taken away to prison. (Courtesy Audrey Edmunds)

The day I was led from court in handcuffs to my life in prison.
(Courtesy Craig Schreiner/Wisconsin State Journal)

My dad helping Allie pick up pine cones at a truck stop on the way to
visit me in prison. The trip was a grueling five-and-a-half hours each way.
(Courtesy Audrey Edmunds)

My dear mother Jean Glassbrenner sent me weekly letters with lots of photos.
She nurtured my children well. (Courtesy Audrey Edmunds)

A woman at the prison took photos with visitors. Not a very clear picture, but one of only a few of me with my children as they grew up. (Courtesy Audrey Edmunds)

The girls visiting me for Christmas in 2003 at Taycheedah Correctional Institute was the only sparkle in the holiday for me. I missed them so much! (Courtesy Audrey Edmunds)

Wisconsin Innocence Project Attorney Keith Findley signs the papers for my release from prison with Assistant Prosecutor Shelly Rusch. (Courtesy Jill Wellington)

The wondrous Wisconsin Innocence Project members after the hearing that set me free. From left: Attorney Keith Findley, students Steve Gaunder, Laura Bayard, and Anwar Regep. (Courtesy Jill Wellington)

Driving out of the prison with my dear and loyal friend Shelley Murphy.
I don't know what I would have done without Shelley's endless support!
(Courtesy Audrey Edmunds)

The day after my release with my dear friend Journalist Jill Wellington who wrote this book so my story could be told. We were going out to lunch for the first time in eleven years. (Courtesy Jill Wellington)

With famed attorney Barry Scheck and Keith Findley at the national Innocence Project Conference in 2008. (Courtesy Audrey Edmunds)

Keith Findley, me and my original trial attorney Steve Hurley at a party Keith hosted for me the summer I was released from prison. (Courtesy Audrey Edmunds)

Carrie's graduation from high school in 2009. I was ripped from her in kindergarten, but felt blessed to be home to celebrate her graduation. My beautiful daughters, from left: Jenny, me, Carrie and Allison. (Courtesy Audrey Edmunds)